Praise for *More Than a Game*

"No one has done more to explore African Americans' connection to sport, or better understands this complex history than David Wiggins. *More Than a Game* will become a cornerstone for courses about sport as well as a jumping off point for countless studies. This is a masterful account, sober but poignant, by the field's preeminent scholar that reveals as much about sport and race as it does about the country's troubled history. Wiggins lays bare the past while leaving me upbeat about the future." —**Rob Ruck,** University of Pittsburgh; author of *Tropic of Football: The Long and Perilous Journey of Samoans to the NFL*

"For decades, David K. Wiggins has been the leading historian on African Americans in sport, and he shows us why in *More Than a Game*. With rich insight and a skilled hand, Wiggins takes us from the era of slavery through the controversy surrounding quarterback Colin Kaepernick as he explores the history and politics of race and sport in America. This is a wonderful and important book." —**Jaime Schultz,** The Pennsylvania State University

"David Wiggins, one of the most respected scholars of African American sport history, brings decades worth of knowledge to *More Than a Game*. This highly readable, engaging, and aptly titled text sheds valuable light on sport's significance to the lives of African Americans and the communities from which they came. This book reminds us that athletic involvement and achievement among African Americans was and is a consistently powerful marker of self-empowerment and collective agency." —**Rita Liberti,** California State University, East Bay

"From the plantation to the professional playing fields, from Molineaux to Kaepernick, David Wiggins weaves his way through the history of the African American athlete. This is an essential synthesis for anybody who wants to learn about the struggle and triumphs of the African American athlete." —**Louis Moore,** Grand Valley State University

"David K. Wiggins has produced an important history about the experiences of African American athletes. He reveals how throughout history black athletes navigated and ultimately erased the color line in American sports. Anyone interested in the complex history of race and sports should read this book." —**Johnny Smith,** co-author of *Blood Brothers: The Fatal Friendship Between Muhammad Ali and Malcolm X*

"In *More Than a Game*, David Wiggins provides a sweeping chronicle of one of the most visible venues for African Americans in American history: sport. Wiggins recounts the challenges African Americans have faced on the nation's playing fields from slave plantations to contemporary arenas, excavating their enduring struggles for equality and illuminating the racialist attitudes that remain entrenched in sport even in an epoch in which black athletes have become global icons. Wiggins celebrates the triumphs of remarkable individuals while illuminating the racial structures and attitudes that have been historically embedded in both sport and the larger society. Wiggins details how African American athletes have served on the frontlines of American debates about race and racism since the early history of the republic, providing a compelling argument that when it comes to the essence of what many historians consider the fundamental 'American dilemma'—race—sporting endeavors have always been much more than mere games." —**Mary Dyreson**, The Pennsylvania State University

More Than a Game

The African American Experience

Series Editors: Jacqueline M. Moore and Nina Mjagkij

This series takes both chronological and thematic approaches to topics and individuals crucial to an understanding of the African American experience. The books in this series, in lively prose by established scholars, are aimed primarily at nonspecialists. They focus on topics in African American history that have broad significance and place them in their historical context. While presenting sophisticated interpretations based on primary sources and the latest scholarship, the authors tell their stories in a succinct manner, avoiding jargon and obscure language. They include selected documents that allow readers to judge the evidence for themselves and to evaluate the authors' conclusions. Bridging the gap between popular and academic history, these books will bring the African American story to life.

Current Titles in the Series

Caring for Equality: A History of African American Health and Healthcare, by David McBride

Between Slavery and Freedom: Free People of Color from Settlement to the Civil War, by Julie Winch

Paying Freedom's Price: A History of African Americans in the Civil War, by Paul David Escott

A Working People: A History of African American Workers Since Emancipation, by Steven A. Reich

Enslaved Women in America: From Colonial Times to Emancipation, by Emily West

Loyalty in Time of Trial: The African American Experience during World War I, by Nina Mjagkij

Enjoy the Same Liberty: Black Americans and the Revolutionary Era, by Edward Countryman

Through the Storm, Through the Night: A History of African American Christianity, by Paul Harvey

The African American Experience during World War II, by Neil A. Wynn

To Ask for an Equal Chance: African Americans in the Great Depression, by Cheryl Lynn Greenberg

African Americans Confront Lynching: Strategies of Resistance from the Civil War to the Civil Rights Era, by Christopher Waldrep

Lift Every Voice: The History of African American Music, by Burton W. Peretti

Bayard Rustin: American Dreamer, by Jerald Podair

The African American Experience in Vietnam: Brothers in Arms, by James E. Westheider

A. Philip Randolph: A Life in the Vanguard, by Andrew E. Kersten

African Americans in the Jazz Age: A Decade of Struggle and Promise, by Mark R. Schneider

Slavery in Colonial America, 1619–1776, by Betty Wood

Booker T. Washington, W. E. B. Du Bois, and the Struggle for Racial Uplift, by Jacqueline M. Moore

More Than a Game

A History of the African American Experience in Sport

David K. Wiggins

ROWMAN & LITTLEFIELD
Lanham • Boulder • New York • London

Published by Rowman & Littlefield
An imprint of The Rowman & Littlefield Publishing Group, Inc.
4501 Forbes Boulevard, Suite 200, Lanham, Maryland 20706
www.rowman.com

Unit A, Whitacre Mews, 26-34 Stannary Street, London SE11 4AB

British Library Cataloguing in Publication Information Available

Library of Congress Cataloging-in-Publication Data

978-1-4422-4896-0 (cloth)
978-1-4422-4898-8 (electronic)

♾™ The paper used in this publication meets the minimum requirements of
American National Standard for Information Sciences—Permanence of Paper
for Printed Library Materials, ANSI/NISO Z39.48-1992.

Printed in the United States of America

For my father

Contents

Introduction

Black athletes have struggled mightily over the years to become full participants in American sport at every level of competition. Continually faced with racial discrimination and racialist thinking, they have encountered roadblocks and a number of various constraints that have made it extraordinarily difficult to find their way into—let alone achieve success—one of America's most important and popular institutions. Black athletes have, however, persevered and carved out an important place in the history of American sport, in some cases garnering national and international acclaim and becoming household names on account of their exploits on the hardwood, track, and playing fields. This success, it should immediately be noted, has not taken place in all sports as black athletes have always been underrepresented in some sports and overrepresented in others as a result of a combination of monetary, cultural, and environmental factors. They have also competed in a sports industry that has largely been controlled by whites. With the notable exception of the separate black sports institutions established behind the walls of segregation during the interwar period, black athletes have plied their trade in an institution that has largely been run by white coaches, administrators, and owners. It has only been recently that a larger number of African Americans have assumed such positions as head coaches, athletic directors, general managers, agents, broadcasters, and owners. Not unexpectedly, the pattern of sport participation for female black athletes was decidedly different than that for their male counterparts in that they had to contend with gender as well as racial issues that have made their journey even more complicated and fraught with difficulties. In spite of this, a number of African American female athletes had outstanding careers in sport, particularly in basketball and track and field rather than such "country club" sports as golf and tennis.

This book provides a brief overview of the participation of black athletes in American sport. Not intended to be exhaustive in nature, the book furnishes insights into the trials and tribulations of prominent African American athletes, the impact of cultural changes over time on the lives of African American athletes, and how African American athletes have negotiated the racial realities of American life while at once influencing the institution of sport. This overview begins with slavery, recounting the differing conceptions of sport among blacks forced to cope with the cruel and inhumane institution. It is clear from the available evidence that the level of involvement and types of sports participated in by slaves were dependent on the size and location of the plantations in which they resided, the attitude of their owner and his or her family, and the types of regular work they performed.

Irrespective of those variables, the pattern of sports among slaves can most accurately be described as those that took place in the slave quarter community and those that were participated in on behalf of the planter. Those sports in the slave quarter community were most meaningful in that they allowed slaves to exercise a much-needed degree of independence and to bond with their fellow slaves, while those engaged in on behalf of the planter allowed the more gifted and trusted slaves to realize a freedom of movement and agency rare for those held in bondage.

Freedom from slavery promised to provide African Americans an opportunity to engage in sport on an unlimited basis depending on their talent level and physical skills. The entry into sport, however, would be arduous and fraught with difficulties for even the most gifted black athletes because of the racial realities of American culture. In spite of this fact, a select number of outstanding African American athletes realized much success in predominantly white organized sport and enjoyed the fame and adulation and monetary rewards that resulted from it. Unfortunately, hardening of the racial lines at the turn of the twentieth century would successfully eliminate black athletes from many predominantly white organized sports. Although a select number of black athletes would continue to distinguish themselves in boxing, predominantly white college sport, and Olympic competition, the largest majority were forced to organize parallel or separate teams, events, and organizations behind the walls of segregation. These were extremely important to African Americans because it allowed them to exhibit their physical skills, take part in high-level competitions, and make clear that they were capable of establishing and maintaining successful sports organizations. While legendary performers such as Jesse Owens and Joe Louis garnered enormous international attention for their athletic exploits, African Americans followed with great interest Negro League Baseball, New York Renaissance Five, and Harlem Globetrotters basketball teams, athletic programs at Historically Black Colleges and Universities (HBCUs), and those who competed in competitions sponsored by such groups as the American Tennis Association, United Golfers Association, and National Negro Bowling Association.

The middle decades of the twentieth century saw prominent individuals and groups clamoring for the reintegration of American sport. The most vocal and prominent of these individuals were sportswriters from notable black weeklies. Dogged in their efforts to once again open up predominantly white organized sport to African American athletes, black sportswriters, who ironically enough were not able to secure their own positions with white dailies because of their color, pricked the consciousness of those with the power to see that integration took place in an institution that resonated so strongly with most Americans. Their efforts, in collaboration with sympathetic white sportswriters and others, would eventually result in the reintegration of predominantly white organized sport. The major event in the reintegration process was Branch Rickey's signing of Jackie Robinson in 1945 to a contract with the Brooklyn Dodgers and the ultimate debut of the great black athlete in Major League Baseball two years later. Robinson's reintegration of Major League Baseball was a landmark event in the civil rights movement, symbolic in that it took place in America's "national pastime" and of practical importance because it led to the entry of black athletes into other predominantly white organized sports. Tellingly, the shattering of the color line in predominantly white organized sport would be a long and slow process as those whites in positions of power were very hesitant to break with tradition and sign African American athletes irrespective of character and skill level.

The initial wave of black athletes to reintegrate sport generally did not publically speak out about racially discriminatory practices and larger civil rights issues. Obviously not wanting to do anything to jeopardize their careers and chances for success, they focused on honing their talents, being good teammates, and refraining from involving themselves in controversial issues. That would begin to change in the 1960s, however, as more black athletes inspired by the larger civil rights movement began to speak out about racial inequality both in and outside of sport. The most famous athlete of this kind was Muhammad Ali, the legendary heavyweight champion who "shook up the world" with his extraordinary accomplishments in the ring, membership in the Nation of Islam, and his refusal to fight in Vietnam. His membership in a religion considered by many to be a hate group and refusal to fight in Vietnam were condemned by many people around the world, but for many others, particularly younger blacks and whites of the era opposed to the controversial war, Ali became an iconic figure for his willingness to live life on his own terms and unwillingness to sacrifice his principles. One of the many inspired by Ali was Harry Edwards, an instructor of sociology at San Jose State College, who led a black athletic boycott of both the New York Athletic Club and the 1968 Mexico City Olympic Games. While the boycott did not materialize in Mexico City, the games witnessed a number of protests, most famously the black glove power salute of Tommie Smith and John Carlos on the medal stand following their first and third place finishes in the 200-meter dash. The protests in Mexico City coincided with a number of black athletic disturbances on predominantly white college campuses across the country. The disturbances typically revolved around conflicts with white coaches, housing arrangements, dating practices, curriculum issues, and the question of black faculty and administrative representation.

The racial disturbances of the 1960s and early 1970s involving black athletes would gradually diminish in the wake of the women's rights movement, civil rights legislation, economic downturn, and a host of other factors. But issues of racial inequality in sport and the treatment of black athletes would continue to exist during what is always termed the post–civil rights era. Taking up the cause for racial equality in sport were often academicians and popular writers who had become sensitized to the interconnection among race, sport, and American culture because of the protests lodged by black athletes during the civil rights movement. Drawing particular attention were inadequate reward structures in sport based on race, the underrepresentation of black athletes in selected sports and overrepresentation in others, and lack of blacks in coaching, managerial, and upper-level administrative positions. There was also the seemingly never-ending debate regarding the reasons for the great athletic performances of black athletes, a debate that essentially pitted biological determinists against those who accounted for athletic success on a combination of carefully honed physical skills, hard work, adequate support systems, and opportunity.

The last number of years has witnessed the continued success of black athletes, most notably in the two most popular commercial sports of basketball and football at the collegiate and professional levels of competition. Black athletes in these two sports, along with those in a select number of other sports, have, in some cases, realized hero status and become global icons because of their success and great performances. Athletes such as

Tiger Woods, Serena Williams, Kobe Bryant, Michael Jordan, and LeBron James became household names and garnered celebrity status as well as much wealth. The celebrity status and extraordinary wealth they garnered as well as their seeming lack of interest in larger societal issues opened these individuals to criticism that—relative to black athletes of yesteryear—they selfishly pursued their career goals while showing no interest in erasing racial inequality and improving the lives of those in the African American community. While those criticisms might not be entirely fair, there is no question that prominent black athletes are now speaking out more forcefully about racial inequality in America. Positively influenced by the Black Lives Matter movement, black athletes have taken a more activist role in publicizing and trying to combat racially discriminatory practices that have ripped at the heart of the black community and America more generally. It is reminiscent of an era in which black athletes took more controversial stands against racial inequality by giving black-gloved salutes, speaking out, and confronting the institution in which they plied their trade and earned their living.

CHAPTER ONE

~

Establishing the
Boundaries of Sport

Slavery's Lasting Legacy

Slavery was a cruel and inhumane institution. Although varying to a degree by the temperament of the plantation owner and the types of jobs the slaves performed, slaves labored long hours, were often separated from family and other loved ones, and suffered from both physical and emotional abuse. In spite of these conditions, slaves adopted various survival mechanisms, including participation in different types of activities that can clearly be classified as a combination of recreation and sport. During holidays, Sundays, weekday evenings, and other periods when they were freed from their regular labor, slaves complemented their housekeeping and other personal chores with participation in leisure pursuits and recreation and sports that helped cement familial relationships with other slaves and provided opportunities to exhibit individual physical prowess, enjoy the pleasures of games and athletic contests, and realize a much needed sense of agency in an inherently restrictive environment. Although never able to completely escape the dictates of planters and overseers who controlled all aspects of plantation life, these activities were both a physical escape and part of a broader slave culture that was necessary for survival.

The recreation and sports of slaves were offset by others that were more closely intertwined with the particular interests of their owner, type of work done on the plantation, and geographical location. Slaves regularly engaged in such traditional communal activities as corn shuckings, log rollings, hog killings, quilting bees, and cotton pickings. In an effort to increase the productivity of their slaves while also undoubtedly realizing satisfaction through a sense of accomplishing selfless service, plantation owners fashioned these occasions as grand social gatherings that typically included different material incentives, lavish dinners, and all night dances. There is little doubt that the strategy helped offset the physical exertion that was required during these occasions. These activities were most meaningful to slaves, however, because it provided them an opportunity to express their distinctive performance style and communicate in a manner that empowered them.

The more physically talented and trusted slaves were also participants in the sporting life of the planter. A class of men who as a group were lovers of various types of sports, planters utilized slaves in an assortment of different ways in their own recreation and sports activities. It is clear that these slaves held a privileged position in the plantation community, different from ordinary field hands and even house slaves in that they typically had more freedom of movement and special opportunities and closer relationships with their owners. They were also able, in spite of never being capable of exerting complete control over the activities they participated in, to exhibit their physical skills in front of large audiences and realize material benefits from their performances. A select few earned their freedom as a result of their good behavior and athletic successes.

Learning Slavery through Play

Slave children experienced periods of leisure and had opportunities to participate in a number of play activities. Prior to assuming agricultural, domestic, or industrial jobs that probably took place after the age of ten, slave children created a world of play apart from the time they spent nurturing those younger than themselves and performing such tasks as carrying water to field hands, cleaning up yards, fetching wood, and tending the family garden. This world had educational implications for slave children and helped them develop physically, emotionally, and socially within a larger plantation community that was based on white power and control. Although they were not able to physically escape this environment, the play of slave children provided opportunities to explore the world around them, discover their particular strengths and weaknesses, and nurture relationships with other children and their own families. Play was also essential to slave children in that it was a means to learn the values and mores of their parents' world, preserve cultural traits from one generation to the next, and liquidate some of their problems by dramatizing those things that troubled them.[1]

Slave children typically had opportunities to visit their peers on neighboring plantations. The slave children on smaller plantations were particularly excited to make these excursions since it was often the only chance they had to play with children of their own age group. Parents typically allowed their children to take these trips as long as they returned before nightfall.

Older boys—and less often girls—relished the chance to contribute foodstuff to their family's table by hunting and fishing with their fathers during evening hours, on Sundays, and during holiday periods. Being able to augment their family's diet through the trapping of small game and catching fish in local streams provided slave children with a great deal of satisfaction and sense of self-worth. These excursions had the added benefit of providing slave children and their fathers an opportunity to enjoy much needed feelings of camaraderie and excitement of participation in common pursuits. Working long hours and having limited opportunities to contribute to the welfare of their families, slave men found these activities especially significant because it gave them a chance to establish bonds with their children while at once teaching them how to hunt and fish.

Slave children participated in a variety of both traditional games passed down from the older to younger children and those improvised on the spot. Very popular among slave children were ring games and dances as well as role-playing and reenacting those events that were most significant to them. Ring games or ring dances, particularly among slave girls, are repeatedly mentioned in the slave narratives. Accompanied by different songs and riddles, the general procedure in these activities was to draw a ring on the ground ranging anywhere from fifteen to thirty feet in diameter, depending on the number of children participating in the game. The players congregated in the ring and danced to various rhythmic clapping. Like the dances among older slaves, during these games slave children often berated whites in song or commented on their particular fears and anxieties.

Role-playing and reenactment of events provide important insights into the lives of slave children and their view of the world. They engaged in representative play that had special meaning to them such as simulated funerals, church activities, and slave auctions. Another representational activity that was sometimes played by slave children was variations of "hiding the switch." In this activity the players hunt for a switch that has been hidden by one of the children. Whoever finds the switch runs after the other children attempting to hit them.

There are differences of opinion among scholars as to what purpose this game served slave children. Thomas Webber, a specialist on education in the slave community, believes the game was a means through which slave children coped with their fear of whippings. Besides participating in the game merely for the excitement and adrenaline rush it provided, slave children who had witnessed the flogging of their parents could certainly be expected to engage in hiding the switch if it assisted them in lessening their fears. Physically reenacting whippings allowed slave children to deal with the terrifying nature of this event through an exploration of their innermost feelings and emotions. American studies scholar Bernard Mergen disagrees with this theory, noting that Arawak Indians in Guiana as well as white children in the United States and Europe played a similar type of game variously referred to as "hide the switch," "rap jacket," and "daddy wacker."[2]

Irrespective of the meaning behind their role-playing, slave children complemented it with a number of more traditional games. Numerous sources indicate that slave children played baseball, marbles, and prisoner's base. It is not easy to assess the nature of some of these games because of limited information regarding rules and methods for determining outcomes, but the evidence is clear that slave children took every opportunity to organize them out of the sense of enjoyment and feelings of satisfaction that resulted. Slave narratives, particularly those completed by the Federal Writers Project, and visitors' travel accounts often mention the playing of baseball. Whether the ballgames mentioned were baseball in the form we know today or some other modification of the older sports of rounders or townball is impossible to determine with any certainty.[3]

Marbles—and apparently to a lesser extent prisoner's base—challenged baseball for popularity among slave children. Marbles was extraordinarily popular among slave children, a game that required little equipment and could be arranged any time two children came together who wanted to test their shooting skills. Prisoner's base, a recreational activity mentioned in some of the earliest books on the history of sports and pastimes, was a running and chasing game without a ball that slave children participated in with great enthusiasm. Slave children evidently played marbles and prisoner's base on the Mount Vernon plantation owned by our first president, George Washington. In 1984 archaeologists discovered clay marbles in the cellar of a two-structure dwelling that housed slaves on Washington's plantation. Julian Ursyn Niemcewicz, a polish visitor to the plantation, described seeing a team activity among some thirty slaves in the summer of 1798. Calling it "prisoner's base," he noted that the slaves were divided into two groups and engaged in an activity that consisted of "jumps and gambols as if they (slaves) had rested all week."[4]

Slave children complemented their participation in baseball, marbles, and prisoner's base with impromptu contests that tested their physical prowess. They delighted in determining who could run the fastest, jump the highest, throw the farthest, and swim with the greatest speed. This spirit of competition does not appear to have spilled over into combative activities or games that required the elimination of players. Although there are some examples in the slave narratives of boxing and wrestling and games excluding players, children in the slave quarter seemingly did their best to avoid these activities. Despite any personal animosities and jealousies that slave children might have had toward one another, they were similar to their parents in that they recognized themselves as a familial group with common problems and concerns that precluded physically harming one another or leaving peer group members out of any activities. Although physical abuse on southern plantations was common as was the separation of family members, these practices were not represented in the play world of slave children. Historian Wilma King suggests that slave children were probably more likely to take out their frustrations and aggressions by "playing the dozens" rather than physically fighting one another. A verbal contest with deep roots in African American folklore, slave boys and less likely the girls, disparaged each other's family members with taunts as group members looked on. The essence of the contest was to publicly display the ability to quickly respond to insults with more witty and sharper retorts than one's adversary.[5]

Tellingly, slave children played with white children on the plantation as well as their own peer group. There is little question that plantation owners placed restrictions on the movements of their offspring and whom they associated with, but white and slave children participated in some of the same games and played together with apparently some degree of harmony. White children of the plantation often sought the companionship of slave children their own age and enjoyed the opportunity to play with them in a variety of different games and recreation.

Much of the leisure time of slave and white children were spent getting into mischief and helping each other out of difficult situations. In addition to playing games together, they roamed the plantation and its environs participating in such activities as fishing, hunting, and swimming. The mutual involvement in these activities fostered, on occasion, close relationships, if not genuine friendships, among white and slave children on southern plantations.

This does not obscure the fact that slave children, particularly as they grew older, understood very well their subservient position in the plantation community and the many disadvantages they faced compared to their white playmates. They were reminded of this on an almost daily basis by the differences in their recreation and sports equipment from those of the white children in the plantation community. While white children had the means to purchase toys and equipment, slave children typically either made their own playthings, obtained toys crafted by their parents, or acquired toys that the white children on the plantation no longer found usable. Slave children were also reminded of their subservient position because of the caste system that was sometimes evident in the representative play they participated in with white children. Candis Goodwin, a former slave from Virginia, recalled that when the Civil War started, the children on the plantation would play "Yankees" and "Federates" with the white boys taking the role of the "Federates." The white boys, noted Goodwin, would "take us black boys prisoners" and threaten to "cut our necks off; guess dey got dat fom dere fathers."[6]

Shadow of the Slave Quarter

The lives of slave children changed significantly once they became old enough to assume the routinized labor essential for the efficient running of the plantation. No longer able to roam the plantation and engage in an assortment of play activities free from the constant surveillance of the plantation owner and overseer, they now entered a world that was generally more circumscribed and laborious. Notwithstanding the differing lifestyles of slaves living in urban settings or those working under the task system in the low country of South Carolina and Georgia or those with highly specialized skills, the majority of adult slaves were destined for an existence that was decidedly routine and prescriptive in nature. It is for this reason that time off from work—weekday evenings, Sundays, and holidays—was extremely important for slaves because it gave them an opportunity to socialize with one another and participate in a number of recreational activities. Although there is much truth that plantation owners granted leisure time in order to ensure a level of contentment, a more productive worker and perhaps even more compliant slave, those moments free from labor were looked forward to by slaves with much anticipation and excitement. It is difficult to dispute Frederick Douglass's contention that the Christmas holidays were utilized by slaveholders as "safety-valves" and a means "to secure the ends of injustice and oppression," but also difficult to deny is that these holidays and other times off from labor were extraordinarily important because it allowed slaves to engage in leisure and recreational pursuits that fostered both individual autonomy and group cohesion.[7]

The physical and emotional demands of routine labor did not necessarily preclude slaves from participating in many of the recreational activities they had engaged in as children. The younger adult slaves in particular continued to engage in traditional games and contests that tested their physical skills. Like all people, however, the advancement in age typically meant a different style and pattern of leisure and recreation among slaves. Much of the difficulty in assessing their style and pattern of leisure and recreation though has to do with what constitutes play and what constitutes work. So many of their recreational activities seemed to result from a mix of intrinsic motivation most often associated with play and extrinsic motivation most often associated with work and survival.

Hunting and fishing provide a good example of this as these sporting activities were regularly pursued by slaves—particularly the men—for both pure pleasure and a way to gather food necessary to supplement their diet. Slave fathers also found hunting and fishing especially satisfying because it gave them an opportunity to bond with their children and teach them the intricacies of the two activities while at once realizing a much needed sense of autonomy.

Although severe laws were passed in the southern states to prevent slaves from hunting, some planters allowed their more trusted slaves to pursue game and use their guns and dogs, particularly if they stood to profit from the kills. Even when not granted permission to pursue game, slaves organized clandestine nightly hunting excursions when the planter and his family had retired for the evening and were out of earshot of the activities. Like so many recreational activities in the slave quarter community, these unauthorized hunting excursions brought particular satisfaction because they required much ingenuity and the mapping of strategy in the face of potentially dangerous consequences. Of the different types of hunting, slaves seemingly loved nothing more than raccoon and possum chases. They also became highly skilled at trapping squirrels, rabbits, and other small animals.

Slaves complemented their hunting excursions with fishing trips. Like hunting, laws were passed to prevent slaves from fishing, but the majority of plantation owners did not prevent them from pursuing the activity since no guns were involved and they often partook from and even paid for the catch. Slaves caught a variety of different fish, the most popular probably being the catfish, and utilized a number of different ways to catch them, including trot lines, nets, baskets, hooks, and seines. These methods were preferred by slaves since they required little time to maintain and did not interfere with their daily labors.

While hunting and fishing provided slaves with important forms of recreation, rural customs linked with the types of work done on the plantation provided another. Quilting bees, log rollings, hog killings, cotton pickings, and corn shuckings were significant cultural events that were looked forward to by slaves with great anticipation and excitement. In an effort to increase the productivity of their slaves, and no doubt another means to convince themselves of their basic goodness and to assist in the maintenance of the plantation regime, slave owners structured these events as grand social gatherings which usually included material incentives, lavish dinners, and all-night dances. These events were important to slaves not only as opportunities to socialize with friends and relatives, but also because they provided them with a space to exert their individuality and become a more central and dominant presence in the plantation community. Slaves took advantage of these events to exhibit an aesthetic style that was heavily infused with African conceptions of movement and performance.

Of all the work-related recreational activities, perhaps none of them were as important to slaves and as culturally significant as corn shuckings. Folklorist Roger Abrahams makes the convincing argument that corn shuckings were symbiotic in nature in that it was a celebration in which white planters and slaves took advantage of each other. United in this singular and dramatic event, planters and slaves learned and benefited from one another while at once exhibiting their respective cultural forms and repertories. Within the context of the event, slaves engaged in a lively contest to determine who could shuck the most ears intermingled with songs and dances and oratorical style woven together with African American features. Planters, in turn, were so impressed with these expressive displays that they attempted to imitate them with varying degrees of success.[8]

Planters invited their neighbors to the corn shucking celebration and on the appointed evening slave gangs traveled to the site of the event carrying lighted torches and singing songs inspired by their African ancestors. They were typically provided liberal amounts of alcohol and helped prepare the dinner that followed the shucking. The corn shucking itself was a good-natured contest, a race between two companies of slaves headed by a "captain." Each "captain" seated himself on top of his pile of corn with his shuckers surrounding him and at a given signal everyone fervently began to shuck while singing various songs. The uncertainty of the outcome, convivial atmosphere, spirited nature of the competition, and ability to dictate the form and structure of the contest all contributed to the slave's enjoyment of corn shucking.

After the last piece of corn had been shucked, it was the custom for slaves to lift the host planter upon their shoulders and carry him to the big house where a lavish dinner and dance awaited them. This part of the celebration could not come soon enough for the slaves because they could spend the rest of the evening dancing in a style that was unique to them. From all indications, slaves loved to dance at almost any occasion, but not the more formalized and sedate minuets, schottishes, and European reels performed elsewhere. Although these are mentioned in slave narratives, the dances in the slave quarter closely mirrored African dancers in regard to methods and style. They were often performed from a flexed, fluid, bodily position with an emphasis on a propulsive swinging rhythm that animated the whole body. Their dances also emphasized satire, improvisation, and freedom of individual expression.

The dance in the slave quarter was often a test of physical prowess and a means of eliciting praise from one's peer group. Slaves took great joy in their ability to perform difficult movements and vicariously appreciate the skills of their fellow dancers. They also used their dances to satirize the cultural mannerisms of whites. Not having the freedom to voice their frustrations and innermost feelings because of the restrictive plantation environment, slaves took pleasure in temporarily reversing social roles and ridiculing the planter and his family and other whites through various dance forms. Shepard Edmonds recalled how the slaves in Tennessee would perform the "cakewalk": "It was generally on Sundays, when there was little work, that the slaves, both young and old would dress up in hand-me-down finery to do a high-kicking, prancing walk-around. They did a take-off on the high manners of the white folks in the 'big house,' but their masters, who gathered around to watch the fun, missed the point."[9] The *South Carolina Gazette* of 1772 described a slave dance on the outskirts of Charleston:

> "The entertainment was opened by the men copying the manners of their masters and the women those of their mistresses, and relating some highly curious anecdotes, to the inexpressible diversion of that company. Then they danced, betted, gamed, swore, quarreled, fought and did everything that the most modern accomplished gentlemen are not ashamed of. . . . Whenever or wherever such nocturnal rendezvous are made, may it not be concluded that their deliberations are never intended for the advantage of the white people?"[10]

Certainly one of the most popular and meaningful dances in the slave quarter was "juba." African in origin and sometimes mentioned in conjunction with the West Indies as a sacred dance, "juba" was originally a competitive game of skill. Two men stepped forward in a circle of dancers and exhibited their ability at the juba step—essentially an eccentric shuffle. At the same time, the men in the surrounding circle performed the same step before and after each performance of the two men in the center while clapping rhythmically and encouraging the participants with song and verse. In the South, it evolved into a dance called "patting juba," which was characterized by a special routine of slapping the hands, knees, thighs, and body in a rhythmic pattern accompanied by different songs.[11]

Several religious denominations in the South implored their slave congregations to give up the sinful practice of dancing. Some slaves even spoke of the inharmonious relationship between their love for dancing and simultaneous devotion to practical piety. For most slaves, however, dancing was simply too important to discontinue.

The same could also be said for many slaves in regard to their love for gambling. Even those owned by more devout planters, placed bets on everything from dice and card games to local horse races and cockfights. Most southern states by 1830 had passed legislation prohibiting the gambling of slaves, but the temperament of their masters as well as the economic and social circumstances of their community was more crucial in determining the extent to which slaves gambled. Slaves, with or without permission, joined whites in placing bets and rooting on their favorite racehorses. Although not always having a great deal of money to wager, they thoroughly enjoyed making their way to the track and gambling on racehorses, many of them which were trained, groomed, and ridden by fellow slaves.

Those slaves who lived closer to urban centers could satisfy their thirst for gambling, alcohol, and other forms of entertainment at taverns and private tippling houses. White tavern owners, intent on turning a profit and maintaining their business operation, circumvented the laws and ran the risk of suffering the wrath of authorities by opening their doors to slaves who were some of their best customers. Although not always having access to more elaborate types of recreation devices such as bowling alleys and billiard tables, slaves could turn to less expensive gaming activities and various blood sports in and around taverns.

Swimmers, Hunters, Pugilists, and "Race Horsemen"

Southern planters thoroughly enjoyed their leisure and as a group were avid and enthusiastic sportsmen. Slave owners throughout the South hunted and fished and gambled on everything from cockfights and boxing matches to card games and horse races. Often playing an integral role in these activities were the slaves themselves. Southern planters employed their slaves as oarsmen in local boat races, profited from their abilities as horse trainers, grooms, and jockeys, used their services during hunting and fishing excursions, and exploited their skills as swimmers, dancers, boxers, wrestlers, and runners. These slaves often held a privileged position in the plantation community and were granted certain rights usually reserved for free men and women. Possessing desired physical skills resulted in an elevated degree of status in the slave quarter while often leading to a more intimate relationship with the planter. Like many of today's athletes, ability in sport was sometimes the means to a more rewarding and satisfying way of life that included more freedom of movement and material benefits. In some cases, it earned slaves their freedom from bondage.

How slaves were used in the sporting life of planters is perhaps best illustrated in swimming, hunting, boxing, and horse racing. Even before their enslavement in America, West Africans had shown great skill in swimming and underwater diving. They would continue to do so as slaves in the New World. In what may come as a surprise to many because of the underrepresentation of blacks in the sport today and deep-seated stereotypical notions about their inability to float let alone move through water, slaves who lived near waterways, both children as well as adults, often exhibited extraordinary skills as swimmers and realized much satisfaction and a sense of enjoyment engaging in the activity with their family and friends. It was seemingly not uncommon for planters to organize competitions among their best swimmers with large amounts of money being wagered on the outcomes. It is also true that slaves were employed as underwater divers who, among other things, cleared riverbeds, helped in the harvesting of pearls, and salvaged cargo from shipwrecks. These slaves were valuable, and while their jobs as divers was seasonal, which often meant they were forced to assume regular plantation work when not engaging in it, their unique skills allowed them to exact some favors from planters and realize a life less burdened than that experienced by their contemporaries.

Hunting had deep roots in southern culture and no group was more passionate about it than plantation owners. Before the sport adopted its more modern trappings in regard to detailed rules and game commissions, southern planters roamed the open fields and woods searching for deer and other animals to kill. Slaves often played an integral role in these hunting excursions, assisting their masters in the search for game. One of their primary responsibilities was the training and handling of dogs used in the hunt for larger animals. The slave narratives are replete with stories of men who trained and cared for the dogs used by their owners for hunting.

In addition to using their slaves to pursue game, some planters pitted their slaves in boxing matches. Although there are questions as to how frequent and popular they were and what purpose they served, these matches did take place on southern plantations. Not unexpectedly, in a culture that placed such a premium on honor, as evidenced by the popularity of eye-gouging contests in the backcountry and dueling matches among the elite, many planters were enthralled with boxing and it was reflected in the exploitation of their stronger and more physically gifted slaves as pugilists. The boxing matches between slaves, like so much of the recreational and sporting life on southern plantations, took place during holiday and seasonal work celebrations when more people were available to watch and place bets on the contests.

By most accounts, the first two notable black boxers in America had their start as slave pugilists. Bill Richmond and Tom Molineaux were outstanding black boxers at the turn of the nineteenth century before the sport had become a national pastime in America. This is why our information about the two boxers comes from English rather than American sources. Notwithstanding, Richmond and Molineaux established the precedent for other outstanding black boxers in America by traveling overseas to seek fame and fortune. The two men became important transnational figures who led transitory lives that frequently intermingled with nomadic laborers, sailors, and performers of all types.

Bill Richmond was born as either a free man or slave in either 1763 or 1765 in Cuckold's Town (now Richmondtown) on Staten Island, New York. On some unspecified date, General Hugh Percy, who was in charge of British forces during the War of Independence, took Richmond as his servant and brought him to England where he first became an apprentice cabinetmaker. Recognizing his enormous physical skills following an insult-induced fight with the soldier Docky Moore, Richmond sought out professional bouts against some of England's most famous pugilists. Richmond, who ultimately became known as "The Black Terror," established his reputation as an outstanding boxer in 1805 when he defeated the Jewish fighter known as "Fighting Youssep." He followed the bout with a twenty-six-round victory over Jack Holmes that, in turn, set him up for a match with the celebrated Tom Crib. He lost to the much younger Crib in twenty-five grueling rounds and then defeated Jack Carter and George Maddox, among others, before retiring from the ring in 1809. After retirement, Richmond married and bought and operated the Horse and Dolphin Tavern where he trained boxers.

Richmond's most famous pupil was Tom Molineaux. Legend has it that Molineaux was born a slave in either Virginia or Maryland in 1784 and was granted his freedom after winning money for his owner in boxing matches. As much as one would like to believe this story, the sources do not indicate whether Molineaux was born a freeman or slave. What we do know is that at some point Molineaux found his way to New York City where he labored as a dock worker and porter while also participating in informal boxing matches with fellow workers and visiting seamen. In 1809, he sailed to England to seek out matches with the world's greatest pugilists. After honing his skills under the tutelage of Richmond, Molineaux fought Tom Crib in 1810 for the world championship at Shenington Hollow in Oxfordshire. Unfortunately, he lost to Crib in a controversial bout in the thirty-fifth round. In the return bout the following year at Thistleton Gap, Molineaux was knocked out in the eleventh round. Molineaux continued to fight until 1815 but, like many pugilists through the years, suffered after his retirement from the ring. Following time in a debtor's prison, he continued to drink excessively and died penniless in

Figure 1.1. Tom Molineaux, one of the first great African American sports heroes, ca. 1810.
Courtesy of National Portrait Gallery, Smithsonian Institution.

Galway, Ireland, before reaching the age of thirty-five. Tellingly, Molineaux's life continues to fascinate people as evidenced by the amount of coverage he has received in articles and books on boxing. The well-known and prolific Scottish author George MacDonald Fraser even wrote a historical novel based on Molineaux's life titled *Black Ajax*.

Besides boxing, slaves served their masters as trainers, groomers, and jockeys in horse racing, America's first national spectator sport. Enthusiastic about the breeding of horses and racing, planters were avid turf men who depended on the specialized skills and expertise of slaves in their efforts to achieve success in a sport that would draw an increasing number of fans and was intently followed by all stratums of society. Those slaves who worked as trainers, groomers, and jockeys, although largely objectified, often not even given the respect of a surname, and according to historian Katherine C. Mooney, important in maintaining the white planter's notion of hierarchical order and human servitude, held a privileged position in the plantation

Figure 1.2. Painting of the horse Tobacconist with slave trainer and jockey. Courtesy of Virginia Museum of Fine Arts, Richmond. Paul Mellon Collection.
Photo: Katherine Wetzel © Virginia Museum of Fine Arts.

community and were treated with some care by their owners who wanted to ensure the health of one of their most important commodities. Freed from the arduous labor performed by field hands, these slaves typically had a closer relationship with their owners, traveled the South without being under constant surveillance, and were sometimes paid and granted freedom for their services. The memories of some of these slaves have been preserved through the paintings of Swiss-born Edward Troye and less well-known artists who were commissioned to depict famous thoroughbreds and their handlers.

The lives and careers of slave horsemen can perhaps be best illustrated through the stories of Austin Curtis, Hark, and Charles Stewart. Curtis, referred to by writer Edward Hotaling as "America's first truly great professional athlete," was a highly skilled trainer, groomer, and jockey who helped manage the racing stable of Willie Jones in Roanoke, Virginia. Curtis's connection to Jones was seemingly less a master and slave relationship than a business arrangement in which Curtis was allowed freedom of movement, some control over his own time, and opportunities to make his own decisions because of his expertise and knowledge of horse racing. In 1791, because of "his fidelity to his master" and "honesty and good behavior on all occasions," Jones officially freed Curtis.[12]

Hark, a highly skilled slave who worked as a trainer at different times for both well-known Virginia bloodstock importer A. T. B. Merritt and the famous South Carolina cotton planter and horseman Richard Singleton, traveled freely without anyone being overly concerned about his whereabouts. He received relatively large sums for travel expenses, sometimes received a share of the winning purse and perhaps even money from bettors who had experienced a good day at the races, and on at least one occasion an exchange of fifty dollars a month was offered between two horsemen for his services. A celebrity whose talents and intelligence were praised in the sporting press, Hark's importance was made clear by Merritt's refusal to send him to South Carolina Lowcountry during the malaria season. While ordinary field hands continued to toil on plantations in the area, Hark was simply too valuable to live in a part of the world during a time when disease was so rampant.

Charles Stewart was one of the great slave horsemen who provided a firsthand account of his life and career. In his "My Life as a Slave" from the autumn 1884 issue of *Harper's New Monthly Magazine*, Stewart details in the dialect-laden language of transcriber Annie Porter the privileges he enjoyed first as a groom then later jockey, trainer, and stable foreman. Owned initially by Virginia's William Ransom Johnson and then Alexander Porter (Annie's uncle) of Louisiana, Stewart, like Austin Curtis and Hark, traveled freely and was paid hundreds of dollars for his services. Part of the racing team that prepared Henry for the famous 1823 North-South match race against Eclipse, Stewart had control of Johnson's stable of horses in Paris, Kentucky, and then beginning in 1841 Porter's horses on his estate in St. Mary Parish in Louisiana.[13]

The privileged careers of Curtis, Hark, and Stewart should not obscure the complex nature of horse racing and the slave system. Historian Katherine C. Mooney persuasively argues that slave horsemen, while realizing some authority, freedom of movement, and autonomy, understood the fragility of their privileged positions and confronted pressures not faced by ordinary field hands and most others held in bondage. Ultimately, slave horsemen were involved in a line of work controlled by whites who viewed the racetrack as a means to maintain a plantation system based on the belief in subordination and human servitude. In many ways, this view was also true regarding the careers of slave swimmers, hunters, boxers and so many other skilled athletic bondsmen in the plantation community. Planters valued the talents of their skilled athletic bondsmen and integrated them into a sporting world in which whites continued to exert their power and control while holding tight to deep-seated stereotypical notions regarding racial differences and inherent physical and mental capabilities of men. This pattern, in which talented black men displayed their athletic skills in a sporting world largely controlled by whites, would continue following emancipation and throughout the first half of the twentieth century and beyond. Exceptions to this were the separate or parallel all-black sporting organizations that sprang up at various levels of competition in the nineteenth century as a result of continuing racial segregation and discrimination in America.

CHAPTER TWO

～

Freedom to Participate on an Unlevel Playing Field

The official end of slavery in 1865 would have a decided effect and result in many changes in America. No one was more dramatically affected than freed slaves. Having lived through the rigors of slavery and been nothing more than human property, they could now search for family and other loved ones who had been sold away and seek out employment that would hopefully lead to financial independence, a happier and more meaningful existence, and full citizenship. Unfortunately, the freed slaves were thwarted in their efforts as southern states passed legislation, commonly known as the Black Codes, which denied them opportunities to conduct business, own property, the right to bear arms, vote, and move freely through public spaces. The legal restrictions encountered by freed slaves were complemented by a host of unwritten rules that circumscribed their dealings with whites and violent acts committed against them that resulted in serious injuries and sometimes death. Some of the more violent acts committed against them came at the hands of the Ku Klux Klan (KKK), a white supremacist group originally founded in 1865 by a group of ex-confederate soldiers in Pulaski, Tennessee. Eventually spreading to other southern states and different locations in the North, the KKK, which would go through periods of decline and revival, evolved into a group that spewed hatred and intimidated not just blacks, but also immigrants, Catholics, Jews, and organized labor.

In spite of these conditions, freed slaves, along with blacks from the North and South who had never experienced slavery, became involved in a number of sports at various levels of competition during the latter half of the nineteenth and early part of the twentieth centuries when sport was evolving from a more informal, less organized activity to a more highly structured and organized phenomenon. In urban settings, where this transformation of sport largely took place, blacks boxed and taught the techniques of pugilism in gymnasiums they owned, founded athletic clubs and Young Men's Christian Associations (YMCAs), organized baseball and basketball teams, and participated in billiards, golf, tennis, pedestrianism, blood sports, horse racing, and bicycling, among other sports.

A select number of outstanding African American athletes realized success in predominantly white organized sport at the amateur and professional levels of competition during this period, garnering national and sometimes international acclaim for their exploits. Talented black athletes, most of them from middle-class families that placed much emphasis on the importance of education, were competing in intercollegiate athletics at some of the most prestigious predominantly white universities in the North. Included among this select group were such outstanding athletes as William Henry Lewis of both Amherst College and Harvard University, George Poage of the University of Wisconsin, John Baxter Taylor of the University of Pennsylvania, Fritz Pollard of Brown University, and Paul Robeson of Rutgers University. At the professional level of sport, Boston's Frank "Black Dan" Hart established himself as one of the greatest pedestrians of the period; Moses "Fleetwood" Walker became the first African American in Major League Baseball (MLB) by playing with the Toledo Mudhens of the American Association; Indianapolis native Marshall "Major" Taylor was one of the outstanding bicycle racers of his era; Isaac Murphy, Jimmy Winkfield, and a host of other jockeys captured many of horse racing's most prestigious events; and such famous boxers as George "Little Chocolate" Dixon, Peter Jackson, and Jack Johnson became champion pugilists.

Unfortunately, by the latter stages of the nineteenth century, many African American athletes were excluded from various levels of white organized sport. It resulted from a combination of factors, including the general deterioration of black rights resulting from the Republican Party's decreasing commitment to African Americans and a number of Supreme Court decisions that legally sanctioned segregation based on race. The response of some African American athletes eliminated from predominantly white organized sport was to travel outside the United States to continue their careers, while others joined previously organized all-black teams or formed their own. Although difficult to discern a specific pattern of exclusion of African

American athletes at this time, it is evident they continued to find some success, albeit while enduring various forms of racial discrimination, in predominantly white college sport, the Olympic Games, and boxing. This was due, in part, to the perceived nature and ability levels of African American athletes as well as the quest for national and international prestige.

Professors of Pugilism and Sports Clubs

Historian Louis Moore provides important details on those African Americans who became integral to the physical culture movement in the early to middle years of the nineteenth century. Noting that scholars of the physical culture movement have traditionally focused on just whites, Moore makes clear that African American men were equally concerned about the lack of good health and exercise and set up gymnasiums where sparring and the teaching of boxing techniques were often central components of the curriculum. Three men that Moore has profiled were Joseph Battis, Paton Stewart, and Aaron Molineaux Hewlett. Battis, who owned a barbershop in Philadelphia, supplemented his salary during the 1830s and 1840s by giving boxing lessons to white clients and putting on exhibitions at the advertised "sparring school" attached to his place of business and other venues throughout the city. Careful to point out he was not a paid prizefighter but a sparring master who could teach gentlemen the art of self-defense, Battis gained a solid reputation for his technical skills and influenced others, including the Baltimore physical culture specialist John B. Bailey, who were interested in learning the intricacies of the sport. Unfortunately, Battis was not able to take full advantage of the increased interest in sparring since he fell out of favor with whites who were angered, among other things, by his association with white women.[1]

Stewart was one of the most influential physical culture specialists and sparring masters in Boston during the 1850s. Owner of his own gymnasium, first on Franklin Street and then later on Boylston Street, Stewart had a flourishing business that catered to some five hundred members that could take part in sparring, calisthenics, gymnastics, and fencing. Stewart, who had such prominent clients as Judge Oliver Wendell Holmes, Boston Mayor J. V. C. Smith, and Massachusetts Governor Henry J. Gardner, offered training at different times for women as well as men with one of his female instructors being his daughter Emma. In 1865 Stewart moved to San Francisco where he first opened the "Boston Gymnasium" and then became head instructor of the new YMCA gymnasium. Hewlett, by whatever measures are used, had an extraordinary career as a sparring master and physical culture specialist. A great boxer and all-around athlete, the first mention of him is in Brooklyn, New York, where he established at his own residence in 1854 a sparring academy called "Molineaux House." The following year he opened a gymnasium in Worcester, Massachusetts, and then in 1859 was hired as the physical education instructor at Harvard University. This was two years prior to Amherst College's hiring of Edward Hitchcock, the Harvard medical school graduate often referred to as the "father of college physical education." Hewlett instructed Harvard students in a variety of activities, including boxing, baseball, rowing, and gymnastics. He also opened up with his wife, an outstanding gymnast in her own right, a prominent gymnasium and was a trustee of a local real estate company and co-owner of a secondhand clothing store. He continued to be involved in these diverse activities until his death in 1871.

Privately owned gymnasiums operated by sparring masters and physical culturists would increasingly face stiff competition for membership from those YMCAs being established across the country by African Americans. Unable to gain membership in other YMCAs, African Americans established their own branches that, by the 1890s, were focused on Christian manliness that emphasized the development of "mind, body, and spirit" through programs in sport, physical education, and religious and moral development. Anthony Bowen, a former slave and the first African American to clerk in the US Patent Office, established the first separate branch of the YMCA in Washington, D.C. Initially titled the "YMCA for Colored Men and Boys" but more popularly referred to as the Twelve Street YMCA because of its location, the programs offered by the branch were enthusiastically embraced by the local African American community. Other separate branches would be established in the latter stages of the following decade in Charleston, South Carolina; Harrisburg, Pennsylvania; Philadelphia; and New York City.

Like their white counterparts, the sport of basketball came to dominate most of the YMCAs established by African Americans. As a team game, it provided a perfect opportunity to teach such concepts as cooperation, teamwork, loyalty, obedience, and self-sacrifice. The Twelve Street YMCA had one of the earliest and most successful basketball teams during the opening decade of the twentieth century. The team went undefeated during the 1909–1910 season, including a victory over the powerful Smart Set Club from Brooklyn, New York. Its success was largely due to the efforts of Edwin Bancroft Henderson, the highly respected civil rights activist and historian of the African American athlete who for many years directed the health and physical education programs in the segregated public schools in Washington, D.C. In 1904, 1905, and 1907 Henderson, a graduate of the famous M Street School (now Dunbar), attended the Dudley Allen Sargent directed

Figure 2.5.   Hampton University women playing the relatively new game of basketball, ca. 1905.
Courtesy of Hampton University Archives.

Harvard Summer School of Physical Education where he was introduced to, among other things, the relatively new game of basketball that had been founded by James Naismith at the YMCA Training School in Springfield, Massachusetts, just a few years earlier. He fell in love with the sport and at some point began to teach the techniques of basketball to African Americans in his hometown while playing and directing the hoop squads for both the Twelve Street YMCA and Howard University. Henderson also incorporated basketball, along with such other sports as swimming, soccer, and track and field, into the program of the Inter-Scholastic Athletic Association of Middle Atlantic States, an organization he established in 1906 to promote competition among African Americans at both the high school and college levels.

While the black community obviously embraced basketball, it was baseball that drew an extraordinary amount of attention from African Americans throughout the latter half of the nineteenth and early part of the twentieth centuries. This is made clear by the hundreds of amateur baseball clubs established by African Americans beginning in the 1860s. Seemingly everywhere African Americans congregated or lived, amateur baseball teams were formed and competitions ensued in the sport historian Ronald Story claims would become a mass cultural movement in the latter half of the nineteenth century and the sport loved above all others in the United States. Richmond had its Reindeer baseball club; Washington, D.C., had its Alert and Mutual baseball clubs; Philadelphia had its Excelsior, L'Overture, and Pythian baseball clubs; and New Orleans had its Boston, Pickwick, Orleans, Dumonts, Aetnas, Unions, and Fischers baseball clubs. Black baseball clubs in cities as diverse as Rockford (IL), New York City, Pittsburgh, Niagara Falls, Chicago, Boston, Baltimore, Camden (NJ), and Carlisle (PA) were also organized, some for just a year at most and some on a more permanent basis. The games played by black clubs were sometimes accompanied by brass bands, festive pregame activities, and lavish meals afterward. Before the racial lines began to harden in the late 1870s, black clubs sometimes played against white clubs in relative harmony, although the white clubs probably determined the time and location and ground rules of the contests.

Perhaps the most notable of the early black amateur baseball clubs, and certainly the most written about and examined by historians, were the Philadelphia Pythians. The club was organized and led by two prominent black Philadelphia men by the names of Octavius Catto and Jacob C. White Jr. Catto, the son of a Presbyterian minister and graduate and later teacher at the Institute for Colored Youth which was the forerunner of Cheyney University, was a lifelong civil rights activist and outspoken critic of racial inequality and discrimination. He was also reputed to be an excellent cricket and baseball player. White was one of ten children born to seamstress Elizabeth Miller White and Jacob Clement White Sr., a highly successful and wealthy dentist, barber, and businessman. He was also a graduate of the Institute for Colored Youth, was the principal for twenty years at the historic Robert Vaux School, and was deeply involved in such organizations as the Pennsylvania State Equal Rights League, Pennsylvania Society for Promoting the Abolition of Slavery, and the Relief of Free Negroes.

Catto, White, and other members of the team adhered to an organizational structure that resembled, according to one historian of the Pythians, the mutual aids societies that sprang up during the 1840s and 1850s. With an eye toward gaining acceptance into American society while at once exhibiting evidence of self-determination, the Pythians elected officers, established bylaws, and were guided by a constitution. Similar to white clubs, the Pythians sent out written invitations to clubs they wished to play that typically requested a two-game "home and away" series. If accepted, Catto, as team captain, would work closely with his counterpart on the other team to select an umpire and to ensure that the press was aware of the upcoming contest.

At the end of a contest, a prize was awarded to the team that won, speeches were made by representatives from both clubs, and players were rewarded for their efforts with a lavish dinner and other festivities.

The Pythians were highly successful on the field, but faced challenges experienced by other separate black clubs in and outside of baseball. One of the challenges they would always encounter—and this would be the case throughout the history of black baseball—was finding an adequate field in which to play their games. For a time, they were able to share the facilities of the white Philadelphia Athletics. An even bigger challenge for the Pythians was finding their way into the higher echelons of organized baseball. In 1858 the four oldest white clubs in New York would form the National Association of Base Ball Players (NABBP), the first important central organization in the sport that would remain in existence for thirteen years. Although not always the most effective of sport organizations, it had more than sixty clubs as members at the start of the Civil War and eventually would exercise its control through state associations.

This would be crucial to the Pythians who sought membership in the NABBP by way of the Pennsylvania Association of Amateur Base Ball Players (PAABBP). On October 16, 1867, the Pythians, through its delegate Raymond Burr, sought membership in the PAABBP at its convention in Harrisburg, Pennsylvania. While some in the organization expressed sympathy for the Pythians, the delegates simply ignored the request for membership and Burr, recognizing the futility of the situation, chose to rescind the black club's application at the convention's evening session. Two months later at the NABBP national convention, the delegates made clear their feelings by adopting a formal resolution excluding black players from membership in the organization. The historical record provides no evidence as to whether the Pythians made another attempt to join the NABBP prior to disbanding in 1872.

The Pythians' quest for membership in the NABBP coincided with the increased commercialization of black baseball clubs and their eventual movement toward professional status characterized by salaried players, recruiting, gate receipts, and barnstorming tours. These clubs were loosely organized by today's standards with seemingly little permanence as evidenced by players moving from one team to another in search of material benefits and special privileges and better treatment. These clubs also began what would become a long tradition among African American teams in a number of sports in that they took extended trips outside the confines of their own home to seek competition. Although at this point still considering themselves an amateur club, the Mutuals of Washington, D.C., for instance, traveled in 1870 to

Maryland and New York to play other black clubs. Characterized by the press as "the most extensive trip that any colored club has ever undertaken," the Mutuals first played in Baltimore where they defeated the Enterprise Club and then beat the Artic Club in Lockport, New York, Rapids Club in Niagara Falls, the Mutuals (another club by the same name) in Buffalo, and a club made up of star players from various nines in Rochester before returning to Washington, D.C.

The Mutuals and Pythians, like other black baseball clubs across the country, not only traveled some distances for their contests, but also occasionally played against whites. One of the most famous interracial contests took place in 1869 between the Pythians and Philadelphia's Olympic Base Ball Club. The game took place through the efforts of Thomas Fitzgerald, the publisher of the Philadelphia *City Item* newspaper, educational reformer, a founding member of the Philadelphia Athletics, and former president of the NABBP. In the summer of 1869, Fitzgerald began a vigorous campaign in the *City Item* in an effort to convince the white baseball clubs in Philadelphia to schedule games against the Pythians. He specifically targeted the Athletics, but the best and most famous team in the city refused to cross the color line and play the Pythians. Finally, the Olympic Club, while no longer competing at the highest levels, agreed to play the Pythians on September 3, 1869. Unfortunately for the Pythians, they lost to the Olympic Club, which was a bitter disappointment to Octavius Catto, who played in the contest, and was confirmation among some that African Americans lacked the skills necessary to play against whites.

The move toward commercialization, of course, would ultimately lead to the formation of black professional baseball clubs. By most accounts, the first black professional baseball club was the Cuban Giants, founded in 1885 at the Argyle Hotel in Babylon, Long Island, by headwaiter Frank P. Thompson in collaboration with S. K. "Cos" Govern, C. S. Massey, and John Lang. The Giants had a roster of great players, many of them originally from the Philadelphia Orions, Washington Manhattans, and Argyle Athletics, which were reflected in their many victories against both white and black teams. Two of their best players were pitcher Sheppard "Shep" Trusty from New Jersey and catcher Clarence Williams who was born in Harrisburg, Pennsylvania. For a time, they had the services of George Stovey, one of the best pitchers of his day who in 1887 would win thirty-three games for Newark in the International League. Future Hall of Fame selections Frank Grant and Sol White were at one time members of the Giants.

The Cuban Giants were a team willing to travel in search of competition. In the winter they entertained guests with their play at the Hotel Ponce de

Leon in St. Augustine, Florida, and became the first professional team to play outside the United States when they participated in a series of games in Havana, Cuba. No distance seemed to be too far as they barnstormed through Maryland, Michigan, Massachusetts, Illinois, Ohio, Connecticut, Pennsylvania, and Vermont, among other states. The majority of their games were against other black teams, but they did play some games against Major League clubs and predominantly white colleges. In their first year of operation, the Giants lost to the Major League New York Metropolitans and Philadelphia Athletics and over the 1887 and 1888 seasons had contests against such famous educational institutions as Princeton, Syracuse University, University of Pennsylvania, Williams College, Trinity College, Lafayette, Cornell, Yale, and Amherst College.

Importantly, while the Giants did play for a time in the Middle States League, Connecticut League, and Eastern Interstate League, they played the majority of their games as an independent club, believing it was in their financial interest to do so. It is also true that the leagues at the time were short-lived, unable to provide the structure and organization that could benefit individual teams and black baseball as a collective. Efforts to provide regional and national oversight to black baseball was unsuccessful as evidenced, for instance, by the failure to form the Southern League of Colored Base Ballists in 1886 and National League of Colored Baseball Players in 1887. Organizational structure in black baseball would not be realized until the second decade of the twentieth century.

Achieving Success at the Highest Levels of Competition

While the largest majority of African American athletes competed in sport among themselves during the latter half of the nineteenth century because of racially exclusionary policies, a select number found success in predominantly white organized sport. Through sheer determination and outstanding talent, and often with the help of white benefactors and being in the right place at the right time, a select number of elite African American athletes triumphed in predominantly white organized sport that resulted, in some cases, in much fame and material benefits. These successes, which took place over careers that varied from very brief to relatively lengthy ones, were most prominent in individual rather than team sports and intermixed with racial confrontations and discrimination. With the major exception of baseball, the popularity at the time of individual sports at the professional level of competition combined with difficulties in establishing team chemistry and dealing with logistical issues regarding travel and housing accommodations of integrated sports teams were partly responsible for African Americans participating in those pastimes in which their success was largely dependent on their own physical skills and competitive spirit rather than those of others.

At approximately the same time as the Cuban Giants and other black clubs were beginning to make their mark in what would become America's national pastime, a small number of outstanding African American players were finding their way onto teams at the highest levels of predominantly white organized baseball. Bud Fowler, born in Cooperstown, New York, the site of baseball's Hall of Fame and referred to by historian Jules Tygiel as the "first black professional baseball player," was an outstanding second baseman that, by most accounts, began his career on the diamond in 1872.[2] After playing with a club in Stillwater, Minnesota, in 1884; Keokuk in the Western League and a club in Pueblo, Colorado, in 1885; and Topeka, Kansas, in the Western League in 1886, Fowler signed a contract and played much of the 1887 season with Binghamton, New York, of the International League where he stole thirty bases and hit .350. Unfortunately, as would befall many African American athletes over time, Fowler was released before the season was over after several outstanding white players threatened that they would leave the league because of the "colored element." This ended Fowler's participation in white baseball and he spent the rest of his career back in black baseball where he formed the Page Fence Giants and All-American Black Tourists, two teams that combined great baseball with an equal amount of showmanship.

The career of Fowler, as important as it is to baseball history, was eclipsed in significance by the career of Moses "Fleetwood" Walker. His story, which has been told many times, is notable because he was the first black to play predominantly white college and MLB. Although not a great athlete, Walker played on the first baseball team at Oberlin College in 1881 and then on the baseball team at the University of Michigan in 1882 and 1883 while in law school at the well-known institution in Ann Arbor, Michigan. In 1884 he became the first black player in MLB when he played for the Toledo Mudhens of the American Association, which at that time had Major League status. His younger brother Weldy, who had also played at Oberlin College and the University of Michigan, signed with the Mudhens shortly thereafter to become the second black man to play MLB. The Mudhens disbanded after just one season and Moses went back to the minor leagues, playing in 1885 and 1886 with Waterbury, Connecticut, in the Eastern League before joining Newark, New Jersey, of the International League in 1887 where he played alongside George Stovey and against several other blacks in the integrated league. Walker experienced various forms of discrimination at the hands of Chicago White Sox manager Cap Anson and other white racists prior to finally leaving the game in 1890. His post-athletic career was turbulent in an assortment of different ways, including being charged with second degree murder after stabbing a man during a bar fight in Syracuse, New York, and spending a year in jail for mail fraud. Ultimately, Walker became involved in the "back to Africa movement," contending in his 1908 polemic *Our Home Colony* that the only solution to the race problem in America was the separation of blacks from whites.

Pedestrian Frank "Black Dan" Hart and bicyclist Marshall "Major" Taylor, while experiencing their own forms of racial discrimination, had longer and much more successful athletic careers than Walker's. Born in 1858 in Haiti with the given name Fred Hichborn, Hart immigrated to America in the 1870s and settled in Boston where he worked at a local grocery store while participating in the "six day go as you please" pedestrian races that had become so extraordinarily popular during this period in the United States and Great Britain. Eventually connecting with and financed by Irish immigrant and sports promoter Daniel O'Leary (thus the name "Black Dan"), Hart won many prestigious races in a sport requiring enormous physical endurance and mental toughness, two qualities that many claimed were lacking among black Americans. His most famous six-day race took place in 1880 when he smashed the world record by covering 565 miles on an indoor track in New York's famous Madison Square Garden.

Marshall "Major" Taylor enjoyed one of bicycle racing's outstanding careers during the latter stages of the nineteenth and early stages of the twentieth centuries. Born in Indianapolis, Indiana, in 1878 and eventually making his home in Worcester, Massachusetts, Taylor was a transnational figure who won many of bicycle racing's most important events in the United States and as far away as France and Australia. Managed, promoted, and guided by bicycle manufacturer Louis D. Munger, Taylor became a hero in Paris, a city where he experienced some of his greatest victories. The Parisians followed his every move, sought his autograph, invited him to various events, showered him with gifts, and rooted for him with unabated enthusiasm. Referred to by writer Robert Coquelle in the illustrated weekly magazine *La Vie au Grand Air* as "le negre volant" (the flying Negro), the Parisians were intrigued by the physical abilities of Taylor, so much so that doctors at the Academy of Sciences x-rayed and conducted anthropometric measurements on him in line with the racial stereotypes that ruled the day. The test determined that Taylor's thighs were slightly overdeveloped because of all his riding, but otherwise he was a "human masterpiece."[3] Unfortunately, like Moses

"Fleetwood" Walker, his post-athletic career was fraught with difficulties and disappointments. He was penniless and estranged from many of his family members at the time of his death in 1932.

One predominantly white organized sport that would continue to have a large number of outstanding African American athletes as participants was horse racing. Following in the tradition of Austin Curtis, Hark, Charles Stewart, Abe Hawkins, and other race horsemen, blacks would continue to be heavily involved as grooms, trainers, and jockeys following the Civil War. Of these men, jockeys would garner much press coverage and in some cases realize celebrity status, particularly after individuals in the sport, including bettors, began to attach more importance to those who rode the horses across the finish line. Black jockeys—while encountering discrimination, racialist thinking, and physical intimidation on the tracks—became part of the free enterprise system by signing legal contracts with wealthy owners and riding in horse racing's most famous events. In some cases, it meant the accumulation of great wealth and lasting recognition and fame.

Two black jockeys who fit squarely into this category were Isaac Murphy and Jimmy Winkfield. Murphy, born in Fayette County, Kentucky, in 1861, rode Salvator to victory in a famous 1890 match race against Tenny at Sheepshead Bay, captured four American Derby titles at Washington Park in Chicago, and won the Kentucky Derby in 1884, 1890, and 1891. Evidence of Murphy's greatness was made clear by the fact he was the first jockey inducted into the Hall of Fame at the National Museum of Racing in Saratoga Springs, New York, in 1955. Winkfield's career mixed important triumphs on the track with interesting life experiences and much travel in the United States and abroad. The youngest of seventeen children born to sharecroppers in Chilesburg, Kentucky, Winkfield captured the Kentucky Derby in 1901 and 1902 and reportedly won 2,600 races during his career. In 1904, supposedly after a falling out with an owner and in an effort to extend his career, Winkfield fled to Russia where he was victorious multiple times in both the Russian and Moscow derbies. When the Bolshevik Revolution broke out in 1917, Winkfield left for France where he raised, trained, and rode horses until his retirement in 1930. He returned to the United States for a short time during World War II when the Nazis took his farm, but eventually came back to France where he spent the rest of his life.

Unfortunately, by the time of Winkfield's Kentucky Derby triumphs in 1901 and 1902, horse racing was already experiencing a significant decline in the number of black trainers, grooms, and jockeys. Why this occurred has been debated with some regularity, but there seems little question that the disappearance of blacks from the horse-racing profession came about because

Figure 2.1. Issac Murphy, one of the most successful and famous jockeys of the late nineteenth century, ca. 1895.
Courtesy of Library of Congress Prints and Photographs Division. LC-USZ62-50261.

of the hardening of the racial lines and increasing segregation of African Americans from all walks of life. Whites took away jobs in the horse-racing profession previously held by blacks and then rationalized their actions along revolutionary lines and with a firm belief in their own superiority and the inevitability of their dominance in the sport. African Americans have never found their way back into horse racing in any significant numbers, now realizing success, and in some cases dominating, other sports.

Jackson, Johnson, and White College Sport

The rate, pattern, and degree of exclusion of African Americans from predominantly white organized sport was largely dependent on the status and prominence of the sport in question as well as the context in which they were held. While MLB had closed its door on African Americans and horse racing was in the process of doing the same, blacks would continue to fight at the upper levels of boxing, participate to a limited extent in predominantly white college sport, and even begin to find their way into the Olympic games.

Boxing became increasingly important to African Americans during the latter half of the nineteenth and early years of the twentieth centuries. The level of importance and meaning they attached to boxing, however, largely had to do with the form it took, the rules involved, and intent of participation on part of the contestants as well as audience. One degraded form of boxing involving black youth were battle royals, a phenomenon largely confined to the South in which dozens of black boys would engage in a bloody free-for-all and crawl on their hands and knees for pennies thrown into the ring by a grateful white crowd. Usually held prior to the main events on a boxing card, variations of the battle royal included tying one arm behind the back of each contestant, blind-folding all the boys and making them fight while in sacks, and enticing boys with disabilities. Battle royals have been firmly embedded in black literary circles and recounted in various levels of detail by some of the most prominent African Americans, including former assistant secretary of the National Association for the Advancement of Colored People (NAACP) Walter White who perhaps provided the first account of the event in an unpublished novel he wrote in the late 1920s and Ralph Ellison who spends several pages describing the event in the first chapter of his classic *Invisible Man*.

Battle royals, as much as anything else, seemingly represented the racial realities of a Darwinian America in which blacks and whites were engaged in a constant battle for survival. It is for this reason why blacks took special delight, not in battle royals, but in organized boxing matches with just two fighters in the ring rather than twelve. Blacks attached great importance to boxing, a sport that has always been about masculinity and fraught with racial symbolism that has fascinated Americans who were both enthralled and ambivalent about the violent and bloody contests in the squared circle. Even those black leaders who spoke of racial uplift and held tight to Victorian notions of propriety, found boxing satisfying and meaningful because it provided opportunities in very public spaces where blacks, in the words of Tiger Flowers's biographer Andrew Kaye, "could openly strike a white man with impunity."[4] Evidence of the pride and deeply emotional responses to the victories of black boxers can be gleaned from the writings of influential black intellectuals and literary figures. These individuals, and others, wrote glowingly of the triumphs in the ring by black boxers, particularly those in the heavyweight division, which garnered the most attention because of the sheer size and strength of the combatants, noting the practical implications and representational importance of those triumphs to the larger black community.

Whites, of course, viewed the triumphs of black boxers much differently. To them, victories by black boxers were bitter disappointments and unsettling because those victories in a sport that at the time resonated so deeply with Americans disrupted the natural social order and challenged the belief in their own superiority and manhood. It is one reason why some white fighters drew the color line and refused to enter the ring with black fighters. It is also one reason why many black boxers fought the same black boxers over and over again until they were too battered and bruised to fight again.

In spite of these circumstances, a small number of talented black boxers successfully navigated the slippery nature of the color line to carve out productive careers marked by memorable fights against outstanding white boxers that brought their fellow blacks the kind of satisfaction that only victories in the prize ring could provide. The stories of two of the most successful black boxers of the late nineteenth century provide important insights into the racial realities of the sport and American society. Although their backgrounds were decidedly different and their careers diverged in a number of different of ways, George "Little Chocolate" Dixon, the great lightweight boxer, and Peter Jackson, the distinguished heavyweight fighter, faced some of the same pressures and difficulties as foreign-born black men who sought fame in America where boxing was quickly becoming a center of the sport. Dixon, a native of Halifax, Nova Scotia, who only stood five feet, three and half inches and in the early part of his career weighed just eighty-seven pounds, became the first black champion of the world in any sport in 1890 when he captured the featherweight title from Nunc Wallace in London. That same year, he would beat Johnny Murphy in Providence, Rhode Island, and in 1891 defeated Cal McCarthy in New York and Australian champion Abe Willis in San Francisco.

Certainly one of the most important fights in Dixon's career was against Jack Skelly in 1892 as part of a "prize-fighting festival" in New Orleans. Organized by the city's prestigious Olympic Club, the triple-header included the Jack McAuliffe and Billy Myer lightweight championship fight on September 5, the Dixon and Skelly featherweight championship fight on September 6, and the September 7 heavyweight championship fight between John L. Sullivan and James J. Corbett. The marquee bout, of course, was the Sullivan and Corbett matchup, which Corbett won ending the great "Boston Strong Boy's" long reign as heavyweight champion. The most controversial of the three bouts, however, was Dixon versus Skelly because of its racial implications. The Olympic Club, which admitted black spectators for the first time and set aside a special section for them to watch the bout, successfully kept order and prevented any violence among those in attendance even as Dixon pummeled and disfigured Skelly in eight violent rounds that ended in victory for the black Canadian. But the press coverage following the fight brought up the question as to the appropriateness of future interracial boxing matches in the Crescent City. Some local commentators voiced the opinion that it was wrong to bring two fighters of different races together on conditions of equality, while others thought it was wrong to admit black fans and fearful that Dixon's overwhelming triumph would result in a false belief among blacks about their own superiority. Irrespective of these differing opinions, there is no question that Dixon's battering of Skelly infuriated white fans and roused local racial prejudices to the point that it speeded up the elimination of black and white boxing matches in a part of the country where racial separatism in all walks of life was increasingly becoming the norm. "The sight [seeing Dixon beat Skelly] was repugnant to some men from the South," noted a correspondent from the *Chicago Tribune*. "A darky is alright in his place here, but the idea of sitting quietly by and seeing a colored boy pommel a white lad grates on Southerners."[5]

Peter Jackson was less fortunate than Dixon in that he was never able to fight for a world title. An Australian by way of Saint Croix, Virgin Islands, Jackson captured the Australian heavyweight championship by defeating Tom Lees in a grueling thirty-round bout in 1886. Unable to find any worthy opponents to fight over the next two years, Jackson left Australia for the United States in 1888 with the expressed intent of proving his worth to fight for the world heavyweight championship. He did everything humanly possible to convince those in boxing he was a legitimate contender to fight heavyweight champion John L. Sullivan, defeating such notable opponents as Joe McAuliffe and Frank Slavin and battling James J. Corbett to a sixty-one-round draw at the California Athletic Club in San Francisco in 1891. But all of these performances went for naught. Sullivan would never get into the ring with him or any other black fighter during his long and storied career. He always drew the color line. Jack Johnson biographer Geoffrey C. Ward noted that Sullivan became very explicit toward the end of his career about his view on fighting blacks. Ward wrote that in 1892 Sullivan was ready "to defend his title against 'All . . . fighters—first come, first served—who are white. I [Sullivan] will not fight a Negro. I never have and never will.'"[6]

Equally frustrating to Jackson was his inability to secure another fight with Corbett after the great fighter from San Francisco defeated Sullivan for the world heavyweight title in 1892 at the Olympic Club in New Orleans. In spite of several challenges made through his manager Charles "Parson" Davies, Jackson could never secure a return bout with Corbett, the "gentleman" boxer who hated blacks and never wanted to see one of them become champion of the world. While Corbett had used his bout with Jackson in 1891 at the California Athletic Club to further establish his reputation in an effort to secure a title fight, he would not return the favor to the great Australian boxer after capturing the world championship. In the end, Jackson finished his outstanding career in the ring frustrated by never having an opportunity to fight for the most prestigious title in boxing.

The inability to secure a heavyweight title fight was a bitter pill to swallow for the very proud and enormously talented Jackson who died in Roma, Australia, in 1901 at just forty years of age. While it probably would have been bittersweet for Jackson, he certainly would have been thrilled when Jack Johnson, the very talented and confident and controversial black boxer from Galveston, Texas, beat Tommy Burns in 1908 in Sydney, Australia, to become the first black heavyweight champion of the world. To say that Johnson was one of the most closely followed, debated, and divisive athletes in the history of sport would be an understatement. A black man who one historian claimed knew no fear of death or danger, Johnson lived life on his own terms, refused to acquiesce to the white power structure, and violated racial mores both in and outside the ring during one of the most racially oppressive periods in American history. He owned his own cafe, drove his high-priced cars at excessive speeds, lavished expensive gifts on loved ones, wore diamond studded cuff links and tailor-made suits, traveled widely and partied until all hours of the night, and refused to bow his head and step aside for anyone. He exploited the myth of black sexuality and played on white fears during training sessions by wrapping his penis in gauze bandages to enhance its size. He infuriated whites by marrying three white women and flaunting his relationships with other white women, many of them prostitutes, in very public settings.

The hatred of Johnson was so intense that not long after he captured the heavyweight title from Burns, a search began for a "white hope," one who could batter the incorrigible black fighter from Galveston and restore the championship to the white race where it rightfully belonged. One possibility was James Corbett who noted in the *Chicago Daily Tribune* of January 3, 1909, that "I am not anxious to fight a Negro, but it galls me to see a black champion."[7] Corbett, however, was forty-two years old at the time of this pronouncement and no one believed he would have a chance to overcome, let alone survive, the punishment that Johnson would mete out in the ring.

The man who finally came forward in an attempt to put Johnson in his place and save the white race from any further embarrassment was Jim Jeffries, the former heavyweight champion from California who had been in the ring with some of boxing's biggest names, including Joe Choynski, Peter Jackson, Tom Sharkey, and Bob Fitzsimmons. After receiving repeated requests to come out of retirement and fight Johnson, Jeffries eventually acceded to the pressure and signed a contract to do battle with Johnson on the Fourth of July, 1910, in Reno, Nevada. He should not have acceded to the requests. Johnson, in the most important fight of his career and one fraught with obvious racial symbolism, pummeled Jeffries with punch after punch until the handlers of the former world champion jumped into the ring in the fifteenth round and stopped the fight. Reporters believed Johnson had purposely strung Jeffries along, keeping the former heavyweight champion upright as long as he could so as to inflict as much damage as possible. Inflicting damage he did, breaking Jeffries nose and pummeling his eyes and face to the point where blood was spewing from his mouth. Johnson accomplished all this while taunting Jeffries throughout the fight. Historian Randy Roberts noted that in the second round Johnson started throwing barbs at Jeffries, telling him at one point, "Don't rush Jim. I can go on like this forever."[8]

The events surrounding the Johnson and Jeffries fight make clear white America's hatred of Johnson and others of his race, but also the philosophical differences in the black community regarding sport's power to effect change and the best means to achieve justice and racial equality. To more conservative African Americans, Johnson's lifestyle was reprehensible, ultimately harmful to the entire race and the struggle for equal rights and full citizenship. Booker T. Washington, one of the most prominent of all

Figure 2.2. Poster produced by the Adolph Friedlander Lithography company in Hamburg, Germany, to advertise the film of the Jack Johnson fight in 1910 against Jim Jeffries.
Courtesy of National Portrait Gallery, Smithsonian Institution.

African Americans, was in this camp. Typically keeping some distance from most forms of an expressive black culture and always strongly condemning anything that would discredit the race in the eyes of whites, Washington was very troubled by Johnson's behavior which he believed had a harmful effect on all African Americans. He noted, for instance, in a 1912 issue of the *African American Ledger* that "in misrepresenting the colored people of the country this man [Johnson] is harming himself the least. I wish to say emphatically that his actions do not meet my personal approval, and I am sure that they do not meet with the approval of the colored race."[9]

To other African Americans, however, Johnson was extraordinarily important from a representational standpoint because of his victories in the ring and refusal to consent to the dominant white culture. W. E. B. Du Bois, the great black intellectual, author, and civil rights activist, was among those in this camp. Although he may have been troubled by Johnson's plethora of illicit relationships with white women and fearful it would alienate some people, Du Bois saw the black fighter's ring triumphs in symbolic terms, believing they were significant examples of possibility that should be admired and celebrated. Unfortunately, Du Bois famously wrote in 1914, the "thrill of national disgust" regarding Johnson was a result of his greatness as a boxer and "unforgivable blackness."[10]

Attracting far less attention than Johnson and other prominent black professional boxers on the national scene were those African American fighters who did battle in the squared circle at segregated US Army camps during World War I. Historian Horace Nash, for instance, explained the prominent role that boxing played among African Americans at Camp Furlong, an Army base just outside Columbus, New Mexico, that by 1920 housed 3,599 black members of the Twenty-Fourth Infantry and 510 white members of the Twelfth Cavalry. A variety of sports, particularly boxing, was especially important to the military in that it provided both black and white soldiers "wholesome" recreation and the strenuous physical activity necessary to keep them in top combat condition. In the very small isolated town of Columbus, that was located just three miles north of the Mexican border, boxing was also important in alleviating boredom while at once contributing to a sense of community. Leaders in the black community and local white civilians, moreover, saw the financial benefits that could potentially result from boxing and arranged fights that matched black on black and interracial matches between local pugilists and those from elsewhere. These bouts, which featured such outstanding black boxers as regimental champions Joe Blackburn and Rufus Williams and the extremely gifted Thomas Hayden, were extraordinarily important, according to Nash, because they "were a source of inspiration and pride for civilian and military blacks, and helped create a more dynamic black community." The boxing matches also "provided means for interracial contact and significantly promoted positive race relations."[11]

While Johnson and other black boxers were plying their trade in the prize ring, a select number of outstanding African American athletes were realizing success in predominantly white college sport. The majority of black athletes at the turn of the twentieth century would participate in sport at one of the Historically Black Colleges and Universities (HBCUs) in the South, but a significantly smaller number of them would realize success in intercollegiate athletics at well-known predominantly white universities in the North. For the most part, these men were scholar-athletes who placed just as much and, in some cases, perhaps even more emphasis on their academic success and educational achievement than they did their performance in sport. These men, many of them coming from middle-class black families who placed an extraordinary emphasis on education and culture, prepared for careers in law, education, business, politics, and any number of other professions by first attending a private academy in New England, a well-known public school, or an HBCU in the South. After completing this stage of their schooling, they matriculated to more racially liberal colleges in the North to participate in sport and receive the education they required to enter professions that affirmed and solidified their middle-class status.

Those African American athletes at predominantly white universities in the North at the turn of the century were largely represented in three sports that would dominate college life for some time: football, track and field, and, to a lesser degree, baseball. In addition to their representation in certain sports, these African American athletes were only permitted to participate of course for those predominantly white universities that allowed African Americans as part of their general student body. African American athletes found early success at such prominent private institutions as Amherst College, Harvard University, Oberlin College, Brown University, University of Chicago, Williams College, University of Dubuque, University of Pennsylvania, and University of Southern California. African American athletes would also realize some success at such larger state universities as Rutgers University, University of Nebraska, University of Minnesota, University of Michigan, Northwestern University, Indiana University, Michigan State University, and University of Wisconsin.

African American athletes were conspicuous by their absence at the turn of the twentieth century at several Catholic universities that would eventually become powers in college sport: both West Point and the Naval Academy, and two of the Ivy Leagues "Big Three": Yale and Princeton.

The few black athletes at Catholic universities stemmed from the fact that a number of these institutions excluded black students from their general student body. The University of Notre Dame, which has one of the most prominent, tradition-laden, and powerful sports programs in the country, did not have an African American athlete representing the university until Frazier Thompson. Although there is speculation that he was only admitted because his surname gave no indication of his race, Thompson came to Notre Dame under the V-12 training program where he lettered in track and field in 1945 and graduated in 1947. The service academies were just as slow as Catholic universities to have African American athletes represent their institutions, with Calvin Huey being the first African American to play football at the Naval Academy in 1964 and Gary Steele doing the same at West Point two years later. Yale did not have an African American on its football team until Levi Jackson, who began playing for the school in 1946 and three years later became its first black captain in the gridiron sport. Princeton, a school with a traditionally very strong connection to southern society and always with a number of southern-born students on its campus, had as its first African American athlete Art Wilson, a star player, on its 1944–1945 basketball team.

Among those outstanding African Americans who distinguished themselves in predominantly white university sport shortly before and after the turn of the twentieth century were George A. Flippin of the University of Nebraska, Moses Fleetwood Walker of Oberlin College, William Tecumseh Sherman Jackson of Amherst College, Edward Gray of Amherst College, William Henry Lewis of both Amherst College and Harvard University, George Poage of the University of Wisconsin, Theodore "Ted" Cable of Harvard University, John Baxter Taylor of the University of Pennsylvania, Howard Drew of the University of Southern California, Bobby Marshall of the University of Minnesota, Henry Binga Dismond of the University of Chicago, Edward Soloman Butler of Dubuque College, Fritz Pollard of Brown University, and Paul Robeson of Rutgers University. These athletes all had long lists of accomplishments and sports performances of which they could be proud, including Poage capturing bronze medals in both the 200- and 400–meter hurdles in the 1904 Olympic Games in St. Louis and Taylor winning the gold medal in the 1600–meter medley relay at the 1908 Olympic Games in London. But it was the careers of William Henry Lewis and Paul Robeson that perhaps most vividly portray both the privileges and difficulties encountered by this first wave of African American athletes to participate at the highest level of college sport.

Figure 2.3.   William Henry Lewis (holding football) with Amherst College teammates in 1891.
Courtesy of Amherst College Archives and Special Collections, by permission of the Trustees of Amherst College.

Lewis had a distinguished career both on and off the playing field. Born in 1868 in Berkeley, Virginia, Lewis moved with his father, the Reverend Ashley Lewis, and his mother to New England at a very early age and at some point returned to his native state to attend Virginia Normal and Industrial Institute. In 1888 he enrolled at Amherst College where he was the outstanding player and captain of the football team, college senator, class orator, and president of the Hitchcock Society of Inquiry. After graduating from Amherst, Lewis continued his football career while a student in Harvard's Law School where he was a dominant force at center-rush (by the late nineteenth century would universally be known as the center position), the position that earned him a place in 1892 and 1893 to Walter Camp's prestigious all-American team. During his initial years as a lawyer, Lewis served part time as a coach at Harvard, establishing a reputation as a great strategist and student of the game. His interest and passion for the sport was such that he authored the book *Primer of College Football* (1896), published an essay on how to develop a football team in Casper Whitney's magazine, *Outing* (1902), and penned a chapter on line play in Camp's coaching manual, *How to Play Football* (1903). Lewis eventually became a prominent lawyer and held a number of influential political positions, including an appointment by President William Taft as assistant attorney general for the United States in 1911.

On the surface, it would seem that Lewis experienced a charmed life as a college athlete and student. He was bestowed with the most prestigious honors for his excellence on the football field and outstanding performance in the classroom. Appearances are deceiving, however. Lewis experienced some of the same forms of racial insensitivity and discrimination experienced by other black students at predominantly white universities during this period and well into the twentieth century. As one of the very few African American students at Amherst and Harvard, Lewis spent much of his time on the two campuses in isolation, forced to seek companionship and nurturing relationships in the local black communities. He forged important relationships with his teammates and developed close ties with white faculty but only found true friendships and a sense of community in the homes of elite black families who had created a necessary social network based on common lifestyles, values, and similar philosophical approaches to the world. In many ways, his college days were similar—with the exception of participation in athletics—to his fellow Harvard alumnus W. E. B. Du Bois in that he found it necessary to think of Amherst and Harvard primarily in instrumental terms. He asked nothing of the two schools except the "tutelage of teachers and the freedom of the laboratories, library," and playing field.[12]

Paul Robeson had some of the same experiences as Lewis during his days as an undergraduate student at Rutgers University between 1915 and 1919. Robeson, a native of Somerville, New Jersey, entered Rutgers on an academic scholarship the same year that Jack Johnson lost his heavyweight championship, saw the revival of the KKK in Alabama, the release of D. W. Griffith's racially charged film *Birth of a Nation*, and the death of Booker T. Washington. Robeson, a black man with extraordinary intellectual, artistic, and athletic abilities, realized enormous success at Rutgers, including being elected to Phi Beta Kappa, chosen as class valedictorian, distinguishing himself in drama and many other cultural activities, awarded twelve varsity letters in four different sports, and twice selected as an All-American in football. Following his graduation from Rutgers, Robeson had a career marked by great successes intermingled with much controversy and bitter disappointments. He became an internationally known singer and actor and civil rights activist whose life eventually took a serious toll at the hands of the US government for his outspoken attacks against racism, praise of the Soviet Union's "experiment in socialism," a close association with Marxism, and the founding of the Progressive Party.

Figure 2.4. Paul Robeson, the great athlete, scholar, activist, actor, and singer.
Courtesy of Rutgers University Libraries.

Robeson, in spite of his great athletic successes at Rutgers, became one of the first African American athletes at a predominantly white university in the North to be excluded from an athletic contest against a southern institution. Similar to what would take place over and over again in intercollegiate athletics throughout the first half of the twentieth century in a number of different sports, Rutgers acceded to the demands of Washington and Lee University and kept Robeson out of a home football game in 1916 against the private institution founded in 1749 in Lexington, Virginia. Washington and Lee made clear to Rutgers their refusal to play against Robeson on account of his color. Rutgers head coach George Sanford, undoubtedly after deliberations with the institution's upper-level administration, agreed to keep Robeson out of the contest and was therefore complicit in the racial discrimination committed against his star player.

There is no evidence of how Robeson responded to being excluded from the game against Washington and Lee, but he must have been terribly disappointed, especially since it denied him the opportunity to utilize his immense physical skills and help defeat one of the racist South's most storied institutions. There was also no apparent outcry from Rutgers' white students or more liberally minded faculty over the Robeson snubbing, perhaps because of their reluctance to speak out against those who had almost unlimited power in regard to student and faculty retention. There was, moreover, seemingly no immediate outpouring of protest over the treatment of Robeson by the local black community, the black press, and civil rights organizations like there was, for instance, when New York University's Dave Myers was kept out of a football game against the University of Georgia in 1929 or when the University of Michigan kept Willis Ward out of a football game against Georgia Tech in 1934 or when New York University kept Leonard Bates out of a football game against the University of Missouri in 1940 or when Harvard University kept Lucien Alexis Jr. out of a lacrosse game against Catholic University of Washington, D.C., in 1941. The time had not yet arrived for these groups, including the NAACP, to become involved in matters relating to racial discrimination in sport.

The first time that anyone openly addressed the treatment of Robeson was nearly three years after the event had taken place. In June 1919, James D. Carr, Rutgers' first black graduate and Phi Beta Kappa honor student who became assistant attorney and assistant corporation counsel of New York City, wrote a very candid letter to then Rutgers' President William H. S. Demarest criticizing the school for acceding to the racist policies of Washington and Lee. Obviously frustrated and bitter about the event, Carr made clear to Demarest that he was "deeply moved by the injustice done" to Robeson and disappointed by Rutgers that "prostituted her sacred principles, when they were brazenly challenged and laid her convictions upon the alter of compromise."[13]

The exclusion of Robeson from the Washington and Lee game took place around the same time that the all-black sports teams and leagues of the nineteenth century were beginning to become far more structured and formalized in nature. A result of a number of factors, including the hardening of the racial lines and movement toward increased racial segregation in society at large, these separate teams and leagues existed at both the amateur and professional levels of competition. While remarkably similar in format, structure, and philosophy to predominantly white organized sport, separate teams and leagues reflected African American life and culture and made evident the vibrancy and strength of the black community between the first and second world wars. It is important to note that the racial lines in sport, just like most other institutions in America, were not always hard and fast which meant that the increasing formalization of separate teams and leagues did preclude some black athletes from continuing to compete against and alongside whites, especially if those in charge of highly organized sport stood to benefit financially or had their own prestige or those they represented enhanced from interracial contests.

CHAPTER THREE

~

Sport behind the Walls of Segregation

The sport programs established behind the walls of segregation were important because it gave highly skilled African American athletes an opportunity to exhibit their skills in front of appreciative black audiences who yearned for entertainment and the opportunity to engage in communal activities. The sport programs established behind the walls of segregation were also crucial to African Americans because it provided them an opportunity to experience a sense of self-worth and exhibit their ability for self-organization and business acumen. The sport programs behind the walls of segregation, moreover, provided an opportunity for black athletes to showcase their talents to a larger audience and convince themselves and others that they deserved the opportunity to participate at the highest levels of predominantly white organized sport. Taken together, the various sports programs behind the walls of segregation combined to form a black national sporting culture covered by a weekly black press that proudly and regularly recounted the exploits of individual African American athletes and performances of teams at both the amateur and professional levels of competition.

A number of important amateur teams and sports organizations were established behind the walls of segregation during the first half of the twentieth century. These teams and sports organizations appeared in high schools and colleges and among private groups and associations. Virtually every sport in America at the time was represented, including track and field, the country club pastimes of tennis and golf, and the big three: football, basketball, and baseball. Providing needed structure were such prominent sports bureaucracies as the Interscholastic Athletic Association (ISAA), Central Intercollegiate Athletic Association (CIAA), American Tennis Association (ATA), and National Negro Bowling Association (NNBA). Most of the amateur sports behind the walls of segregation would also be represented at the professional level, most notably Negro League Baseball, which has been the most written about and researched of all separate black sports organizations. As America's most popular sport during the first half of the twentieth century and the game considered the "national pastime," Negro League Baseball held special significance to African Americans as they strove for equal rights and full participation in American life. To play baseball was to be an American and this was not lost on blacks mired in poverty during this period and confronted on a daily basis with racial discrimination.

Sport in Historically Black
Educational Institutions

Edwin Bancroft Henderson's establishment of the ISAA in 1906 and Public Schools Athletic League (PSAL) in 1910 were watershed events in the history of black high school sports. They provided needed structure, including codified rules, eligibility requirements, and formal administration, which led to more educationally sound and competitively balanced athletic programs for black high school students. The ISAA, consisting of schools from Indianapolis, Wilmington, Delaware, Baltimore, and Washington, D.C., organized contests in baseball, football, basketball, and track and field. The Washington, D.C.-based PSAL was modeled after the white public schools athletic leagues and included a variety of sports for children of varying physical skills at the grammar school and high school levels of instruction. The league organized, among other events, high school cross country meets, an intercity soccer league, a grammar school baseball tournament, Saturday night basketball games, and dances during the winter months at the city's famous True Reformer's Hall.

The ISAA and PSAL would be followed several years later by other black high school sports organizations of various sizes and focus and organizational structure. In 1924 fourteen high schools organized the West Virginia Athletic Union, an extremely important event in that it was the first black statewide athletic association in the South. Over the next six years other black state high school athletic associations would be formed in Virginia, North Carolina, Missouri, Kansas, Illinois, Indiana, and Florida. Not unexpectedly, most states in the lower South were much slower in establishing athletic associations. Mississippi did not establish a black athletic association until 1940, two years later Arkansas followed suit by forming a separate organization, and in 1948 Alabama finally established their own athletic association for black high school students.

Black high school athletic associations sponsored a variety of sports, but nothing seemed to generate more interest and enthusiasm among the African American community than their year-end basketball tournaments. The year-end basketball tournament organized by the West Virginia Athletic Union (WVAU) is a case in point. Held for the first time in 1925 at West Virginia State College, the WVAU tournament was intended to determine each year the best team in the state and showcase the skill level of individual players who had spent countless hours on the basketball court honing their talents. Over time, however, the WVAU tournament evolved, like the Howard and Lincoln Thanksgiving Day football game, East-West All-Star game in Negro League Baseball and so many other sporting events in the African American community, into a grand cultural affair in which blacks could exhibit the racial pride so characteristic of the "New Negro" at the time. The style and efficient running of the tournament had significant implications for African Americans because it was one way to overcome stereotypes of black inferiority while at once fostering black community building.

The WVAU tournament, and those organized by other black state high school athletic associations, would be greatly enhanced by the National Interscholastic Basketball Tournament (NIBT) that was founded in 1929. The brainchild of Charles H. Williams—the noted physical educator, coach, and administrator from Hampton Institute who would be instrumental in the founding and implementation of other black sporting events and organizations—the NIBT experienced some initial success by hosting such traditionally powerful teams as Chicago's Wendell Phillips; Gary, Indiana's Roosevelt High School; and Washington, D.C.'s Armstrong Technical High School. In 1933, however, Hampton Institute, citing the difficulties of supporting such a financially exorbitant event amidst the Great Depression, stopped its sponsorship of the tournament. As a result, the tournament was held in Gary, Indiana, in 1934 and 1935, at Roanoke, Virginia's Lucy Addison High School in 1936, and back to Gary, Indiana, in 1937 and 1938. Beginning in 1939 the tournament was held at various locations until World War II put a temporary halt to the event in 1942.

In 1945 Tennessee A&I President Walter Davis and Athletic Director Henry Arthur Keane resurrected the tournament. First held in Nashville and later moved to Alabama State under the auspices of the newly established National High School Athletic Association, the revised edition of the tournament was very successful and would continue to be so until 1964. It was obvious long before 1964, however, that a number of factors combined to change the nature and overall quality of the tournament. Indianapolis' Crispus Attucks High School and Gary, Indiana's Roosevelt High School, two of the most dominant basketball schools in the country, stopped entering the tournament in 1943 because they both elected to play instead in the recently desegregated Indiana High School Athletic Association championships. The *Brown v. Board of Education* decision in 1954 would have a decided impact on the tournament just as it would other athletic events among black high schools. The famous Supreme Court decision set in motion a number of individual and collective challenges to separate interscholastic athletic programs. These challenges would ultimately result in the desegregation of various sports in high schools in the South, first in the District of Columbia and later all states in the region.

The vibrant athletic programs established at black high schools would be duplicated at HBCUs. First appearing in the latter stages of the nineteenth century, sports would become an integral part of campus life among most black colleges, irrespective of size, geographical location, and whether private or state supported. These athletic programs were decidedly similar to those at predominantly white institutions in regard to organizational structure, philosophy and purpose, relationship to academics, types of sports offered, and kinds of controversial issues and ethical decisions encountered. Prominent black institutions of higher learning, including such famous schools as Lincoln University and Hampton Institute in the upper South and Tuskegee Institute and Grambling College in the lower South, organized elaborate programs in football, basketball, and other sports that brought them various degrees of attention and prestige and financial resources. Accompanying these sports programs were an assortment of different issues and problems that had always plagued those at predominantly white institutions, including inadequate coaching, poor officiating, player injuries, inappropriate fan behavior, academic eligibility concerns, and game scheduling issues.

The issues and problems that accompanied the growth of sport in black colleges became a serious concern to many faculty and upper-level administrators in those institutions. Following closely on the heels of the creation of the National Collegiate Athletic Association (NCAA) in 1906, a number of very prominent individuals were calling for the creation of a national organization to oversee black college sport. Samuel H. Archer and John Brown Watson, colleagues at Morehouse College and both later presidents of black colleges, spoke out vehemently for a national organization to govern athletics among black colleges. Writing in a 1906 issue of *The Voice of the Negro*, Archer argued for a national organization with a constitution and rules that would guarantee a positive athletic environment and ensure that all eligibility requirements were met and that no professionalism pervaded black college sport. The following year in an essay in *The Voice*, Watson maintained that an "Intercollegiate Athletic Association" was needed to overcome the many evils connected to college sport and to make sure that "college athletics was given a higher tone."[1]

In spite of the pleas of Archer, Watson, and others, no national organization was established to govern black college sport. This did not mean, however, that there was no interest among African Americans in bringing more organizational structure to black college sport as evidenced by the creation of several regional athletic associations among HBCUs. The first of these organizations was apparently the Georgia-Carolina Athletic Association (GCAA), which was founded in 1910. It would be followed by the Colored (later Central) Intercollegiate Athletic Association (CIAA) in 1912; Southern Intercollegiate Athletic Conference (SIAC) in 1913; Southwestern Athletic Association (SWAA) in 1920; South Central Athletic Association (SCAA) in 1923; Middle Atlantic Athletic Association (MAAA) in 1931; and Midwestern Athletic Association (MWAA) in 1932.

Of these organizations, it was the CIAA that was perhaps initially most important and influential and culturally significant. Organized just six years after the founding of the NCAA, original members of the CIAA included Hampton Institute, Howard University, Shaw University, Virginia Union University, and Lincoln University. Acting as representatives to the CIAA from these five prestigious HBCUs were a close-knit group of prominent coaches, athletic directors, and upper-level administrators who, like many middle-class African Americans, believed in the principle of racial uplift. Confronted by different forms of racial discrimination and forced to live in a segregated society, the founders of the CIAA hoped to establish through quality sports programs positive images of highly educated and dignified African Americans with unimpeachable character and unmatched organizational skills. To the founders, the CIAA would offer sports programs characterized by fairness and equality, good sportsmanship, strict allegiance to rules, fiscal responsibility, and pristine bureaucratic structure. This would guarantee, thought the founders, the appropriate conditions for athletic competition and, by extension, help in overcoming deep-seated stereotypical notions of black inferiority and moral depravity.

Unfortunately, the CIAA quest for racial uplift through sport did not include women for much of the twentieth century. Although not officially excluding African American women, as the prestigious American Negro Academy did for example in its bylaws of 1897, no black women competed under the auspices or served as officers or in any other capacity in the association. In 1928, Hampton Institute's Charles H. Williams, a long-time officer and driving force in the association, wrote in *The Southern Workman* that the CIAA had made provisions for women's participation, "but this innovation has met with little success."[2] Why there were no women in the organization is open to speculation since the sources are silent on the matter, but certainly playing a part were the needs of leaders in the CIAA to exert authority over an institution always considered a male domain and deep-seated stereotypical notions in America regarding the physical and emotional capabilities of women and their suitability for participating in sport.

Notwithstanding the lack of women in the organization, the CIAA paid an extraordinary amount of attention to seemingly every aspect of college sport as evidenced in the *C.I.A.A. Bulletin* they began publishing in 1923. Printed and distributed by Hampton Institute, the *Bulletin* was a high-quality publication that recounted in much detail the organization's yearly activities. Each issue typically included the names of delegates and minutes from the previous year's two-day CIAA meeting; lists of certified officials for each sport; extensive financial statements; a listing and summary of scores and team champions; essays written by sports experts on a variety of topics; and photographs of individual athletes and victorious teams in each sport. On occasion, issues would also include reports of presentations made by members of the black press, summaries of one-day coaches and referee conferences, testimonials from former CIAA athletes, and a section titled "In memoriams" for athletes and other individuals who had been affiliated with the organization.

The *C.I.A.A. Bulletin* was matched in quality by the organization's outstanding leadership, coaches, athletes, and sports programs. Highly respected academicians and professional educators led the fight against the varied problems inherent in college athletes while at once administering excellent programs in a host of sports. Examples of the organization's leadership included the likes of William A. Rogers, secretary of Virginia State University who was president of the CIAA from 1920 to 1924, and Walter G. Alexander, a 1899 graduate of Lincoln University and medical doctor in Orange, New Jersey, who was president of the CIAA from 1925 to 1928. Great coaches roamed the sidelines for CIAA schools, some who had achieved enormous success as players at predominantly white institutions but were unable to coach at those same institutions after the completion of their athletic careers. Examples of the organization's coaches included the likes of Fritz Pollard, the great running back from Brown University, who was briefly the head football coach at Lincoln University; John B. McLendon, the outstanding basketball coach who introduced the "fast break" style of play to the sport, led his North Carolina College Eagles to a 88–44 victory over the Duke School of Medicine in the famous "secret game" in 1944, and coached Tennessee State to three consecutive NAIA national championships; and Winston-Salem University's Clarence "Big House" Gaines who garnered many basketball coach of the year honors in the CIAA and had on his squad such brilliant players as Earl "The Pearl" Monroe. Outstanding athletes graced the playing fields in a number of sports for CIAA institutions. Examples of the organization's great players included the likes of Lincoln University's outstanding running back Alfred "Jazz" Byrd, Virginia State track star John Borican, Hampton University basketball standout Rick Mahorn, and West Virginia State basketball standout Earl Lloyd who had the distinction of breaking the color line in the National Basketball Association in 1950 along with Chuck Cooper and Nat "Sweetwater" Clifton.

The CIAA offered programs in football, basketball, baseball, track and field, and a number of other sports. While all these sports were of interest to CIAA followers, it was track and field, football, and basketball that were seemingly most important to the organization. Track and field was extraordinarily popular among members of the CIAA and African Americans throughout the South. The number of images and column space in the C.I.A.A. Bulletin make clear the love affair that association members had with the sport. The man who was perhaps most important in promoting the sport among association members was Charles H. Williams. In 1922 Williams organized and Hampton Institute hosted the first CIAA track and field meet. This inaugural meet, which included both college and high school divisions, proved to be a huge success and others would follow on a yearly basis at different locations that required greater oversight because of the event's increased importance and stature. The growing importance and stature of the meet was made evident when it was held in 1942 at Morgan State University. Honorary referees for the meet included Morgan State president D. O. W. Holmes, Baltimore mayor Howard W. Jackson, and Maryland Governor Herbert R. O'Connor. Serving as the meet's formal starter was Howard P. Drew, the former recordholder in the sprints from the University of Southern California. Jesse Owens, who realized lasting fame by capturing four gold medals in the 1936 Olympic Games in Berlin, was featured in an exhibition of the broad jump and 100 yard dash.

Football was seen by CIAA institutions as a way to make money, build character, toughen young men, garner alumni support, and foster school spirit and loyalty. Like predominantly white institutions, football rivalries developed among schools in the CIAA and none were bigger than the annual Thanksgiving Day game established between Howard University and Lincoln University. This rivalry, which was most intense and closely followed between 1919 and 1929, preceded such other football classics among black colleges as the Aggies Eagles Classic between North Carolina A&T and North Carolina Central (1924), Turkey Day Classic between Tuskegee Institute and Alabama State (1924), State Fair Classic between Grambling State and Prairie View A&M (1925), and Morehouse-Tuskegee Classic between Morehouse College and Tuskegee Institute (1935).

The Howard University and Lincoln University Thanksgiving Day football classic, like so many sporting events behind the walls of segregation, was part athletic contest and part spectacle. It was a three- to five-day affair with a series of parties, dances, dinners, and other social events accompanying the game between two prestigious black colleges that were decidedly different in regard to enrollment, curriculum, faculty, and history. These differences, combined with the fact that both institutions included middle-class African Americans with similar aspirations, lifestyles, and philosophical approaches to the world, fueled a rivalry that was simultaneously about community building and competition. Unfortunately, by 1929 the Howard University and Lincoln University Thanksgiving Day football classic had declined in popularity, largely a result of the Great Depression and the fact that Howard had begun to deemphasize sport under the leadership of President Mordecai Johnson.

There were few sporting events in the CIAA that could immediately take the place of the Howard University and Lincoln University Thanksgiving Day football classic in regard to popularity and fan interest and media attention. That would dramatically change in 1946, however, when the CIAA held its first year-end basketball tournament to determine the association's champion. Initiated to bring more money into CIAA coffers and taking place during a period of time in which college basketball was beginning to challenge college football for popularity, the inaugural tournament was held in Washington, D.C.'s famous Turner's Arena and proved to be a resounding success in every way and continues to be so to this very day. The tournament, which began with sixteen league teams, drew large crowds, much press coverage, and generated almost $934 in revenue. The highlight of the tournament was the championship game in which the North Carolina College Eagles, coached by John B. McLendon, defeated the Virginia Union

Panthers 64–56. Sportswriter Lem Graves Jr. wrote that the tournament was his "all-time sports 'thrill-of-a-lifetime.'"[3]

The CIAA was truly a pioneering organization. But as the years progressed during the first half of the twentieth century, more and more HBCUs around the country with great athletes, coaches, teams, and organizational structure would emerge. There were, indeed, pockets of athletic excellence that would materialize at black colleges throughout different parts of the South. It was certainly evident in the quality of coaches at HBCUs. For instance, Cleveland "Cleve" Abbott, a South Dakota native, arrived at Tuskegee Institute in 1923 where he served as long-time athletic director and led the school to many victories as football and track and field coach. William "Big Bill" Bell, an outstanding lineman at Ohio State University from 1929 to 1931, started a great tradition of football at Florida A&M when he became head coach in 1936. Jake Gaither, a Knoxville College graduate, took over as head coach of the program in 1945 and led it to greater successes while for a time also in charge of the school's basketball and track and field programs. Ed Temple, born in Harrisburg, Pennsylvania, was the head women's track and field coach at Tennessee State University from 1953 to 1994. Many of his athletes achieved Olympic stardom, most notably Wilma Rudolph because of her gold medal–winning performances in the 1960 games in Rome. Eddie Robinson realized enormous success as head football coach at Grambling State College beginning in 1941. By the time of his retirement in 1997, Robinson had won 408 games and coached over 200 men that would play professional football, including Super Bowl Most Valuable Player Doug Williams and Hall of Famers Willie Davis, Buck Buchanon, Willie Brown, and Charlie Joiner.

Notwithstanding the outstanding men's athletic programs at black colleges, the women's athletic programs at these institutions perhaps tell us even more about race, gender, and conceptions of the black body and guiding principles of sport. Although some scholars have contended that the black community was more supportive of women engaging in organized sport than the white community, there seems little question that there were decidedly different opinions among African Americans regarding the appropriateness, extent, and level of participation of women in high-level athletic competitions. There were always concerns, and in some cases even alarm, expressed by segments of the black community that women ran the risk of compromising their femininity and respectability by participating in highly organized competitive sport. One group that took this philosophical position was the National Association of College Women (NACW), a very prestigious group founded in 1910 by civil rights activist and suffragette Mary Church Terrell.

In 1929 and 1940, the NACW took official stands against highly organized competitive sport for women, arguing instead for intramural sports and less competitive activities. There were others in the black community, however, who supported it, if not always enthusiastically endorsing African American women's participation in highly organized sport, viewing it as important for allowing the display of physical skills and fostering moral development and discipline. Edwin Bancroft Henderson, the well-known physical educator, civil rights activist, and historian of the black athlete, was highly critical of "the narrow limits prescribed for girls and women," noting in 1939 that the outstanding performances of African American women athletes should be applauded as "the race of man needs the inspiration of strong virile womanhood."[4]

These divergent opinions would result in a complex pattern of sport among African American women in black colleges that would change over time depending on the social and historical context. There were, for instance, a select number of African American women at black colleges who were highly successful in the white country club oriented sport of tennis. African American women found much satisfaction representing their schools in a sport that required a finely tuned combination of speed, agility, power, finesse, and grace, although for many of them their most important and prestigious triumphs were those that occurred in the national tournaments sponsored by the black ATA. One of the earliest and most well known of these players was Lucy Diggs Slowe, the valedictorian of her 1908 graduating class at Howard University and first dean of women at Howard University as well as first president of the NACW. Although little is known about her early tennis career as an undergraduate student, she was president of the women's tennis club and was obviously extraordinarily skilled as she captured the women's singles title in 1917 at the first ATA national tournament in Baltimore. Sisters Margaret and Matilda Roumania Peters, natives of Washington, D.C., who were nicknamed "Pete and Repeat," were star tennis players at Tuskegee Institute in the late 1930s and initial years of the 1940s. Roumania Peters captured a singles championship and teamed with her sister Margaret to win a number of doubles championships in the Southern Intercollegiate Athletic Conference (SIAC). The legendary Althea Gibson dominated her college opponents while competing for Florida A&M during the late 1940s and early 1950s. Gibson's triumphs at Florida A&M combined with those she experienced in national ATA tournaments certainly helped in preparation for her historic victories in the French Open, US Open, and Wimbledon.

Perhaps the sports that were most important to women at black colleges were basketball and track and field. African American women college students took to these two sports with much enthusiasm. Especially noteworthy is that basketball and track and field have traditionally been thought of as two of the most masculine of sports, which affected the kind of press coverage that African American women basketball players and track and field athletes received, the way their performances were described, and how they dealt with the inevitable questions raised about their femininity and appearance. Also noteworthy was the large number of women's basketball and track and field programs at black colleges that were established and coached by men. Unable to take positions at predominantly white universities, some black male coaches were highly supportive of the sports programs for women at black colleges as indicated by their time commitment, dedication, and length of service. Black male coaches of women's sports, like black male coaches of men's sports, viewed their positions as careers, many of them taking graduate degrees in physical education to learn the principles of human movement in more depth and regularly attending coaching clinics sponsored by black colleges as well as predominantly white institutions.

There were several outstanding women's basketball programs at black colleges during the first half of the twentieth century. One of the best known of those programs was at Bennett College in North Carolina. The private all-female Methodist school which fashioned itself as the "Vassar of the South," enthusiastically supported basketball, providing an environment where the women students could freely exert their physicality and competitiveness on the court while at once maintaining the decorum and proper feminine behavior expected of them by the larger society. Led for much of the time by coach William Trent, Bennett College players came from different parts of the country, alumni and others always searching for new talent to ensure the continued success of the team. Highly organized and disciplined and well coached, the Bennett College team had such talented players as Almeda Clavon, Amaleta Moore, Lucille Townsend, and Ruth Glover. Like other women's basketball teams at black colleges, the Bennett College women played against other schools and club teams. One of their most famous series of games took place against the famous *Philadelphia Tribune* girls' basketball team, led by the extraordinarily talented all-around athlete Ora Washington.

The Tuskegee Institute women's basketball team also realized enormous success on the court. Led by Booker T. Washington, Tuskegee Institute established an outstanding athletic program and an environment that encouraged women to participate in a number of sports. The driving force behind the program was Cleveland "Cleve" Abbott, an outstanding high school and college athlete from South Dakota who was hired as Tuskegee Institute's athletic director in 1923. He established a model athletic program by virtue of his organizational skills and the financial resources made available by Washington. He oversaw an upgrade of the school's athletic facilities, including expansion of the tennis facilities to eight clay courts that qualified Tuskegee Institute to host the prestigious ATA national championship tournament in 1931, 1938, and 1941. He coached the football team for thirty-two years, accumulating a record of 205–98–27 and capturing multiple Southern Intercollegiate Athletic Conference (SIAC) titles and bowl victories over a career that stretched between 1923 and 1954. His most famous player was Ben Stevenson, the powerful running back originally from Liberty, Kansas, who played some eight seasons at the school and was named to several black college All-American teams. Besides his football duties, Abbott helped attract to Tuskegee Institute outstanding women athletes in basketball and track and field. Showing an unusual interest in women's sports, Abbott saw the educational value of women's participation in highly organized competitive sport and understood that their success could potentially bring regional, national, and international prestige to the school.

The Tuskegee Institute women's basketball team included great players, many of them who were also outstanding track and field performers. The team became a dominant force in women's basketball, capturing many SIAC titles during the 1930s and 1940s. As important as their accomplishments on the hard court were to Tuskegee Institute, they paled in comparison to the attention and national prestige that the women's track and field team would bring to the school. In 1927 Abbott established a two-day track and field competition for men called the Tuskegee Carnival (eventually referred to as Tuskegee Relays), which attracted outstanding athletes from high schools and colleges throughout the South. In 1929 Abbott added women's events to the Tuskegee Relays and began putting together a team of highly skilled women track and field athletes that he would coach along with the assistance of Christine Petty and later Nell Jackson. The team would soon become a powerhouse, competing against women's track and field squads from such institutions as Alabama State College, Florida A&M, Alcorn College, and Fort Valley State College. Including such outstanding athletes as Lula Hymes (Glenn), Leila Perry, and Alice Coachman, the Tuskegee Institute women won eleven Amateur Athletic Union (AAU) outdoor titles between 1937 and 1948. The most famous of the Tuskegee Institute women track and field performers was

Coachman who became the first African American woman to capture a gold medal in the Olympic Games when she won the high jump competition in 1948 in London. Not unexpectedly, because of their exclusion from southern regional AAU competitions, the Tuskegee Institute women were limited to participating each year in the Tuskegee Relays and the indoor and outdoor AAU national championships.

Succeeding Tuskegee Institute as the best women's track and field team in the country was Tennessee State University (at that time Tennessee A&I). Established in 1945 under the leadership of Jessie Abbott, the daughter of Cleve Abbott, the Tennessee State women's track and field program, commonly known as the Tigerbelles, would be a dominant force in the sport between the 1950s and early 1980s. A turning point in the program came in 1953 when Ed Temple became the coach of the Tennessee State women's track and field team. A charming man with a thorough knowledge and love of the sport, Temple lured some great talent to Tennessee State and it resulted in much success for a women's track and field program that would realize international acclaim. His early group of athletes in particular, which included Barbara Jones, Lucinda Williams, Martha Hudson, Willye White, Shirley Crowder, and the indomitable Wilma Rudolph, among others, electrified fans with their many victories at the national level and in Olympic competition. Jones, Williams, Hudson, and Rudolph combined to capture the gold medal in the 4X100 relay at the 1960 Olympic Games in Rome. Rudolph became the darling of the Rome Olympics as she captured gold medals in the 100 meters, 200 meters, and 4X100 relay. The supremely talented Rudolph achieved legendary status for her performances, made all that more remarkable since she had to overcame paralysis in her left leg as a young child to become the world's greatest sprinter. For some two years, Rudolph's mother took her to Meharry Medical College in Nashville one day a week for physical therapy and alternated "rubbing Wilma" with three older children in the family in four-hour shifts during the remaining six days of the week. By the time Rudolph was eight, she was walking with a brace and gradually regained full strength in her once "wasted small leg."[5]

Heightening Rudolph's popularity was her appearance. The tall, lean, and attractive Rudolph defied the masculine image of track and field, a beautiful athlete who exuded feminine charm as opposed to the tomboyish and heavily muscled look that fit the stereotypical image of women in the sport. Although the press resorted to jungle animal imagery by referring to her as the "black gazelle," Rudolph was seen as a unique woman athlete who did not have overdeveloped muscles or exhibit unattractive mannishness

Figure 3.1.　Wilma Rudolph mesmerized track and field fans with her spectacular performances in National and International competitions.
Courtesy of the Stanford Athletics Photograph Collection (PC0010).

attributed to such notable female track and field athletes as Mildred "Babe" Didrikson, Stella Walsh, and Tamara Press. In addition to her appearance, Rudolph's enormous popularity was enhanced by the fact that her victories were witnessed through the relatively new medium of television. The timing could not have been more perfect as Rudolph's triumphs could not just be heard, but also seen since CBS devoted for the first time several hours of coverage to the games in Rome. The victories of Rudolph, along with those of her teammates, were also that much more significant because they took place amid the Cold War. Rudolph and her teammates were, in the words of one historian, "Cold War Warriors" since their triumphs were symbolic in nature, representing, ironically enough, the American way of life and democratic principles.[6]

Sport Beyond the Walls of Academia

In addition to the sport programs established at the interscholastic and intercollegiate levels of competition, there were a large number of amateur and professional teams and leagues established outside the walls of academia that were enthusiastically supported and garnered much media attention in the African American community. Many of the most significant of these organizations came about during the decade of the 1920s, partly a result of the Great Migration that brought over a million southern blacks north by "exodus trains" where they settled in New York, Chicago, Philadelphia, Cleveland, Detroit, Pittsburgh, and other great metropolitan areas. Important examples of self-organization, racial pride, and commercial astuteness, these separate black leagues and teams were established in sports ranging from bowling and car racing to golf and baseball. The integration of sport in the post–World War II period was essentially the death knell for these professional teams and leagues, but some of the amateur teams and leagues remained intact and have prospered to the present day. Although now less important symbolically or as crucial in providing needed examples of self-organization, racial pride, and business acumen, these amateur sport programs continue to provide opportunities for people to engage in friendly competition and realize the sense of satisfaction and communal spirit that often results from participation in sport.

One relatively little known separate sports organization was the Colored Speedway Association (CSA). Established in 1924 in Indianapolis, Indiana, a city with a long heritage of car racing and home of the famous Indianapolis 500–Mile Race, the CSA was organized by an integrated group made up of three prominent African Americans and two white racing promoters. Not uncommon to have white benefactors involved in the world of black sport because of limited financial resources in the African American community, the five men set up the organization in order to provide opportunities for black drivers who had been denied access to races on account of their color to test their skills on the track. The major event sponsored by the CSA was the "Gold and Glory Sweepstakes," a 100–mile race held at the Indiana State Fairgrounds that brought together outstanding black drivers who tested their mettle on the dusty dirt track in front of hundreds of screaming fans. Covered closely by some of the leading black newspapers, the "Gold and Glory Sweepstakes" was, like so many sporting events in the African Community, a grand social affair as well as an athletic contest.

Although there were a number of individuals who contributed to the success of the "Gold and Glory Sweepstakes," no one associated with the event was more popular and influential than Charlie Wiggins. An Evansville, Indiana, native who moved to Indianapolis in 1922, Wiggins was a garage owner and gifted mechanic as well as a superlative car racer who was labeled by the *Indianapolis Recorder*, "The Negro Speed King." He captured the 1926 "Gold and Glory Sweepstakes," was second in the 1929 race, and then won the event in 1931, 1932, and 1933. He would be the only driver to win the prestigious race four times.[7]

The expertise and organizational skills shown by African Americans in car racing would also be evident in the country club sports of golf and tennis. African Americans, particularly from the upper reaches of society, took to these two sports with great enthusiasm as evidenced by the creation of the United Golfers Association (UGA) and ATA. Unable to play on most courses and compete in major tournaments, African Americans organized their own golf clubs and in 1925 established the UGA. A national organization that included many prominent African Americans, the UGA supported the development of new clubs, helped attract and served as a breeding ground for the best black players, and sponsored local tournaments and the annual Negro National Open. The Negro National Open, which by 1930 included a women's division, was the centerpiece of the UGA, attracting the country's best black players and receiving much coverage in the black press. Eventually serving as a tune-up to the Negro National Open was the Joe Louis Open, a tournament organized by the famous heavyweight champion and avid golfer. By 1954 the Negro National Open had to share the spotlight with the North and South tournament that became a major event on the black golf circuit.

The ATA realized just as much success in their respective sport. One of the older separate black sports organizations, the ATA was founded in 1916 in Washington, D.C., to lend support and provide administrative structure for African American men and women who desired to play competitive tennis. The annual ATA national tournament, the first of which was hosted by the Monumental Tennis Club of Washington, D.C., in 1917 at Druid Hill Park in Baltimore, brought together the greatest black players in the game. Those who regularly played in the tournament and garnered multiple titles were such outstanding players as Reginald Weir, Nathaniel Jackson, Jimmy McDaniel, Tally Holmes, Lucy Diggs Slowe, Isadore Channels, Ora Washington, Lulu Ballard, and Althea Gibson.

The ATA tournaments were sometimes held at HBCUs. Although only a select number of HBCUs had tennis programs, there were some real benefits that resulted from their hosting of ATA tournaments. HBCUs, including such prestigious schools as Hampton Institute, Morehouse College, Wilberforce College, and Tuskegee Institute, benefited from having wealthy African Americans on campus, using the tournament as an opportunity to showcase their institutions and connect with potential benefactors who could contribute to university coffers. HBCUs, some of which had quality courts in which to play, could also accommodate more participants than individual black tennis clubs and provided lodging and meals—that was extraordinarily important in the South where segregated housing and public accommodations were the norm.

Complementing the separate organizations that contributed to the growth of a national African American sporting culture were a number of highly successful independent black teams that garnered much attention and, in some cases, lasting fame because of their athletic skills and numerous victories. Sometimes competing against white as well as black clubs, these teams were constantly on the road, barnstorming across the country searching for games to play and audiences to entertain and money to be made. Seemingly every popular sport in America was represented, including basketball, that had an intense following and its share of famous teams and players. Three of the most famous independent basketball teams were the Philadelphia Tribune Newsgirls, New York Renaissance Five, and Harlem Globetrotters. The Newsgirls, organized in 1931 by former Hilldale baseball great and *Philadelphia Tribune* circulation manager Otto Briggs, were loaded with great talent as reflected by their many victories against some of the best black and white teams in the country. Included on the roster at various times were such outstanding players as two-sport stars Ora Washington, Inez Patterson, Rose Wilson, Sarah Latimere, and Bernice Robinson. Like other independent black teams, the players on the Newsgirls had relatively small salaries and typically supplemented it by taking part-time jobs. They fulfilled Briggs's wishes, however, by bringing attention to the *Philadelphia Tribune* and perhaps even increasing its circulation through their outstanding performances on the hardwood.

The New York Renaissance Five garnered national attention for their exploits on the basketball court. Founded in 1923 by Robert L. "Bob" Douglas, a West Indian immigrant and successful businessman, the team took its name from Harlem's Renaissance Ballroom. The team spent countless hours on the road, barnstorming through the East, Midwest, and the South playing against such famous clubs as the Original Celtics, Philadelphia SPAHS (South Philadelphia Hebrew Association), Harlem Globetrotters, Detroit Eagles, Akron Firestones, and Chicago Collegians. Having on their roster at various times such great players as Clarence (Fats) Jenkins, James (Pappy) Ricks, Eyre (Bruiser) Saitch, Charles T. (Tarzan) Cooper, and Bill Yancey, the Renaissance Five garnered some 2,400 victories during twenty-seven years of play. A testament to the Renaissance Five's greatness is that in 1933 they beat the vaunted original Celtics in seven of eight games, the following year were victorious in eighty-eight consecutive games and amassed an overall record of 127–7, and in 1939 captured the first World Championship Tournament for Professional Basketball. On account of their great record and contributions to the game, the Renaissance Five were selected as a team to the Naismith Memorial Basketball Hall of Fame in 1963.

Far better known to sports fans today are the Harlem Globetrotters. Originally known as the Savoy Big Five and founded and owned by Jewish entrepreneur Abe Saperstein, the Globetrotters had their start in the late 1920s and were for many years a very serious basketball team. Evidence for this is the fact that in 1940 they won the World Championship Tournament for Professional Basketball. Among the most important of their many victories was against the National Basketball League's Minneapolis Lakers at Chicago Stadium in 1948. With a starting lineup that included such legendary players as Reece "Goose" Tatum and Marques Haynes, the Globetrotters defeated the Lakers and their star center George Mikan 61–59 in front of approximately eighteen thousand fans in a game that made clear to some observers that blacks were capable of playing at the highest levels of the sport.

Ironically, as a result of the integration of professional basketball in the early 1950s and his inability to no longer attract the best African American players, Saperstein transformed the Globetrotters from a very serious team into one that emphasized trick ball handling, comedy routines, and clownish behavior. This transformation brought harsh criticism from some observers who believed the Globetrotters had been turned into a team that embodied the stereotypical notion of black men as lazy and comedic fools, but the change in style only seemed to heighten interest in the team that began traveling the world and playing in front of thousands of fans of all ages. The increased popularity of the Globetrotters was so great and their political value so apparent, that the State Department sent the team on goodwill tours during the Cold War to help spread the belief in American democracy while at once counteracting the negative perceptions of race relations in sport. Unlike most independent black professional teams, the Globetrotters are still in operation, continuing to perform their warm-up drills to the sounds of "Sweet Georgia Brown," raising the pitch of their voices, uttering wild screeching sounds, and humiliating the Washington Generals on the hardwood and other white foils.

Irrespective of its success, fan interest, and media attention, basketball was not as important and culturally significant to African Americans as baseball during the first half of the twentieth century. While the recent past has seen a dramatic decrease in the number of African Americans in the sport, for many years the black community embraced baseball with much enthusiasm, organizing many teams and leagues with a large number of participants and a great deal of press coverage. African Americans flocked to the sport like seemingly everyone else during the first half of the twentieth century, but participation in baseball was especially important to them symbolically since it was fashioned as the national pastime and a great leveler in a society that was open to everyone regardless of race and color.

As noted before, the Cuban Giants are considered by most to be the first black professional baseball team. Founded in 1885 at the Argyle Hotel in Babylon, Long Island, by headwaiter Frank P. Thompson in collaboration with John Lang, C. S. Massey, and S. K. "Cos" Govern, the Cuban Giants were a highly successful club that continued to compete up through the second decade of the twentieth century. Other outstanding black professional baseball teams of the period included such clubs as the New York Gorhams, Pittsburg Keynotes, Norfolk Red Stockings, Philadelphia Giants, Harrisburg Ponies, and Leland Giants.

While leagues were formed among the first black professional baseball teams, they were typically short-lived with weak organizational and administrative structures. That all changed in 1920, however, when Rube Foster, a Texas native and owner and manager of the Chicago American Giants, organized the Negro National League (NNL). The NNL initially consisted of eight teams with two franchises in Chicago and one each in Detroit, Dayton, Indianapolis, St. Louis, Kansas City, and Cincinnati. The NNL, along with the Eastern Colored League (ECL) that was founded in 1923, brought needed organizational structure to black baseball and created excitement among African Americans for the sport. Teams representing each of the two leagues played the first Negro World Series in 1924, with the Kansas City Monarchs capturing the initial title by defeating the Hilldale club of the ECL over ten games. Unfortunately, in 1928, the ECL folded and three years later, largely as a result of the Great Depression and death of Foster, the NNL closed its doors. In 1933, Gus Greenlee, a Pittsburgh numbers racketeer, bootlegger, and nightclub owner, restored the NNL. In 1937, a rival Negro American League (NAL) was formed that was comprised of franchises in the South and Midwest. The rejuvenated NNL and new NAL guided negro league baseball through some of its best years.

Negro league baseball, even during its heyday of the 1930s, faced major financial difficulties and a host of other problems. The large number of African Americans who had made their home in major cities in the North following the Great Depression did not always have the time or discretionary money to support the Negro Leagues. As a result, teams did not play a full

Figure 3.2.   Team picture of the Philadelphia Giants, who for a time were one of the most dominant teams in Negro League Baseball. Sol White, who wrote a 1907 book on the history of black baseball, is in the back row, third from left.
Courtesy of the National Baseball Hall of Fame and Museum.

slate of league games, competing instead against a variety of different teams, both black and white and pro and semipro, on barnstorming tours throughout the United States, Central America, Mexico, and the Caribbean. If more money could be made, it was not uncommon for teams to refuse to play scheduled league games. In addition to a financially limited black fan base, few Negro League teams owned their own ballparks so they were forced to rent those owned by white minor and Major League teams. This created both monetary and logistical problems since paying rent was costly and minor and Major League ballparks could only be used when those teams that owned them were out of town on away games.

In spite of these constraints, Negro League Baseball became a very important cultural institution in the African American community. An important example of black pride and entrepreneurship and providing much enjoyment and sense of fulfillment during the harsh years of Jim Crow, Negro League Baseball had some great players and teams who fashioned their own style of the game. The racially exclusionary policies of MLB meant that Negro League teams had access to the best black talent. Although most students of the game would agree that there was a decidedly different level of talent in Negro League Baseball, a fact partly attributable to not teaching the proper techniques and fundamentals of the sport, there were a large number of outstanding black players with the requisite skills to play at the very highest levels of competition. Those included the likes of such legendary players as

Josh Gibson, Satchel Paige, Oscar Charleston, Buck Leonard, John Henry "Pop" Lloyd, Turkey Stearnes, Ray Dandridge, Mule Suttles, Cool "Papa" Bell, and Willie Wells. Of all the players in black baseball, no one was more famous than Paige, the enormously skilled pitcher from Mobile, Alabama, who became a "larger-than-life" figure by virtue of his performances on the mound, personality, and showmanship. His pitching prowess alone would have garnered him celebrity status. He had amazing control, an assortment of pitches, and threw with great velocity. Hitters accounted for their failures against the extraordinarily gifted right-handed hurler by explaining that: "You can't hit what you can't see." As physically gifted and successful as he was on the mound, however, Paige became a folk hero by supplementing his many victories as a hurler with comedic routines, free and easy-going life-style, tall tales, and quotes that have become part of the American lexicon. "Don't look back. Something might be gaining on you" is probably Paige's most oft-repeated quote.[8]

The decidedly different talent level among the players in Negro League Baseball was also true of its owners. The best of them, however, were highly skilled business people who adroitly guided their teams under less than optimal circumstances. Rube Foster was certainly one of those people as owner of the Chicago American Giants, as was Effa Manley of the Newark Eagles, J. L. Wilkinson of the Kansas City Monarchs, Cumberland Posey Jr. of the Homestead Grays, and Gus Greenlee of the Pittsburgh Crawfords. Each one of these owners has an interesting story, but Manley's stacks up with any of them as a woman who struggled to find success in the male world of baseball. Always a question about her racial background since she was so light in complexion, Manley was co-owner of the Eagles for a time with her husband, Abe, a racketeer who was some twenty years her senior. Upon his death, she assumed total control of the Eagles and led them to great success on the playing field during the 1940s and one of the NNL's most profitable franchises. During her tenure, the Eagles had such outstanding players as Larry Doby, the first black to integrate the American League, and two other future Major Leaguers in Monte Irvin and Don Newcombe. Besides running the Eagles, Manley was heavily involved in the civil rights movement, serving as treasurer of the Newark, New Jersey, chapter of the NAACP and an active member of the Citizen's League for Fair Play.

Like many other separate black sports organizations, including the previously mentioned Philadelphia Tribune Newsgirls, Harlem Globetrotters, and Renaissance Five, Negro League baseball teams on occasion played white teams. African Americans took great pride in these contests, particularly when black teams came out on top against supposedly superior white teams.

Figure 3.3. Satchel Paige was the biggest drawing card in Negro League Baseball.
Courtesy of the National Baseball Hall of Fame and Museum.

For a time, Major League teams played Negro League teams on a yearly basis until Commissioner Kenesaw "Mountain" Landis put a stop to the games. Embarrassed by the increasing number of victories by Negro League teams in these interracial contests, believing they gave MLB a "black eye," Landis eventually ruled that only all-star teams of major leaguers could play black teams.[9] This ruling also came with the stipulation that these games could only be played in the off-season and that major leaguers could not play in the uniforms they wore during the regular season.

A common form of these games pitted a team of Major League all-stars against one of the intact teams from the Negro Leagues, whether it was the Chicago American Giants, Kansas City Monarchs, or one of the many other black clubs. Perhaps creating even more fan interest and publicity were those games in which Major League all-stars went up against a contingent of Negro League all-stars. People thronged to see the games between the Dizzy Dean all-stars and Satchel Paige all-stars during the mid-1930s because they centered on the matchup between the great white hurler from the St. Louis Cardinals and the Negro Leagues' best pitcher and most famous player. Available accounts indicate that Paige's team was victorious in two-thirds of those games. Drawing enormous amount of attention in 1946 were the series of games played between the Bob Feller all-stars and Satchel Paige all-stars. While the two great hurlers were primarily used for publicity purposes, typically pitching just the first few innings of a game, the contests drew thousands of spectators as the two teams traveled across the country on their way to California.

In addition to these all-star games, a small number of Negro League teams, most often the Kansas City Monarchs, ventured west to play black and white teams in the well-known Denver Post Tournament and National Baseball Congress Tournament in Wichita, Kansas. Organized in 1915 as a semi-professional event to determine the best team in the city, the Denver Post Tournament ultimately expanded to an invitation only double elimination affair that by the 1930s was attracting teams from all across the country. In 1934 the Kansas City Monarchs became the first black team invited to the tournament and represented themselves very well, coming in second to the long-bearded House of David baseball team, a club that originated among a Midwestern religious cult. The ultimate irony was that the Monarch's pitcher Chet Brewer was outdueled in the game 2–1 by Satchel Paige who had been recruited for the tournament by the House of David. The Monarchs captured the championship on a number of occasions following their second place finish in 1934, sometimes beating one of the many black clubs that were now receiving invitations to participate in the tournament.

The National Baseball Congress Tournament invited black teams from the time of its inception in 1935. Run by Ray Dumont, president of the National Baseball Congress and close friend of Monarchs owner J. L. Wilkinson, the tournament offered $10,000 for the champion in an effort to lure the best teams from across the country irrespective of race. The tactic worked as outstanding clubs traveled to Wichita to participate in the highly contested games. The champion of the first tournament was a black team from Bismarck, North Dakota, made up of Paige and such other legendary players as Chet Brewer, Quincy Trouppe, Hilton Smith, and Double Duty Radcliffe. Various black clubs from different parts of the country would capture the tournament championship in subsequent years. Like the Denver Post Tournament, the National Baseball Congress Tournament was crucially important in that black players were placed on an equal footing with white players in a highly organized setting that allowed them to exhibit their talents for all to see.

These tournaments aside, Negro League Baseball, like its Major League counterpart, sponsored both a World Series and All-Star Game. Since 1924, a World Series had been played on a sporadic basis by Negro League teams and was an event that generally attracted few fans and was a financial failure. The lack of success stemmed from the fact that black fans could not afford to attend a consecutive number of games that made up the World Series. The event was also at a disadvantage because of limited franchise identity, no permanent playing site, and that it was frequently held after the Major League season when white players were available to play against barnstorming Negro League players looking for larger paychecks than could be realized through a long series of games against one opponent.

Far more important than the World Series was the Negro League East-West Classic. Referred to by historian Rob Ruck as "Black America's Baseball Fiesta," the East-West Classic was the brainchild of the *Pittsburgh Courier* sportswriter William G. Nunn and Pittsburgh Crawfords's traveling secretary Roy Sparrow who early in 1933 proposed the idea of a black all-star game to Homestead Grays owner Cumberland Posey Jr.[10] Looking for ways to promote the revival of Negro League Baseball while in the midst of the Great Depression and undoubtedly aware of *Chicago Tribune* sports editor Arch Ward's success in convincing the owners in MLB to hold an all-star game, Nunn and Sparrow hoped to have their proposed black all-star game at Yankee Stadium in support of the New York Milk Fund. When their plan to hold the event in New York fell through, they approached Gus Greenlee with the idea of a black all-star game. Greenlee, recognizing the worthiness of the idea and the potential publicity and marketing value of such a contest, embraced the idea and immediately began planning, with the assistance of Chicago American Giants owner Robert Cole, for the first East-West Classic to be held in 1933 at Comiskey Park in Chicago.

The inaugural East-West Classic, held in a historic ballpark and in a city with a large black population and love for baseball, was a resounding success. Some eight thousand fans watched the West's 11–7 victory over the East squad. The East-West Classic would continue to be played until 1962, with Chicago always serving as host city. When two East-West Classics were played during the year, which happened on five different occasions, the second games were hosted either by Cleveland, Washington, D.C., or New York City.

The East-West Classic, which by 1936 was drawing an estimated twenty-one thousand fans and becoming a major source of revenue for Negro League owners, was important to the African American community because it provided an opportunity to showcase the talents of black baseball's best players. Perhaps most importantly, the East-West Classic was a grand social event, "a holiday for at least 48 hours," according to famous sportswriter Sam Lacy.[11] Special trains were chartered to bring fans from New Orleans, New York City, and other cities across the country to share in the excitement of the game itself and take in the many sights and sounds of Chicago. People would party with friends, listen to great jazz, and enjoy the many cafes, bars, and ballrooms located close to Comiskey Park.

The most prominent African Americans from seemingly all walks of life attended the East-West Classic. It was important for people to be there to confirm their social standing, rub shoulders with the rich and famous, make business deals, and cement relationships with new and old friends. Among the many notable people who attended the East-West Classic, perhaps none stood out more than the famous athletes from other sports who attended the event. Joe Louis, the great heavyweight boxing champion, attended the East-West Classic, as did the lesser-known but extraordinarily talented fighter Henry Armstrong, Olympic broad jump medalist DeHart Hubbard, and the celebrated and widely popular Harlem Globetrotters Marquis Haynes and Goose Tatum.

The East-West Classic would continue to be played until 1962. It had lost its appeal far before that time, however. The attendance figures for the games at Comiskey Park in the late 1940s made clear that the East-West Classic had lost its attraction for African Americans. Attendance for the game in 1949 was estimated at 31,097, but just two years later had fallen to 21,312

Figure 3.4. The East-West All-Star Game was a grand athletic and social event that showcased the greatest players in Negro League Baseball.
Courtesy of the National Baseball Hall of Fame and Museum.

and by 1956 was listed at just 8,567. The East-West Classic had simply gone the way of the Negro Leagues more generally as a result of Jackie Robinson's breaking of the color barrier in MLB in 1947 and the gradual entry of other African Americans into the highest levels of the sport. Black fans were deserting their own version of the sport and flocking to Major League ballparks to watch with pride as African American players competed alongside and against white players. This did not come as a surprise to Effa Manley and the other owners in Negro League Baseball who were, like other African Americans, always faced with the difficult choices of individual success, group loyalty, and integrationist ambitions.[12] They wanted the best for their race, but found it difficult to support the efforts to integrate MLB because they understood full well that it would mean the death of their own teams and leagues.

Negro League owners were correct, of course, as the integration of organized baseball effectively put an end to their business operations. The same thing would happen to many other separate black teams and leagues at both the amateur and professional levels of competition that had prospered behind the walls of segregation. As integration unfolded and the most talented African American athletes found their way into predominantly white organized sport, black fans began to patronize in increasing numbers Major League ballparks, NFL stadiums, NBA arenas, and big-time college sport venues and frequented less often those separate sports programs that had served them so well for so long because they were interested in watching and rooting for athletes who were the very best at what they did. The result was the collapse of many separate sports programs, particularly professional ones, and deterioration in the quality of play and diminishing prestige of others on account of a decidedly inferior athletic talent pool and host of other issues. One classic example of this transformation were the sports programs at HB-CUs which declined dramatically in regards to quality of play as physically gifted athletes who often had little choice but to attend a black institution during the era of segregation were now being recruited in greater numbers by prestigious predominately white institutions. Although the CIAA and other leagues among HBCUs, albeit with different member schools over the years, would remain important and serve as a coalescent force in the African American community, their sports programs are Division I in name only, suffering from a lack of athletic talent and persistently meager financial resources, poor support systems, and inadequate facilities.

CHAPTER FOUR

~

Striving to Be Full
Participants in America's Pastimes

While the majority of African American athletes were forced to satisfy their competitive impulses primarily behind the walls of segregation between the first and second world wars, a select number of them overcame the racial realities of the period and played alongside of and against white athletes at both the amateur and professional levels of sport. Some talented African American athletes played a number of different sports at integrated high schools located in small towns and cities in the northeast, upper Midwest, plain states, and far west. The more talented of these athletes went on to distinguish themselves in sport at some of the most well-known and prestigious predominantly white colleges and universities in the United States. The most highly skilled of these athletes, most notably those in track and field, garnered international attention and lasting fame for their triumphs in Olympic competition. Not unexpectedly considering their long history in the sport, there were some extraordinarily gifted African American boxers during this period at various weight divisions who realized hero status in the black community for their triumphs in the ring.

Participating in integrated sport was both a blessing and a curse since it allowed African American athletes to regularly test their abilities against those of their white teammates and opponents, but also opened them up to some of the worst forms of racialist thinking and discrimination. The discrimination they experienced was both subtle and overt, running the gamut from racial slights and epitaphs to physical violence and exclusionary practices. The South, of course, posed a major problem for African American athletes in regard to segregated travel accommodations and whites-only housing, restrooms, restaurants, and other public facilities. Perhaps most importantly, the South, primarily through its segregated educational institutions and regional amateur sports organizations, maintained racially discriminatory policies that precluded interracial athletic contests in the region and negatively impacted African American athletes in all regions of the United States.

Athletes Who Made Their Alma Maters Proud

An increasing number of outstanding African American athletes would distinguish themselves on the playing fields at integrated high schools and predominantly white colleges and universities during the interwar period. The decade of the 1930s in particular would see a noticeable increase in highly skilled African American athletes who would make their way onto the campuses of prestigious predominantly white colleges and universities. Although a variety of factors were responsible for this growth, it was largely attributable to the continued, though reduced, migration of southern blacks to northern urban centers and the resulting increase in the number of African American students attending college. Coupled with this fact was that predominantly white colleges and universities were seemingly now more willing to disregard an athlete's skin color and accept physically talented individuals who could contribute to their school's institutional prestige through success in sport.

Although some of these men were far more interested in their performance on the playing field than in the classroom, perhaps most notably Jesse Owens who struggled academically and never did graduate from Ohio State, many of them were outstanding students who would go on to very productive professional lives once their athletic careers came to a close. Taking a balanced approach to academics and sport that characterized the lives of William Henry Lewis and many of the other African American student-athletes at the turn of the twentieth century, these men took their studies seriously in preparation for careers in education, business, law, and other prestigious professions. For instance, Jerome "Brud" Holland, an outstanding football player at Cornell University and member of the College Football Hall of Fame, took his BS and MA degrees from Cornell and PH.D from the University of Pennsylvania. He spent his post college career in a number of prestigious professional positions, including serving as president of Delaware State College and Hampton Institute, US Ambassador to Sweden, Director of the New York Stock Exchange, and Head of the American Red Cross. Willis Ward, football and track and field star at the University of Michigan, was an excellent student who took his law degree from the Detroit College of Law. He went on to a distinguished career as a lawyer and judge, serving for a time as chairman of the Michigan Public Service Commission. George Gregory, Jr., honors student and basketball star at Columbia University, took his law degree from St. John's University and became heavily involved in New York City politics, civil rights, and an assortment of activities related to youth development and curbing of juvenile delinquency. He was a founding member of the New York City Youth Board and directed the Harlem Youth Center and Forest Neighborhood House in the Bronx. James LuValle, track and field star and Phi Beta Kappa student at UCLA, took his Ph.D. at Cal Tech before teaching at Fisk University and then later conducting research for Kodak. He completed his career as director of undergraduate chemistry labs at Stanford University. Homer Harris, football star at the University of Iowa who became the first African American captain in the Big Ten, took his medical degree from Meharry Medical College and set up a dermatology practice in his hometown of Seattle, Washington where he worked for 43 years. His dermatology practice supposedly became the largest west of the Rocky Mountains.

The academic and athletic success of the previously mentioned African American athletes and many others at predominantly white universities were made during an era that was still fraught with some of the worst forms of racialist thinking and discrimination. Not one of these athletes was immune from it. In fact, as members of an extremely small minority group in an overwhelmingly white setting, these African American athletes were constantly reminded of their inferior status in an assortment of different ways. They certainly felt a sense of social isolation, living in an environment made up almost entirely of white students, coaches, faculty, and administrators. Those African American athletes who attended predominantly white universities located in small rural towns with limited or no black communities—and these were the locations for many of the great college sports programs in the United States—were especially susceptible to this sense of social isolation, as they had no black support system to nurture them and offer them counsel and a shoulder to lean on during difficult times.

The sense of social isolation experienced by African American athletes at predominantly white universities during the interwar period was, in many regards, the least of their worries. Although not always easy to ascertain whether the mistreatment they experienced was racially motivated or the result of personality differences or jealousy of their athletic skills, many of them experienced mistreatment at the hands of their white teammates, coaches, and opponents. They had teammates who refused to support them, coaches who used disparaging racial comments as motivational tools, and opponents who seemingly took special delight in inflicting punishment on them outside the normal bounds of fair play.

The most written about and most obvious form of racial discrimination experienced by African American athletes at predominantly white universities involved southern institutions, especially those in the Deep South, that refused to compete against them on account of their color. These incidents, which garnered far more media attention and public outcry than the snubbing experienced by Paul Robeson in 1916, occurred with remarkable regularity and at a cost to African American athletes caught between the rigid racial segregation of southern institutions and unwillingness of northern schools to stand up for principle and fair play. Although there are examples of southern institutions refusing to compete against northern schools with African American players in every sport, including the famous snubbing in 1941 of Harvard's African American lacrosse player Lucien Alexis by the US Naval Academy, the black and white press covered most often and in greater detail those incidents involving intersectional football games that had taken place in the United States since at least 1890. "King football" was the dominant sport on university campuses and any time a northern institution acquiesced to southern institutions and kept their African American players out of a contest, commonly known as gentlemen's agreements, the incidents were magnified and drew an enormous amount of attention and heated controversy.

Examples of northern schools agreeing to keep their African American athletes out of gridiron contests against southern schools are numerous and provide insights into the pernicious nature of race and simultaneous growth of college sport as big business in the United States during the interwar period. They also furnish important insights into the increasing influences of coaches, cooperation between black and white students, the power of protests and community engagement, and enormous influence of university presidents. The gentlemen's agreement was on full display in 1929 when New York University (NYU) agreed to keep its African American player Dave Myers (another NYU black player William O'Shields was not part of the controversy because he seldom played) out of its scheduled November 9 game against the visiting University of Georgia. When the decision became public, a storm of protests was lodged about the exclusion of Myers, a talented running back who had actually been kept out of an earlier game in the season against West Virginia Wesleyan under the pretense that he was suffering from a cold. Black and white students at NYU joined forces and made public their anger over the decision by gathering support from community groups, holding rallies, and confronting the university administration.

Well-known sportswriters from black and white newspapers, along with the NAACP and other groups and individuals, hammered away at NYU coach Chick Meehan and both NYU president Elmer E. Brown and University of Georgia president Charles M. Snelling for entering into the agreement and maintaining rigid segregation on America's playing fields. Noted sportswriter Heywood Broun blasted Meehan by referring to him as "the gutless coach of a gutless university."[1] Unfortunately, all of the protests proved ineffective as several days before the contest NYU proclaimed that Myers would not play against Georgia because of a supposedly recurring shoulder injury. If being excluded from the Georgia game was not bad enough, Myers incurred the wrath of many influential African Americans for his refusal to quit the team following the incident.

Equally distasteful and, in some ways even more outlandish, was the gentlemen's agreement entered into by the University of Michigan and Georgia Tech in 1934. Willis Ward, the great football and track and field star at Michigan, received much acclaim for his athletic exploits, but he is probably best remembered for a game in which he was not allowed to participate. As early as the fall of 1933, word leaked out that Georgia Tech football coach and athletic director William A. Alexander had written to Michigan athletic director Fielding Yost, the offspring of a confederate soldier, that Georgia Tech would refuse to play in the following year's game in Ann Arbor if Ward was in Michigan's lineup. As the game approached, it was apparent that Michigan would likely accede to Georgia Tech's demand and keep Ward out of the contest. The realization that the popular, academically gifted, and athletically talented Ward would suffer such a fate resulted in a major controversy on the Michigan campus. Faculty expressed their frustrations to the upper-level administration, students led demonstrations and mass meetings, and the NAACP, Ann Arbor Ministerial Association, and other organizations filed formal protests and circulated petitions to the university committee. As was the case with Dave Myers some five years earlier, Michigan did not allow Ward to play and supposedly restricted him from sitting on his team's bench or watching the game from the press box. An interesting, and some might say bizarre, twist to the story was the compromise struck by the two universities prior to the contest. In an effort to maintain competitive balance while also not forcing anyone to violate its racial policies, Michigan elected not to play Ward in exchange for Georgia Tech's benching of star end Hoot Gibson. In the end, the teams two best players, one white and one black, were forced to sit out the intersectional contest because of southern tradition and northern capitulation.

Boston College's Lou Montgomery suffered the same fate as Dave Myers and Willis Ward, but several times over and with even more extended press coverage. Historian Charles H. Martin writes that Boston College treated Montgomery in an "especially egregious" fashion, keeping him out of "more games [against southern institutions] than any other football player in the annals of the sport."[2] Montgomery, a Brockton, Massachusetts, native who had seriously considered playing at UCLA after an illustrious high school football career, ultimately decided to take his gridiron talents to Boston College where he enrolled in 1937. A running back, Montgomery played on the freshman team in 1937, was used sparingly on the varsity squad in 1938, but blossomed the following season under new coach Frank Leahy who had been hired to upgrade the football program at Boston College. Leahy, a protégé of the famous Notre Dame coach Knute Rockne, recruited outstanding local talent and sought out the best teams to play so as to improve Boston College's football ranking and national profile. With the eastern football powers unwilling to play Boston College, Leahy scheduled contests against schools from different parts of the country, including the segregated schools of the South. This would have a deleterious effect on Montgomery's playing career. Boston College, willing to sacrifice their Jesuit ideals to achieve national prominence in the sport, capitulated to the demands of southern institutions and kept their star running back out of both regular season and year-end bowl games. Montgomery would encounter the gentlemen's agreement for the first time in just the third game of the 1939 season. In a pattern that had become all too familiar in gridiron contests between northern and southern institutions, the University of Florida insisted that Boston College follow through on the contract the schools had inked which stipulated that Florida would refuse to play against a black player and if the game were canceled would not forfeit the money they had been promised. Boston College ultimately refused to buck Florida and sat Montgomery for the contest. Some of Montgomery's teammates contemplated sitting out the game and Montgomery apparently threatened to quit the team, but eventually decided to stay with the club. History would repeat itself three weeks later when Boston College benched Montgomery in their home game against Auburn University, once again unwilling to stand on principle and break the secret agreement it had made with the southern institution to bar black athletes from participation. Montgomery would be barred from playing for a third time that season when he was benched for Boston College's Cotton Bowl game against Clemson in Dallas, Texas. Montgomery did not even make the trip to Dallas, staying back home in Boston as his Boston College teammates struggled in a 6–3 loss to the Clemson Tigers.

The 1940 season did not result in any better treatment of Montgomery. While Boston College enjoyed a glorious year on the gridiron, winning all ten of their games and packing the stands at historic Fenway Park for home contests, he was not allowed to participate in all those victories. Montgomery was left out of the second game of the season against Tulane in New Orleans. He traveled with the team, but was forced to watch the game from the press box rather than be seen sitting on the bench with his white teammates. Later in the season, Auburn returned to Boston for a rematch with the Eagles and once again Montgomery was benched for the contest. Boston College's undefeated season was rewarded with an invitation to play Tennessee in the 1941 Sugar Bowl in New Orleans. Boston College accepted the invitation, but again capitulated to southern prejudices and had Montgomery watch from the press box as they beat the previously undefeated University of Tennessee Volunteers. All told, in two seasons, Montgomery had been forced to miss six games, not because of injury or playing ability but because of deeply entrenched racial mores that were slow to dissipate.

Montgomery was obviously frustrated with being benched on multiple occasions, but throughout his two-year ordeal exhibited extraordinary composure and loyalty to his teammates. Tellingly, while Montgomery and other African American athletes were being humiliated by southern racial practices, there were a number of schools that began to schedule intersectional football games irrespective of the racial composition of the teams. These contests, albeit sometimes entered into grudgingly, took place among schools in the border-states and southwest and not in the Deep South. Although these contests were about upholding principles and defying racial mores, they were also about schools pursuing athletic prominence and reaping financial rewards. They also serve as examples of how important particular individuals were in overcoming the Jim Crow policies associated with intersectional athletic contests.

In 1936 the University of North Carolina became the first prominent southern institution to participate in an integrated football game when they played NYU who had on its roster the African American sophomore running back Ed Williams. Played at the Polo Grounds, the game, narrowly won by North Carolina 14–13, caused no apparent outpouring of protests with Williams playing significant minutes and without incident. The two schools played each other again in New York in 1937 and 1938 with Williams performing well despite NYU being on the losing end of both contests. Although the three games came about for a variety of reasons, the two schools would not have played each other if it were not for the efforts of president Frank P. Graham of North Carolina. Graham, a liberal and staunch supporter of civil rights and racial equality, actually wrote to chancellor Harry W. Chase of NYU prior to the first game of the series indicating that North Carolina would play the contest irrespective of who "The Violets" put on the field. The show of goodwill and sportsmanship on Graham's part was extraordinary in the world of intercollegiate sport at the time and was not lost on African Americans who followed the racial travails surrounding intersectional football games. His decision evidently did not result in any outpouring of public protests from southern whites, which perhaps can be partially explained by the fact that all three games were played in New York City.

The University of North Carolina's willingness to participate in integrated intersectional football games was taken up by a select number of other predominantly white universities. Among those were the decisions by the University of Oklahoma and University of Missouri in 1939 to play in the North against Big Ten institutions with African Americans on their squads. Oklahoma played against the integrated Northwestern University football team in Evanston, Illinois, that year, thrashing the Wildcats who had on their squad African American James Smith. On the very same day, Missouri was shut out by Ohio State who had on their team the black running back Charles Anderson who contributed significantly in the Buckeyes' 19–0 victory.

Garnering less attention from the eastern press but equally important in moving toward the elimination of Jim Crow policies in college sport was the decision by several predominantly white universities in Texas to play intersectional football games against integrated squads from schools in the west. White universities with differing affiliations and stages of development in Texas, a state with relatively less rigid approaches to racial matters, sought out these contests so as to improve their athletic reputations, and by extension, the reputations of their individual institutions. Two years prior to North Carolina's historic first contest against NYU, Texas Tech University, at the time a small and little known regional institution, lost 12–6 to Loyola Marymount and its outstanding African American tackle Al Duval.

Three prominent Texas schools in the Southwestern Conference made the long trek west to play UCLA, an institution that would establish a reputation for welcoming and providing a supportive environment for African American athletes. Southern Methodist University (SMU), Texas Christian University (TCU), and Texas A&M University, looking to add money to their coffers, enhance their reputations, and potentially secure a bowl appearance, all made their way to California to play the Bruins. SMU, which was experiencing serious financial problems in its athletic department and university more generally, first played UCLA in 1935 and overwhelmed a Bruin squad that at the time was all white. Circumstances would be decidedly different, however, when SMU returned to California in 1937 and 1940 to play the Bruins. Two of the outstanding players on the UCLA team were African Americans Woody Strode, a standout end, and Kenny Washington, a very gifted halfback. The two talented players were Los Angeles natives and close friends who had the distinction of reintegrating the National Football League in 1946 when they signed with the Los Angeles Rams. From all indications, UCLA volunteered to keep Strode and Washington out of the lineup if SMU asked that they be benched, but the Mustang's coach Matty Bell and his players insisted that the two players participate in the game so that it would prove to be a meaningful contest with all the best athletes on both clubs participating. Despite one of Washington's greatest games, SMU pulled out a come from behind victory over the Briuns 26–13. The return game in 1940 was won again by SMU, this time against a Bruin team that had two different African Americans on its roster, end Ray Bartlett and multitalented halfback Jackie Robinson who would realize hero status when he became the first black to play modern MLB.

TCU made only one trip west to play UCLA. In 1939 they played an outstanding Bruins team that included Bartlett, Strode, Washington, and Robinson. The Horned Frogs, who had claimed the unofficial national championship the previous season with Heisman Trophy winner Davey O'Brien at quarterback, lost to the Bruins 6–2, which put an end to their hopes for a Rose Bowl bid. The UCLA victory, on the other hand, put the Bruins into the conversation about a Rose Bowl appearance, but their hopes were dashed when they lost to the University of Southern California (USC) in an exciting contest in the last game of the season. A victory over USC would certainly have caused a national controversy and the ire of southerners since the University of Tennessee was expected to receive an invitation to play in the Rose Bowl. Texas A&M, a powerhouse in the Southwest Conference who were anointed the unofficial national champion in 1939, defeated UCLA 7–0 at the Los Angeles Coliseum in 1940. The game resulted in angry reactions from UCLA fans and sportswriters who accused the Aggies of dirty tactics and intentionally trying to knock Jackie Robinson and other Bruins out of the contest.

Running for Uncle Sam

The public debate and struggles encountered regarding intersectional intercollegiate athletic contests make clear the regional racial differences and paradoxes of racial customs in America. What institutions were willing to play against integrated teams varied by place, with schools in the Deep South steadfastly refusing to do so and those schools in the border states with less firmly established racial policies consenting to competing against African American players. These regional differences as well as the complexities of racial mores became clear in track and field, a sport in which African Americans became so closely identified. What marked track and field, however, is that leaders of the sport at the national and Olympic levels of competition had always insisted that their events be integrated. Unlike the NCAA, which has rarely broached questions regarding racial issues, the AAU and American Olympic Committee (AOC) clung to the principles of fair play and allowed African Americans to compete in track and field at the highest levels of competition. Although representing regional members that took diverse approaches to racial matters, including those in the Deep South devoted to strict racial segregation, these national organizations sponsored meets in places where legal segregation was firmly entrenched and monitored. There is little doubt that this racially inclusionary approach was to some extent guided by the need to ensure that America was represented by the best athletes in the most important of all international sporting events irrespective of color. The Olympic Games were about national prestige and international reputations, so it was imperative that Uncle Sam be represented by the most talented and highly skilled athletes who could win medals and preferably gold.

A testament to the more progressive position taken by the national organizations that controlled track and field were their staging of meets in the South and refusal to condone racially discriminatory practices on the part of regional associations when it came to national championships and selection of American Olympic teams. The AAU, which annually held its very prestigious national track and field championships, and the AOC, which insisted on fair competitions at all Olympic trials, stood firm on racial inclusion at the national level so as to ensure that the best athletes could participate at the highest level of competition. As early as 1907, the AAU held its national track and field meet in Norfolk, Virginia, where John B. Taylor, the great runner from the University of Pennsylvania, became the first African American to capture a national title by winning the quarter-mile race. Although some local AAU clubs chose not to participate because of the presence of Taylor and other African American athletes, leaders of the national organization insisted that all athletes be allowed to compete regardless of race. In 1927, the AAU showed its commitment to open competitions when it decided to pull its national track and field championships out of New Orleans after the mayor of the city and officials from the regional association made it clear that they would not allow African American athletes to participate in the meet. Another show of commitment to racial inclusion was the AAU's sponsorship of a track meet at the 1936 Centennial Fair in Dallas, which included as participants Eddie Tolan and Ralph Metcalfe who garnered fame for their great performances in the Los Angeles Olympic Games four years earlier.

The AAU national championships, while enormously important events that garnered much media attention, would never challenge the Olympic Games in sheer magnitude and international acclaim. African American athletes had some important successes in some of the earliest Olympic Games as evidenced by George Poage's two bronze medals in the 200– and 400–meter hurdle races in 1904 in St. Louis, John B. Taylor's gold medal as a member of the 4x400–meter relay team in 1908 in London, DeHart Hubbard's gold medal in the long jump, Edward Gourdin's silver medal in the long jump, and Earl Johnson's bronze medal in the 10,000 meters in 1924 in Paris. Although perhaps not that noticeable at the time, it quickly became apparent that the large majority of African American male Olympians would come from predominantly white institutions rather than HBCUs. This seemingly resulted from the fact that for much of the twentieth century, or at least prior to the passage of Title IX in 1972, predominantly white institutions recruited only the very best African American male athletes while the most talented African American female athletes were forced to compete at HBCUs.

The 1932 games in Los Angeles was a watershed event in regard to African American participation in Olympic competition. A highly successful Olympic festival, all the more remarkable since it was held in the midst of the Great Depression, the Los Angeles games witnessed some outstanding individual performances by African American athletes in track and field's marque events. Eddie Tolan, the diminutive sprinter from the University of Michigan known as the "Midnight Express," captured gold medals in the 100 and 200 meters; Ralph Metcalfe, the Marquette University star, won silver in the 100 meters and a bronze in the 200 meters; and Edward Gordon, an outstanding athlete from the University of Iowa, garnered the gold medal in the long jump. Of these triumphs, it was Tolan's victories in the sprints that captured much of the attention from the black press who wrote glowingly of the performances of the "Midnight Express." As the newly crowned "world's fastest human," Tolan's triumphs, while not approaching the representational importance of the heavyweight championship or even subsequent Olympic performances, were symbolic in nature and elicited enormous racial pride from black commentators. Through newspapers, periodicals, and other outlets, many black commentators juxtaposed Tolan's great performance with his inferior status as a black man in a segregated society as part of the larger efforts aimed at racial uplift. He became, like many black athletes to follow, an example of achievement and symbol of possibility.

The triumphs of Tolan and his black teammates in Los Angeles in 1932, while truly significant to the African American community and society at large, would fade into the background and forever be replaced in the public consciousness by the confluence of events surrounding the Berlin Olympic Games four years later. The 1936 games in Berlin, often referred to as the Nazi Olympics, was a major international sporting event that garnered an extraordinary amount of media attention and controversy and an equal amount of soul searching. As historians have made clear, a worldwide debate ensued among countries prior to the games as to whether they should send their athletes to Berlin to compete or keep them home. With knowledge of Adolph Hitler's belief in Aryan racial superiority and increasing realization of the torture and deaths taking place in Germany, countries had to weigh the benefits of participating in the games and the implications resulting from a boycott. Perhaps nowhere was the debate more intense than in the United States, especially between July and December 1935. The debate was so intense that it split the AAU right down the middle with one faction led by AAU president Jeremiah T. Mahoney arguing for a boycott and another faction led by AOC president Avery Brundage arguing for participation. Mahoney's central argument was that participation in the Berlin games would at least give implicit approval of the carnage in Nazi Germany, while Brundage believed—and this philosophy would guide him his entire career—that sports and politics should never mix and that the games must go on.

The black press freely entered into the debate, regularly offering its opinion on whether the United States should send their athletes to Berlin or keep them at home. With the expectation that the United States would be represented up to that time by the largest contingent of African American athletes in Olympic history, well-known black newspapers ranging from the *Chicago Defender* and *Pittsburgh Courier* to the *Cleveland Gazette* and *New York Amsterdam News* took a special interest in the debate regarding participation in the Berlin games. There was never unanimity of opinion among black newspapers regarding the boycott issue, but a common theme that ran through all of them was what they viewed as the hypocritical stance taken by many leaders of the Olympic movement. It was difficult for them to comprehend how some Olympic officials could argue for a boycott on account of Germany's racial policies while not speaking out against the discrimination of African Americans. Although certainly not condoning the mistreatment of Jews and other groups in Nazi Germany, black newspapers astutely pointed out that every argument made against holding the games in Berlin could just as easily be used to rationalize why they should not be held in the United States.

A select number of black newspapers took the same philosophical position as the pro-boycott faction of the AAU and argued that the United States should keep their athletes at home, contending that it was the principled stance to take considering the horrible conditions in Nazi Germany. The strongest advocate of this position was the *New York Amsterdam News*, which was perhaps influenced by the large number of individuals and groups in New York City that were pushing for a boycott. Not unexpectedly, the majority of black newspapers were strongly opposed to a boycott, contending that the best way to fight the Nazi's belief in Aryan racial superiority was to send African American athletes to Berlin and have them be victorious in Olympic competition. It was the best way, noted one black newspaper, to raise the prestige of the "despised darker races and lower the prestige of the proud and arrogant Nordic."[3] Interestingly, black newspapers as well as influential African Americans leaders on both sides of the boycott debate tried to persuade black athletes expected to participate in the games to adopt their respective positions on the issue of participation or nonparticipation. In one well-known letter dated December 4, 1935, NAACP Secretary Walter White implored Jesse Owens not to participate in the Berlin games. "It is my first conviction," wrote White in his letter to Owens, "that the issue of participation in the 1936 Olympics, if held in Germany under the present regime, transcends all other issues. Participation by American athletes, and especially those of our own race, which has suffered more than any other from American race hatred, would, I firmly believe, do irreparable harm."[4]

White's letter, which may never have gotten to Owens, would probably have fallen on deaf ears anyway as the Ohio State star had spent much time honing his talents and the Olympic Games was too important for him to pass up. This all became a moot point when the AAU decided at its December 6–8, 1935, meeting to send American athletes to Berlin, a decision only made possible by Avery Brundage who used his influence—though some might contend underhanded tactics—to persuade members to vote for participation. The AAU decision was certainly a disappointment to pro-boycott forces but a relief to athletes from the United States who were anxious to display their talents to the world. The games themselves, which were filled with great pageantry and symbolism and forever etched in the public consciousness because of Leni Reithanstahl's famous documentary *Olympia*, saw Germany win the all-important medal count but also witnessed a dominating performance by black athletes from the United States in the track and field competitions. A fabulous contingent of extraordinarily gifted African American athletes hailing from predominantly white institutions in the upper Midwest, northern plain states, and California, garnered multiple medals in a variety of events in Berlin's newly constructed stadium. Mack Robinson, older brother of Jackie Robinson and Pasadena Junior College student, captured the silver medal in the 200 meters; Archie Williams, from the University of California at Berkeley, won the gold medal in the 400 meters; John Woodruff, from the University of Pittsburgh, garnered the gold medal in the 800 meters; Cornelius Johnson, from Compton Junior College in California, won the gold medal in the high jump; David Albritton, from Ohio State University, captured the silver medal in the high jump; Fritz Pollard Jr., from the University of North Dakota, won the bronze medal in the 100 meter hurdles; Ralph Metcalfe, from Marquette University, captured the silver medal in the 100 meters and a gold medal as part of the 400 meter relay team; James LuValle, from UCLA, won the bronze medal in the 400 meters; and Jesse Owens captured gold medals in the 100 meters, 200 meters, long jump, and as a member of the 400 meter relay team.

The star of stars was Owens because of the four gold medals he won in some of track and field's most glamorous events. He realized immediate hero status following his four gold medal–winning performance with people clamoring for his autograph, searching him out for photographs, and positioning themselves to be in the presence of the great African American sprinter who almost single-handedly shot a hole in the Nazi's theory of Aryan racial superiority. Not unexpectedly, black America lionized Owens, swelling with pride over his accomplishments and heaping praise on him for overcoming the odds faced by all African Americans to achieve greatness in his chosen sport. His name still resonates with people around the world, completely overshadowing his black teammates, many of whom, in spite of distinguished professional careers, would go on to live lives of relative anonymity once their athletic careers were over. While Ralph Metcalfe, John Woodruff, and the other "black auxiliaries," a phrase coined by the German press to describe the African American athletes competing in Berlin, have largely faded from national memory, Owens secured his place in history with an unparalleled performance in a controversial Olympic festival fraught with symbolism and the specter of race and evil always close at hand. In the words of historians John Gleaves and Mark Dyreson, "Owens remains an icon in American visions of national identity, a vision of speed and an emblem of the complexities of segregation and racism."[5]

One of the great myths perpetuated by American sportswriters regarding the 1936 games was that Adolph Hitler refused to shake Owens's hand following each of his triumphs. "Like George Washington's cherry tree and Abe Lincoln's log cabin, rail splitting youth," noted Owens's biographer William J. Baker, "Owens's snub at the hands of Hitler is the imaginative stuff of hero worship."

Figure 4.1.   Jesse Owens at the start of his gold medal–winning performance in the 200-meter race at the 1936 Olympic Games in Berlin.
Courtesy of Library of Congress Prints and Photographs Division. LC-USZ62-27663.

The tale spun by American scribes, one that was accepted as fact for so many years, fit neatly into the need for people "to believe in a moral order: the evil Hitler insulting the innocent Owens."[6] In reality, as Baker and other historians have pointed out, on the first afternoon of track and field competition in Berlin, Hitler publicly congratulated German gold medalists Tilly Fleischer and Hans Woellke and later a Finnish gold medalist in his private box. Late in the afternoon, with rain beginning to fall, Hitler and his entourage left the stadium just before the playing of the American national anthem as Cornelius Johnson was being awarded his gold medal in the high jump after edging out his teammate David Albritton. Whether Hitler intentionally snubbed Johnson or not, which could have been the case considering his hatred of blacks, Jews, and other minorities, President of the International Olympic Committee Henri de Baillet-Latour made clear to Der Fuhrer that as head of the host country he had to be impartial and either congratulate all winners or none at all. Hitler chose the latter approach and beginning the next day of competition—the day in which Owens captured his first gold medal—stopped congratulating victors in his private box and received German medalists in private. The press, unaware of Baillet-Latour's edict, began spinning the yarn that Hitler had intentionally snubbed Owens when in fact it was Johnson who could legitimately claim to have been slighted by Der Fuhrer.

Owens's spectacular victories in the Berlin games, along with his other athletic exploits, including his shattering of three world records and the tying of another at the Big Ten championships in 1935, would not only ensure him a place in the pantheon of African American cultural heroes, but would help reignite questions regarding the supposed superiority of black athletes resulting from unique genetic makeup and innate physical skills. The outstanding sprint times of Howard Drew earlier in the decade, along with the great performances of Eddie Tolan and Ralph Metcalfe in the 1932 Olympics and now the earthshaking display of speed by Owens and the other "black Auxiliaries" at the Berlin games, all combined to fuel speculation about the connection between race and sport performance that would, in one form or another, continue to this very day. Defenders of white supremacy turned to science and theories of natural endowments by arguing that the extraordinary exploits of Owens and other African American athletes stemmed from unique mental, emotional, and physical characteristics of their race. These theories, which essentially denied that the accomplishments of Owens and his black teammates had anything to do with hard work, discipline, and the other character traits so admired in the United States, were grounded in racialist thinking and the need to prove the crucial nature of heredity and hierarchy of the human races. Among the many who espoused this deep-seated stereotypical view was famous USC track coach Dean Cromwell who once noted that the success of African American sprinters and jumpers resulted from the fact they were more primitive than whites. "It was not long ago," wrote Cromwell, "that his (African Americans) ability to sprint and jump was a life-and-death matter to him in the jungle. His muscles are more pliable, and his easy-going disposition is a valuable aid to the mental and physical relaxation that a runner and jumper must have."[7]

Those who turned to racial science and theories of natural endowments would have their critics. The most outspoken of these was W. Montague Cobb, a noted physical anthropologist from Howard University and long-time editor of the journal of the all-black National Medical Association. So taken with the subject of race and athletic performance, Cobb conducted anthropometric measurements on Owens and other black athletes with the results being published in a 1936 issue of the *Journal of Health and Physical Education*. In an article titled "Race and Runners," Cobb made clear his position on the subject, convincingly arguing that the outstanding performances of African American sprinters and jumpers resulted from environmental factors rather than racially distinctive physical characteristics postulated by some such as the "Negroid type of calf, foot, and heel bone." Cobb noted that as an anthropologist, he could find no racial homogeneity among black sprinters, let alone between black and white sprinters. "If all of our Negro and white champions were lined up indiscriminately for inspection," wrote Cobb, "no one except those conditioned to American attitudes would suspect that race had anything whatever to do with the athlete's ability."[8]

Not unexpectedly, Cobb's investigations did not put an end to a debate that has, in one form or another, continued to this very day. Evidence for this can be gleaned from discussions involving the performances of African American athletes in Olympic track and field competitions following World War II. Although receiving relatively limited scholarly attention, there was a large contingent of outstanding African American track and field athletes who captured medals in the 1948 Olympic games in London and in Helsinki in 1952 and Melbourne in 1956. Ironically, perhaps the best known of these athletes was Alice Coachman, the Albany, Georgia native who became the first African American to win a gold medal in Olympic competition when she captured the high jump in London. But there were also the notable victories of such individuals as Harrison Dillard, the Baldwin Wallace College product and World War II veteran who is the only athlete to ever capture gold medals in both the sprints and hurdle competitions in Olympic competition; Mal Whitfield, the Ohio State star and member of the famed Tuskegee Airmen who garnered multiple medals in the 400 meter, 800 meter and 4 x 400 relay races in both London and Helsinki; and Milt Campbell, the great Plainfield, New Jersey and Indiana University athlete whose decathlon performances, a silver medal in Helsinki in 1952 and Gold medal in Melbourne in 1956, have always been overshadowed by Bob Mathias, Rafer Johnson, and others who have won the prestigious event.

The great performances of these African American athletes and many more in the Olympic games as well as in national and other international track and field competitions resulted in further speculation about the connection between race and sporting success. These discussions, it is important to note, took place at a time when efforts were being made at the highest levels of government to combat racial discrimination, most notably President Harry Truman's executive order barring discrimination in federal employment, and at the beginning of the Cold War period when well-known black athletes were being sent on goodwill tours by the State Department to combat the Soviet Union's criticism of the United States for its mistreatment of African Americans. Two essays published in 1952 by people who could not have been more different in regards to educational backgrounds and professional careers provide examples of the range of opinions as to the connection between race and athletic accomplishments. British medical doctor Adolph Abrahams comes down on the side of many scientists by postulating in his essay "Race and Athletics" in *The Eugenics Review* that the outstanding performances of African American athletes were the result of innate physical differences. "I think there is some special quality in his [African Americans] muscles," wrote Abrahams, "a more rapid contractibility or reduced viscosity. Alternatively, there may be a superior co-ordination related to his nervous system."[9] G. P. Meade, manager of the Colonial Sugars Company in Gramerey, Louisiana, who had a fascination with records and sport performances, expressed a different view than Abrahams in his essay "The Negro in Track Athletics" in the *Scientific Monthly*. Indicating "the question naturally arises as to why such a small segment of our population [African Americans] has provided such a large proportion of extremely high-class performances" and that "some anthropologists" had accounted for it by "racial difference in the comparative lengths of the leg bones and in the foot structure," Meade claimed that it was "difficult to believe that anatomical differences are the principal reason. Possibly the explanation is sociologic rather than ethnologic."[10]

The "Brown Bomber" and Other Black Fighting Men

Black boxers found it extremely difficult to secure championship fights after the reign of Jack Johnson. "Papa Jack," because of his refusal to acquiesce to the white power structure, insistence on living his life on his own terms, and violation of racial mores by marrying white women and having relationships with many others, did not make it any easier on those black fighters who followed him. The Johnson legacy, combined with a color line that showed no signs of weakening, would result in a continued pattern of black boxers fighting one another on multiple occasions while being denied the opportunity to compete for championships against white pugilists. This was especially true in the heavyweight division that was always the most prestigious and symbolic of all the weight classifications in the sport. All things considered, the heavier the fighters, the more important the fight.

One black boxer who deserved a title shot, but was unable to secure one because of the color line was Harry Wills, the very talented fighter from New Orleans known as "The Black Panther," whose career spanned some twenty years. A great puncher who won a total of seventy-nine fights, many of them against such well-known black fighters as Sam Langford, Joe Jeanette, and Sam McVey, Wills had a number of supporters who made concerted efforts to secure him a title fight with the great white champion Jack Dempsey. The black press tried in vain to get the soft-spoken and highly intelligent African American boxer a championship fight with Dempsey, the fighter who drew the ire of many for his refusal to enter military service in France. Nat Fleischer, founder and editor of Ring Magazine, used his influence in an attempt to raise public support for a championship bout between Wills and Dempsey. In 1925, a match between the two fighters seemed to be eminent after the New York State Athletic Commission (NYSAC) ruled that Dempsey must face Wills in the ring, but politics, race, business, and certainly personality differences would eventually doom the bout in the "Empire state." For unknown reasons, Commissioner George B. Bower changed his mind, deciding instead to support a subsequent vote by the NYSAC that approved a fight instead between Dempsey and the "fighting Marine" Gene Tunney. In New York, however, a committee independent of the NYSAC, which was responsible for issuing licenses to individual fighters, granted Tunney his license but refused to do the same for Dempsey until he agreed to fight Wills. This wrangling doomed any Dempsey and Tunney fight in New York, but Philadelphia seized on the opportunity and agreed to host the first fight between the two boxers on September 23, 1926. Tunney won the fight and did the same in the rematch a year later at Soldier Field in Chicago, a bout famously known as the "battle of the long count" resulting from Dempsey's refusal to go to a neutral corner after knocking Tunney to the canvas in the seventh round.

The reason for Wills's inability to secure a fight with Dempsey is complicated. Dempsey did vow to never cross the color line, but his actions and attitudes regarding race seemed to be far more fluid than his public pronouncements. He did fight black boxers prior to capturing the world title from Jess Willard in 1919 and would do the same in exhibition matches after his professional career in the ring was over. More likely—and historians have broached this question—Dempsey never entered the ring against Wills not necessarily because he refused to, but because others were making his choice of opponents for him. And this is where George "Tex" Rickard entered the picture. Rickard, the smart and not always scrupulous boxing promoter who staged the Johnson and Jeffries fight in Reno in 1910 as well as the Dempsey and Tunney battles, swore that he would never again promote a championship fight involving a black boxer. Dempsey, always the opportunist and a shrewd man, was perfectly willing to submit to Rickard's wishes regarding interracial boxing matches if it would lead to a big pay day and career advancement. As it turned out, Dempsey realized—in spite of his losses to Tunney—big pay days, with Wills left wondering what could have been.

Wills's disappointment in not securing a match with Dempsey for the heavyweight championship did not deter other African American boxers—many of them from lower class backgrounds—from continuing to hone their pugilistic skills and pursuing fame and fortune in the squared circle. Of those who followed Wills, none of them caught the imagination and became such beloved and idealized figures as Sugar Ray Robinson and Joe Louis. Born Walker Smith Jr. in Ailey, Georgia, in 1921, Robinson moved with his parents and two sisters to Detroit at a very early age and eventually to Harlem with his mother after her split from Robinson's father. After dropping out of De Witt Clinton High School in the ninth grade, Robinson focused his life on boxing and never looked back. He was undefeated as an amateur boxer, winning all eighty-five of his bouts, with sixty-nine of the victories coming by way of knockouts. Robinson turned professional in 1940 and went on to a career marked by world titles in different weight divisions and a number of highly publicized and memorable fights against the world's best boxers. He was unbeaten in ninety-one straight fights between 1943 and 1951, held the world welterweight title from 1946 to 1951, and was five times the world middleweight champion between 1951 and 1958.

Robinson, commonly referred to as the best boxer in the world "pound for pound," was a consummate fighter with great instincts, speed, and technique who could seemingly fight any style depending on his opponent. To many, he was simply the best boxer of all time. Versatility was a key to Robinson's success as he possessed the skill to throw a punch with both hands, use hooks and uppercuts with lightning quickness, and deliver knockout blows while moving backward. These skills were all on display in his first professional fight in 1940 against Joe Echevarria and up through his many bouts with Jake LaMotta and tussles with the likes of such bruisers as Bobo Olson, Gene Fullmer, Randy Turpin, Joey Maxim, and Rocky Graziano. There were a number of very memorable fights among the two hundred in Robinson's long career, but perhaps none of them are better known than his six bouts with LaMotta. Robinson beat the tough and hard charging LaMotta five times, most famously perhaps in the 1951 world middleweight title fight known as "The St. Valentine's Day Massacre." Unleashing a barrage of powerful combination punches, Robinson won a thirteen-round technical knockout with LaMotta hanging on the ropes. This fight and others from the Robinson and LaMotta series of battles were depicted in Martin Scorsese's Academy Award–winning film *Raging Bull*.

Robinson's fame in the ring was enhanced by a flamboyant lifestyle outside of it. He lived up to his name Sugar Ray. Possessing good looks, charisma, and a larger than life personality, Robinson owned his own restaurant, Sugar Ray's, where he hosted such stars from the entertainment industry as Lena Horne, Nat King Cole, Jackie Gleason, and Frank Sinatra. Parked outside was his prized flamingo-pink Cadillac, where people could admire the shiny and sleek automobile owned by the great champion. Robinson never traveled alone, always accompanied by an entourage that included gorgeous women, trainers, masseur, secretary, voice coach, barber, secretary, and his manager George Gainford. He was as "cool as the other side of the pillow," arguably the first celebrity athlete, an entrepreneur who sang and danced with a style all his own. He was so influential that others emulated his every move and younger boxers honored him by taking his name. None other than Muhammad Ali idolized him because of his extraordinary boxing skills and style both in and outside the ring.

Realizing even greater fame was Joe Louis, the enormously talented black fighter who held the heavyweight championship from 1937 to 1949 and fought some of the most celebrated and symbolically important bouts during the tumultuous period of World War II. Louis became a heroic figure, his triumphs in the ring inspiring black musicians to honor him through ballads, jazz, gospel, and the blues. Famous African Americans from every walk of life took pride in Louis's ring triumphs, speaking and writing glowingly of the great champion's importance to boxing, the black community, America, and the world at large. Individuals as diverse in temperament, personality, family background, and religious and political affiliations as Marcus Garvey, Lena Horne, Richard Wright, Lofton Mitchell, and Maya Angelou revered Louis and each in their own way remarked on his cultural impact in and outside the ring. Angelou, in her famous memoir *I Know Why the Caged Bird Sings*, provides insight into the meaning that Louis had for black America and the state of race relations in the United States during the 1930s. Recalling the coming together of seemingly the entire black community at the local store in tiny Stamps, Arkansas, to listen on the radio to the Louis and Primo Carnera fight, Angelou makes clear the jubilation that came over the gathering when Louis knocked Carnera to the canvas to win the fight. "When Louis was declared 'Champion of the World,'" wrote Angelou, "People drank Coca-Colas like ambrosia and ate candy bars like Christmas. Some of the men went behind the store and poured white lightning in their soft-drink bottles, and a few of the bigger ones followed them. Those who were not chased away came back blowing their breath in front of themselves like proud smokers."[11]

Louis, born in Alabama and raised in Detroit, Michigan, where his family had moved in search of a better life like so many other African Americans from the South who had made their way north following World War I, began his boxing career in 1932 at the age of seventeen and soon established himself as one of the country's outstanding amateur fighters with a number of victories in Golden Gloves and AAU tournaments. After accumulating an amateur record of 50–4 with forty-three knockouts, Louis turned professional under the guidance of an African American management team consisting of promoters John Roxborough and Julian Black and trainer Jack "Chappy" Blackburn. Eventually, well-known white boxing promoter Mike Jacobs signed Louis to an exclusive contract with Roxborough and Black continuing to serve as his managers and cashing in on his earnings in the ring. From the outset of his professional boxing career, Roxborough and Black carefully crafted a public image of Louis that ran counter to that of Jack Johnson. Both men made it clear to Louis that he should, among other things, never have a picture taken with a white woman, always be polite and soft-spoken irrespective of his accomplishments, never gloat after a victory in the ring, make clear his love for his mother and scripture, and always treat others with dignity and respect regardless of their station in life. For the most part, Louis adhered to this specific code of behavior, largely because it did not veer too dramatically from his true personality and genuine self.

Louis's first significant professional bout was against Primo Carnera, the gigantic six-six 265–pound former world heavyweight champion from Italy. The bout, held in Madison Square Garden on June 25, 1935, was fraught with symbolism. It was a fight between Louis, a black man representing an America that espoused democratic principles and equality of opportunity, and Carnera, representing the brutal regime of Benito Mussolini and fascist Italy. While the irony of a black fighter representing a country that had yet to live up to its democratic ideals was not lost on African Americans,

Louis's sixth-round knockout of Carnera brought them unadulterated joy, particularly because of their sympathy with Ethiopia which was trying desperately to maintain its independence amid the encroachment of Mussolini's Italy.

The fight with Carnera would, in many respects, pale in comparison to Louis's two epic fights with Germany's Max Schmeling in 1936 and 1938. In their first fight, held in New York's Yankee Stadium, Schmeling shocked the boxing world by knocking out the much younger Louis in twelve rounds. Schmeling, who was thirty years of age at the time of the bout, trained extraordinarily hard for the fight, while Louis, obviously underestimating his opponent, spent far too much time playing golf for which he had a lifetime passion and not enough in serious training at his Lakewood, New Jersey, retreat. Louis eventually recovered from the devastating loss and in 1937 captured the heavyweight championship by defeating James Braddock at Comiskey Park in Chicago. After defending the title on three separate occasions, Louis secured a rematch with Schmeling at New York's Yankee Stadium exactly one year to the day of defeating Braddock for the heavyweight championship.

The buildup to the second Louis and Schmeling fight was enormous. After defeating Louis the first time, Schmeling had become a hero in Germany, his twelve-round victory over the black American boxer used by the Nazis to promulgate their belief in Aryan racial superiority. For Louis's part, his status had risen dramatically since his devastating loss to Schmeling by virtue of his triumph over Braddock and the fact he had defended his title by defeating Tommy Farr, Nathan Mann, and Harry Thomas. Adding interest to the bout was the increasing tension worldwide resulting from Hitler's push toward war as evidenced by his takeover of Austria in March 1938. The combination of these factors generated much anticipation for a fight that would be a culturally significant event in sport history, one fueled by issues of race, politics, and international conflict. One legend, a dubious one according to author David Margolick, has it that on a visit to the White House shortly before the fight, President Franklin Roosevelt reputedly told Louis, "Joe, we need muscles like yours to beat Germany."[12]

The bout itself was far shorter than the buildup to it. Those late to their ringside seats missed it as Louis knocked out Schmeling in just two minutes and four seconds of the first round. The emotion that broke out following the bout, not just from the seventy-thousand-plus fans in attendance at Yankee Stadium but also the tens of millions listening to it over the radio in various languages, was overwhelming and palpable. The outpouring of emotion in the African American community could not be contained, black folks from Harlem and Los Angeles to points in between bursting with pride over Louis's quick work of Schmeling. Perhaps no one expressed more eloquently the emotions of African Americans following the fight than Richard Wright, the author of *Black Boy* and other famous works on the black experience who had a fascination with boxing. Shortly after the fight, Wright, who had previously written a piece on the significance of Louis's 1935 triumph over Max Baer, wrote two essays assessing the enormous impact that Louis's victory had on black America. In the second of those two essays titled "High Tide in Harlem: Joe Louis as a Symbol of Freedom," Wright makes clear the pure joy that came over the African American community in Harlem after Louis had put Schmeling on the mat. "In Harlem," notes Wright, "that area of a few square blocks in upper Manhattan where a quarter of a million Negroes are forced to live through an elaborate connivance among landlords, merchants, and politicians, a hundred thousand black people surged out of tap-rooms, flats, restaurants, and filled the streets and sidewalks like the Mississippi River overflowing in flood time. With their faces to the night sky, they filled their lungs with air and let out a scream of joy that seemed would never end, and a scream that seemed to come from untold reserves of strength."[13]

Louis successfully defended his heavyweight title on multiple occasions following his defeat of Schmeling. From January 1939 through May 1941, Louis defended his championship thirteen times against boxers collectively known, because of the pace and success at which Louis was fighting, as members of the "Bum of the Month Club." Included among this group were such top ranked boxers as "Two Ton" Tony Galento, John Henry Lewis, Gus Dorazio, Buddy Baer (brother of Max), Abe Simon, Al McCoy, and Bob Pastor. On June 18, 1941, Louis faced off against Billy Conn, the Light Heavyweight Champion who proved to be nobody's bum. Conn, in one of boxing's greatest fights, was up on points through the first twelve rounds, stinging an increasingly tired, dehydrated, and concerned Louis with repeated jabs. In the thirteenth round, however, Louis knocked out Conn who had made the mistake of exchanging blows with the stronger and heavier champion. By some measures, this fight with Conn would prove to be the apex of Louis's boxing career.

In 1942, Louis's boxing career was put on hold when he enlisted in the US Army. Like some other celebrities, the army assigned Louis to its Special Services Division rather than sending him into combat. In this role, he helped in the army's recruitment campaign and traveled thousands of miles on celebrity tours where he staged boxing exhibitions in an effort to lift the spirits of battle-worn soldiers. Unfortunately, like Sugar Ray Robinson and Jackie Robinson, Louis experienced instances of racial discrimination in the

Figure 4.2.   Oil painting of Joe Louis by Betsy Graves Reyneau (1946).
Courtesy of National Portrait Gallery, gift of the Harmon Foundation.

army. He also emerged from military service in serious financial trouble with the IRS taxing him over $100,000 for his charitable fights and Mike Jacobs claiming that Louis owned him $250,000 for his services. These financial difficulties, which haunted Louis for the rest of his life, forced him to continue to fight long past his prime and eke out a living with an assortment of jobs and other activities.

Following military service, Louis fought a rematch with Conn on June 19, 1946. In front of only forty thousand fans at New York's Yankee Stadium, Louis dispatched Conn, whose physical skills had deteriorated significantly since their first fight, in the eighth round. He defeated Jersey Joe Walcott, a veteran fighter with a 44–11–2 record, in a split decision on December 15, 1947, in Madison Square Garden and some six months later knocked out Walcott in the eleventh round in a rematch at Yankee Stadium. He did not defend his championship again before retiring from the ring on March 1, 1949.

The announcement, however, by the IRS that he owed more than $500,000 in back taxes combined with the fact he was very generous to his family with the small amount of money not spent on his handlers, forced Louis out of retirement. Working out an arrangement in which the IRS would receive the net proceeds from his fights, Louis's camp negotiated a title bout for September 27, 1950, with Ezzard Charles who the year before had wrested the heavyweight championship from Walcott. At the age of thirty-six and his reflexes gone, Louis was battered with one eye swollen shut at the end of his loss to Charles in fifteen rounds. After several fights with mediocre opponents, Louis secured a bout for October 26, 1951, with Rocky Marciano, an extraordinarily strong and hard punching heavyweight contender. Although being favored 6–5 to win the fight, many experts in the sport not only believed Louis would lose, but feared the younger and more powerful Marciano would inflict serious damage on him. The experts were right. Marciano punished his boxing idol, knocking Louis down in the eighth round with a vicious left hand and then a few seconds later through the ropes. In the dressing room following the fight, "Sugar Ray Robinson wept. Marciano came in crying too. He told Louis 'I'm sorry Joe.'"[14] Unfortunately, with no ring prospects left, Louis retired from the sport for the second time. Although similar to many boxers in that he possessed few marketable skills, Louis would retain celebrity status to the very end of his life, competing for a time as a professional wrestler, greeting tourists at Caesars Palace in Las Vegas, and playing and encouraging other African Americans to take up golf that had been his passion since being introduced to the sport early in his boxing career.

CHAPTER FIVE

~

Reintegration of Sport and Its Aftermath

While elite African American athletes distinguished themselves in a select number of amateur and professional sports, campaigns were being waged to reintegrate MLB and other sports at the highest levels of competition that had drawn the color line. Not unexpectedly, the most publicized and culturally significant campaigns focused on MLB. Racially segregated since the latter stages of the nineteenth century and representing the highest levels of competition in a sport considered America's most popular national pastime, prominent individuals and groups fought in an assortment of different ways to eliminate the color line in MLB. No group was more important in this effort than sportswriters from well-known black newspapers. Such notable sportswriters as Sam Lacy, Frank Young, Joe Bostic, Wendell Smith, and Chester Washington wrote regularly about racially discriminatory practices in MLB and other pastimes and that African American athletes deserved to play at the highest levels of sport.

Black sportswriters and those sympathetic to their cause, including liberal white sportswriters, Jewish Americans, and the communist press, were helped by World War II because it provided an opportunity to prick the consciousness of those in charge of professional sports by pointing out the hypocrisy of discriminating against African American athletes while the country was engaged in a war justified by upholding the Four Freedoms. The first crack in sport's color line came in 1946 when the Los Angeles Rams of the National Football League offered contracts to Kenny Washington and Woody Strode, former teammates of Jackie Robinson at UCLA. The signing of Washington and Strode, while certainly drawing national attention and leaders in the sport, did not generate the same level of euphoria among African Americans as did the entry of Robinson into MLB the following year because of professional football's relatively limited popularity at the time.

Robinson's entry into MLB with the Brooklyn Dodgers in 1947 represented an important symbolic victory for African Americans and had practical implications for racial integration in baseball specifically and sport more generally at all levels of competition. As MLB's first black player since Moses Fleetwood Walker in 1884, Robinson represented the possibility of an integrated America, while indicating that baseball was perhaps indeed the great leveler in society and open to everyone regardless of race, creed, or color. Robinson's integration of MLB would also lead to the entry of other African Americans into the sport and stimulate the shattering of the color line in other professional and amateur sports.

The rate of integration in these sports would be a slow and uneven process as African Americans continued to experience resistance from those who controlled sport. It would not be until 1959, twelve years after Robinson's debut with the Brooklyn Dodgers, that all the MLB teams would have an African American player on their roster. The Washington Redskins became the last team in the National Football League to integrate when it signed Bobby Mitchell in 1962, some fifteen years after Robinson's inaugural season with the Brooklyn Dodgers. The Deep South, of course, remained steadfast in its opposition to integrated sport, even in the adult directed athletic programs established for pre-adolescent children. The interscholastic and intercollegiate athletic programs in the Deep South would not become integrated until the latter part of the 1960s and very early 1970s. The integration of these athletic programs would gradually drain HBCUs of its most talented athletes just as the shattering of the color line in MLB would put an end to Negro League Baseball.

Jim Crow and America's Game

Baseball had special meaning for African Americans just as it did white Americans. It was the national pastime, a game played by boys and young men and watched and followed by many Americans who were enthralled with its unique emphasis on individuality within a team concept. The fact that the national pastime was lily-white at the Major League level of play was abhorrent to African Americans who spoke out loudly and consistently against the exclusionary policy. The group that was best suited to speak out about the color line was black sportswriters who valiantly campaigned to see that African American players were permitted to play MLB. Excluded from writing for white dailies for much of the first half of the twentieth century, these talented scribes, in addition to covering Negro League Baseball and other sports behind the walls of segregation, hammered away at MLB for its exclusionary policies through such prominent black newspapers as the *Chicago Defender, Baltimore Afro-American, Pittsburgh Courier, New York Amsterdam News, Indianapolis Recorder, Kansas City Call, Los Angeles Sentinel, Philadelphia Tribune,* and *St. Louis Argus.* These writers, who were supported in their efforts by Lester Rodney of the Communist Party's *Daily Worker* and a host of other more liberally minded white Americans, used every means at their disposal to see that African Americans were allowed to participate at the highest levels of the sport. These included appealing for common decency and fair play, pricking the consciousness of the leaders in baseball, convincing people of the talent level of black players, conducting interviews with Major League players and managers, and ultimately arranging tryouts for promising black players with big league clubs.

Black sportswriters faced a difficult task as they campaigned on behalf of black players. They had to confront obstinate and racially conservative owners as well as commissioner Kenesaw Mountain Landis who were determined to keep their sport white and out of reach for African American players irrespective of talent level. Black sportswriters were faced with the equally difficult task, however, of being supportive of black baseball while at once fighting for the integration of MLB. It was a conundrum since black sportswriters understood that the integration of MLB would likely doom the Negro Leagues. They were, like other African Americans in every walk of life, faced with the burden of balancing the need for individual recognition, group loyalty, and integrationist ambitions.

One black sportswriter who conducted a long-running campaign against MLB's exclusionary policies was Wendell Smith, a Detroit native and West Virginia State College graduate who began his career in 1937 with the *Pittsburgh Courier.* A close observer of sport and talented writer that had a gift for proffering logical arguments and not mincing words, Smith began attacking MLB for its refusal to sign African American players almost immediately after joining the *Courier* staff. In his first column on the segregation of MLB, written on May 14, 1938, and titled "A Strange Tribe," Smith castigated African Americans for continuing to patronize and spend money on MLB while not paying adequate attention to their own leagues. He strongly believed that the campaign to integrate MLB was only possible if black baseball was a thriving institution with a pristine organizational structure that adequately showcased the talents of African American players. "We know they [Major

League Baseball] don't want us, but still we keep giving them our money," wrote Smith. "Keep on going to their ball games and shouting till we are blue in the face. Oh, we're an optimistic, faithful, prideless lot—we pitiful black folk."[1]

Smith followed this column with many others dealing with the campaign effort. He also proposed by 1939 that a NAACP be established on behalf of black players, conducted an interview with National League President Ford Frick and eight managers as well as forty players in that league to assess their views on the color line in baseball, called on President Franklin Roosevelt to create a "Fair Employment Practice Policy" in MLB, and offered suggestions regarding those African Americans who had the talent level to play at the highest level of the sport. He organized, moreover, a meeting between commissioner Landis and the Black Newspaper Publishers Association, helped arrange a tryout for black players with the Boston Red Sox, and recommended to the Brooklyn Dodgers' Branch Rickey that he sign Jackie Robinson to a contract.

Smith and others involved in the campaign effort were helped, ironically enough, by the US entrance into World War II. The war provided an ideal opportunity for those involved in the campaign effort to point out the hypocrisy in baseball specifically and the United States more generally. Taking their cues from the *Pittsburgh Courier*'s "Double V" campaign that stressed victory abroad against the Axis powers and victory at home against racial discrimination, those fighting for the inclusion of African Americans in MLB effectively pointed out how illogical it was to maintain the color line in the supposedly most democratic of all sports while the United States was involved in a war for the Four Freedoms against a country espousing a belief in Aryan racial superiority. Fortunately, while difficult to assess the direct impact that Smith and his fellow campaigners had on the power brokers in MLB, there were a select number of individuals in the senior circuit who were seriously considering the signing of black players.

One of those individuals was Brooklyn Dodgers' general manager Branch Rickey. An Ohio Wesleyan University graduate who had invented and made popular the farm system in his previous position with the St. Louis Cardinals, Rickey had considered for some time signing a black player. A deeply religious man who was focused on putting the best players on the field for the Dodgers, Rickey considered many black players to integrate the sport but finally settled on Jackie Robinson whom he signed to a minor league contract on August 28, 1945. Robinson was the perfect choice. He possessed all the attributes Rickey deemed essential for the first African American to integrate the sport. He was intelligent, possessed great athletic talent, had lived most of his life in a predominantly white environment, and was smart and disciplined enough to withstand the racial epithets and discrimination he would likely encounter as he made his way through white organized baseball.

Robinson's signing in 1945 and debut with the Brooklyn Dodgers two years later was extraordinarily important to African Americans and the larger civil rights struggle. Historian Jules Tygiel claimed that Robinson's integration of MLB was a "tale of courage, heroics, and triumph. Epic in its proportions, the Robinson legend has persevered—and will continue to do so—because the myth, which rarely deviated from reality, fits our national perceptions of fair play and social progress."[2] Tygiel's assessment was not mere hyperbole as Robinson's shattering of the color line caused much excitement among African Americans who viewed it as a sign that the United States was finally living out the true meaning of its creed. Robinson, for his part, proved Rickey correct, garnering rookie of the year honors in 1947 and going on to an outstanding ten-year career that culminated in his selection to the Baseball Hall of Fame in 1962.

Figure 5.1. Jackie Robinson on dugout steps between Dodgers teammates Pee Wee Reese (on his right) and Billy Cox (on his left).
Courtesy of the National Baseball Hall of Fame and Museum.

Larry Doby, who only recently has been adequately acknowledged for his role in the integration of baseball, became the first African American player in the American League when he signed with the Cleveland Indians in the same year that Robinson began his career with the Dodgers. Robinson and Doby would be followed into MLB by an initial wave of African Americans that included such legendary players as Ernie Banks, Hank Aaron, Roy Campanella, Willie Mays, Frank Robinson, Monte Ervin, and Elston Howard. The process of integration in the national pastime, however, would be a very slow and uneven process with not every team in MLB having a black player on its roster until the Boston Red Sox signed Pumpsie Green in 1959. The slow rate of integration partly resulted from the fact that some of the best players from the Negro Leagues were past their prime and no longer possessed the skills necessary to participate at the highest level of the sport. The leaders in baseball were also careful, as were the leaders in other sports at all levels of competition, to maintain racial quotas so as to minimize racial hostility on their teams and against opponents with mostly white players.

Shattering the Color Line in Other Professional Sports

The history of African American involvement in professional football was decidedly different than that in MLB. Several black players competed in the sport prior to the establishment of the National Football League (NFL) in 1920 and even more would distinguish themselves in the twelve years that followed. Charles W. Follis, a halfback who competed for the Shelby Athletic Club between 1902 and 1906, was the first African American professional football player in the pre-NFL era. He was followed into professional football by such outstanding black players as Charles (Doc) Baker of the Akron Indians, Henry McDonald of the Rochester Jeffersons, and Gideon (Charlie) Smith of the Canton Bulldogs. The first two African Americans in the NFL were Fritz Pollard, the former Brown University star who played for several teams and Robert (Rube) Marshall, a former University of Minnesota end who played for Rock Island and Deluth. Pollard and Marshall would be joined in the NFL in the ensuing years by African American players Paul Robeson, Jay (Inky) Williams, John Shelbourne, Fred (Duke) Slater, James Turner, Sol Butler, Dick Hudson, Harold Bradley, David Myers, Joe Lillard, and Ray Kemp.

These athletes, most of them who had been great performers on predominantly white college teams, distinguished themselves for the various clubs that made up the new league. Although confronted by racial discrimination on and off the playing field, they were integral to the success of the fledgling NFL. Fritz Pollard would even serve as a head coach in the new league for the Akron Pros. Unfortunately, NFL owners decided in 1933 to draw the color line. Although the sources are not clear as to why NFL owners made the decision to exclude African American players at this time, most of the blame has been laid at the feet of George Preston Marshall, the southern-born owner of the Washington Redskins who once noted when asked why there were no African Americans on his team that he would "start signing Negroes when the Harlem Globetrotters start signing whites."[3] Other reasons given for the new Jim Crow policy were simply efforts to rationalize a decision made by NFL owners that was indefensible. Some argued that the league did not have enough money to scout African American players, while others feared that African American players would be targeted and suffer injuries at the hands of southern-born players who were intent on hurting them. Others spoke of the logistical problems in finding separate travel, dining, and hotel accommodations for African Americans when they were on the road, while still others claimed, absurdly so, that there were few African American players at the college level who had the requisite skills to play in the NFL.

The color line drawn by NFL owners in 1933 would not be toppled until 1946. In that year the NFL was reintegrated when the Los Angeles Rams signed former UCLA teammates Kenny Washington and Woody Strode to contracts. It came about through a confluence of factors. As was the case in the integration of organized baseball, black sportswriters, in this case primarily at the more local level, played a very important role in the reintegration of the NFL. Almost from the moment they relocated from Cleveland to Los Angeles, the Rams began to receive pressure to sign African American players from noted *Los Angeles Tribune* sportswriter Halley Harding. A great all-around athlete who had played with both the Harlem Globetrotters and Kansas City Monarchs, Harding's seminal moment in his efforts to see that the Rams were reintegrated took place on January 15, 1946, at a meeting of the Los Angeles Coliseum Commission (LACC). Harding, in the company of two supportive Los Angeles County Board of Supervisors and black sportswriters Edward Robinson of the *California Eagle* and Herman Hill of the *Pittsburgh Courier*, made an emotional speech in which he accused George Preston Marshall of drawing the color line, recounted the exploits of African Americans who had played in the NFL, questioned why a player as talented as Kenny Washington had never been drafted, and most importantly argued vehemently that no team that discriminated against African Americans should be permitted to play in the publically funded Los Angeles Coliseum. The LACC agreed, telling the Rams they would have to have at least one African American on their team in order to lease the Coliseum.

The Rams, now with little choice in the matter regarding the use of the Coliseum yet intent on adding additional talent to their roster, finally rid themselves of their segregated status a couple of months later by signing Kenny Washington and then several weeks after that inking a contract with Washington's ex-UCLA teammate Woody Strode. Several months after the Rams signed Washington and Strode, the Cleveland Browns of the All-America Football Conference, a league founded in 1944 by *Chicago Tribune* sports editor Arch Ward, signed contracts with the outstanding black running back Marion Motley from the University of Nevada, Reno, and Ohio State's lineman Bill Willis. Although the names of Motley and Willis resonate more fully now with football fans than those of Washington and Strode because of their outstanding careers and the fact that they were chosen to the Professional Football Hall of Fame, the initial signing of the four African American players garnered little attention compared to the Brooklyn Dodgers signing of Jackie Robinson. The relatively smaller media coverage had nothing to do with the skill level or personal characteristics of the four African American players, but resulted instead from the limited popularity of professional football at the time. The professional game had yet to become a national pastime with a consistently large following, a fact that would not change until the 1950s when television would spark increasing interest in what is now perhaps the United States' most popular commercialized sport.

Although there was limited fanfare regarding the signings of the four African American players by the Rams and Browns, the pace of integration in professional football was similar in some ways to that in professional baseball. No NFL team would sign another African American player until 1948 when the Detroit Lions inked contracts with Mel Groomes and Bob Mann. It would be 1949 before the NFL drafted an African American player, the Chicago Bears taking Indiana University running back George Taliaferro in the thirteenth round. Before 1950 only three of the ten teams in the NFL had African Americans on their rosters. The All-America Football Conference fared better in regard to integration with six of the league's eight teams having black players at the time it merged with the NFL in 1950. By 1952 every team except one in the newly reconfigured NFL had an African American player, the lone holdout being the Washington Redskins.

The Redskins, owned by the Grafton, West Virginia–born George Preston Marshall, steadfastly refused to sign an African American for some sixteen years after the initial signing of black players in the NFL. Marshall, a highly opinionated self-promoter and racially insensitive man who had turned his family's small laundry into a million dollar business, continually turned a deaf ear to those who pressured him for years to sign an African American player. No one could guilt Marshall into signing a black player, even legendary *Washington Post* sportswriter Shirley Povich. Perhaps Marshall's number one nemesis, Povich hammered away at the Washington Redskins owner for paltry player salaries, cheating a charity out of money (for which Marshall unsuccessfully sued Povich and the *Post* for libel), and interfering with the coaching of the team. He even threw barbs at Marshall's wife, trashing her 1947 book *My Life with the Redskins* for its sappiness and self-serving approach. Povich saved much of his criticism, however, for Marshall's refusal to sign black players. He was appalled by Marshall's white supremacist views and insistence on maintaining Jim Crow policies in an effort to appease his white southern television and radio audience. The shame of it all for Povich is that there were many outstanding African American players available who could vastly improve the Redskins and make them a far more competitive and successful team. Among those mentioned were such great players as Roosevelt Brown, Lenny Moore, Jim Brown, Roosevelt Grier, and Jim Parker. "Jim Brown, born ineligible to play for the Redskins," wrote Povich after one memorable game in which the amazingly gifted Cleveland Browns running back had almost single handedly beat the hometown team, "integrated their end zone three times yesterday."[4]

While Povich and many others were not able to convince Marshall to integrate his team, the obstinate owner who on more than one occasion ran onto the field to protest an official's call or would shamelessly confront a heckler was ultimately no match for the Secretary of the Interior Stewart Udall. Born into a Mormon family and a former basketball player at the University of Arizona who took his law degree from the same institution and had been a member of the US House of Representatives, Udall's primary responsibilities as Secretary of the Interior under newly elected President John F. Kennedy were public lands, national parks, and the lives and conditions of Native Americans. He also decided, however, to take dead aim at George Preston Marshall for his refusal to integrate the Redskins.

Udall, who had a deep commitment regarding equality of opportunity and was greatly affected by the increasingly influential civil rights movement, was upset with Marshall's segregationist ways, viewing the Redskins' owner as "one of the few remaining Jim Crow symbols in American sports."[5] In obvious reference to the new DC Memorial Stadium, Udall wrote to Marshall on March 24, 1961, and made it clear that the Interior Department would not countenance any racial discrimination by anyone using a public facility in a designated park. He followed it up with a news conference on the very same day in which he made it explicit that Marshall would not be allowed to use the DC Memorial Stadium if Marshall continued his ban on African American players. Four days later at another news conference, Udall gave Marshall an ultimatum, explaining that if the Redskins did not adhere to the Kennedy administration's policy of antidiscrimination by signing a black player by October 1, the team would lose its lease and face possible criminal charges.

The stand taken by Udall would garner national as well as local attention and receive much support from a number of different individuals and groups. Edwin B. Henderson, local physical educator, civil rights activist, and chronicler of African American athletes, urged a boycott of all Redskins games until the team signed a black player. In 1961, the Congress of Racial Equality (CORE) and NAACP boycotted Redskin's games and picketed both DC Memorial Stadium and Marshall's home. Owners of other sports franchises urged Marshall to comply with Udall's order to integrate the Redskins.

Marshall responded in an assortment of different ways to Udall's edict to integrate the Redskins, at first making light of the order and then questioning, among other things, why the Secretary of the Interior would get involved in such a trivial issue and did the government also plan to exert pressure on segregated football squads at predominantly white colleges and the White House press corps that was all white? Notwithstanding these responses, it became apparent that Marshall, no doubt influenced by NFL Commissioner Pete Rozelle who urged him to accede to Udall's order so as not further embarrass the league, would make an effort to integrate the Redskins. Told by Udall that he could field an all-white team in 1961 in the DC Memorial Stadium if a promise was made to integrate the Redskins the following season, Marshall set about searching for an African American player. Finally, at the December 2, 1961, NFL draft at Chicago's Shoreham Hotel, the Redskins' head coach Bill McPeak selected Heisman Trophy–winning black running back Ernie Davis from Syracuse University and black fullback Ron Hatcher from Michigan State. Shortly after the draft, however, it was announced that Davis had been traded to the Cleveland Browns for its first-round pick Leroy Jackson from Western Illinois University and a player to be named later that turned out to be the Browns' outstanding black halfback Bobby Mitchell. In the spring of 1962, the Redskins traded with the Pittsburgh Steelers for the black guard John Nisby. This brought the number of African American players to four for the 1962 season, with a fifth, wide receiver Joe Hernandez from the University of Arizona, joining the club in 1964. Of these players, Nisby and Mitchell were unquestionably the best. Nisby spent eight seasons in the NFL and played in three Pro Bowls. Mitchell had an even more distinguished

NFL career, making 521 receptions for a total of 7,954 yards, playing in four Pro Bowls, chosen as one of the seventy greatest Redskins of all-time, and being chosen to the Professional Football Hall of Fame in 1983. He served in the front office of the Redskins, including a stint as assistant general manager, for some thirty-four years following his playing career.

The desegregation of the Washington Redskins took place during a period of time in which professional football was experiencing unprecedented growth and increased popularity in the United States. African American players would contribute significantly to this process, particularly following the creation of the American Football League (AFL) in 1960. The brainchild of Texas oilman Lamar Hunt, the AFL welcomed African American players from the time it was founded, providing increased opportunities for athletes from HBCUs. Athletes from HBCUs joined white and black players from predominantly white universities on the rosters of AFL franchises in such cities as Houston, Dallas, Oakland, San Diego, and Denver. At the time of the official merger of the AFL and NFL in 1970, it was apparent that black players had become a dominant force in professional football with some 30 percent of them participating at the highest level of the sport. The trend upward would continue with blacks now constituting some 68 percent of all the players in the NFL.

The integration of professional basketball, while not without its difficulties, seemed far easier to accomplish than that in professional baseball and football. The more loosely organized structure of professional basketball and the fact that black teams had always played against white teams seemingly played a part in this difference. The two most famous black teams, the New York Renaissance Five and Harlem Globetrotters, barnstormed the country, including the South, playing against both black and white teams. Both clubs participated in and realized success in the World Professional Basketball Tournament, an invitational tournament made up largely of white teams sponsored by the *Chicago Herald American* and held each year from 1939 to 1984 at various sites. An indication of their talent levels is the fact that the Renaissance Five captured the first tournament in 1939 with a 34–25 victory over the Oshkosh All-Stars and the following year the Globetrotters captured the championship with a 31–29 triumph over the Chicago Bruins. In 1943 the all-black Washington Bears, with many Renaissance Five players on their roster, won the title by beating the Oshkosh All-Stars 43–31.

African Americans also realized important opportunities in the National Basketball League (NBL). Established in 1937, the NBL was for over a decade the most prominent professional basketball league in the United States with great players on the rosters of teams located largely in small markets in the Great Lakes area. In addition to giving professional basketball some much-needed stability, the NBL was more progressive on matters of race than leagues in other sports. Although largely motivated by money concerns rather than altruism, the league did nonetheless open its doors to black players. In 1942, with a number of the league's players in the armed forces, the Toledo Jim White Chevrolets and Chicago Studebakers signed African American players. One of the black players signed by the Chevrolets was Bill Jones, a former star at the University of Toledo. Unfortunately, both the Chevrolets and Studebakers, who had a number of Harlem Globetrotters on their squad, were eventually forced to disband because of financial problems, partly a result no doubt of the effects of World War II. The Renaissance Five, playing as the Dayton Rens, disbanded in 1949 after competing for one year in the NBL.

This level of involvement by African American players in the NBL was important in setting the stage for integration when the NBL merged with the short-lived Basketball Association of America (BAA) in 1949 to create the National Basketball Association (NBA). It did not take long for the new league to tap into black talent. In 1950, Chuck Cooper became the first black to be taken in the NBA draft when he was selected by the Boston Celtics, Nat "Sweetwater" Clifton became the first black to sign with an NBA team when he inked a contract with the New York Knicks, and Earl Lloyd became the first black to play in a regular NBA game with the Washington Capitols. The three players, while realizing various levels of success on the court, set the stage for the many other black players that would follow them into the league. Cooper, who played collegiately at Duquesne, spent four years with the Celtics before being traded for one-year stays with the Milwaukee Hawks and then later to the Fort Wayne Pistons. He played 409 games in his NBA career, scoring a total of 2,725 points for a 6.7 per game average. Lloyd, who played four years at West Virginia State, had a nine-year NBA career split among the Capitols, Syracuse Nationals, and Fort Wayne Pistons. He played in over 560 games, scoring a total of 4,682 points for an 8.4 per game average. He was selected in 2003 to the Basketball Hall of Fame. Clifton, who played for a brief time with the Renaissance Five and Globetrotters and one season with Negro League Baseball's Chicago American Giants, spent six seasons with the Knicks and one season with the Fort Wayne Pistons. He scored a total of 5,444 points for an average of 10 points per game.

There was no immediate flood of black players into the NBA following the debut of Cooper, Lloyd, and Clifton into the league. It was initially a slow trickle, but by the latter part of the 1950s and early stages of the 1960s a steady stream of outstanding black players would enter the NBA and help transform it into a very large, important, and influential sports organization. By 1965, blacks made up 51 percent of the players in the league. Among those 51 percent were some of the greatest players in basketball history, including the likes of Don Barksdale, Oscar Robertson, Walt Bellamy, Bill Russell, Wilt Chamberlain, Elgin Baylor, Hal Greer, Sam Jones, and Lenny Wilkens. This initial wave of black players were followed by such great hoopsters as Dave Bing, Earl Monroe, Nate Thurmond, Elvin Hayes, Walt Frazier, Willis Reed, Julius Erving, Kareem Abdul Jabbar, Isiah Thomas, Magic Johnson, Michael Jordan, Shaquille O'Neal, David Robinson, Tim Duncan, Kobe Bryant, and LeBron James. By 2014, close to 77 percent of the players in the NBA were black.

The integration of the NBA, while apparently hurting the league's attendance levels for some time, would result in a more expressive playing style that placed a premium on creativity and improvisation. Like the integration of other professional sports, it also meant the death knell for many all-black basketball teams and organizations. For one famous all-black basketball team, however, the integration of the NBA did not result in its demise but was an opportunity to continue to reinvent itself. Harlem Globetrotters' owner Abe Saperstein, losing out on the best black talent and playing on deep-seated prejudices, turned his once seriously competitive team into a troupe of performers who adopted comedy routines and clownish behaviors to please predominantly white fans. Cognizant of the racial attitudes in the United States, the Saperstein-led Globetrotters performed their routines to "Sweet Georgia Brown" and moved on the court while making high-pitched shrieking sounds and engaging in physical antics that fit neatly into the stereotypical notion of black men as lazy and comical. To Saperstein, this was good business, but to many African Americans the Globetrotters were no different than the Hollywood movie characters that portrayed black men as comedic fools and less than human.

The integration of other professional sports would follow on the heels of the elimination of the color line in baseball, football, and basketball. Two of those sports were ice hockey and golf. While they are different in an assortment of different ways, the two sports are similar in that they have remained largely white. Art Dorrington, a center from Truro, Nova Scotia, was the first black to sign with a National Hockey League (NHL) franchise when he inked a contract in 1950 with the New York Rangers, but never played in the league in spite of some impressive statistics at the lower levels of the sport. The first black to actually play in the NHL was Canadian Willie O'Ree, an outstanding winger who made his debut with the Boston Bruins in 1958. Often referred to as the "Jackie Robinson of ice hockey," O'Ree had a long career with the Bruins, staying with the club for over two decades. He would be the only black in the league until 1974 when Mike Marson began his seven-year career with the Washington Capitals. The first black American to play in the NHL was Valmore James who made his debut in 1981 with the Buffalo Sabres. Born in Ocala, Florida, and raised in Long Island, New York, James's career lasted just two years and was marked, as he noted in his autobiography *Black Ice*, by racial taunts from white fans who threw bananas on the ice and hung monkey dolls from a noose in the penalty box. James would be followed into the NHL by a small number of black players such as Mike Grier, Grant Fuhr, Jarome Iginla, Wayne Simmonds, and Kevin Weekes. The number of blacks in the NHL, however, would continue to remain small with current figures estimating they still only make up 5 percent of the league. This is particularly significant when you consider that the recent past has seen a drop in the number of Canadian players and simultaneous increase in the number of American and foreign-born players in the NHL.

The rate of integration and participation levels of blacks in the Professional Golfers Association (PGA) and Ladies Professional Golfers Association (LPGA) was even more dismal than that in the NHL. In 1943, the PGA officially implemented a "Caucasian only" clause in its constitution, which prohibited blacks from entering sanctioned tournaments. This policy would be buttressed by the fact that most PGA tournaments were held at private golf courses that did not allow blacks as members. Not unexpectedly, the black press, like it had done with all forms of racial discrimination in sport, hammered away at the exclusionary policies of the PGA. They were supported in their efforts by African American golfers themselves who took an active role in trying to break down the racial barriers in the sport. Through direct confrontation and litigation, Joe Louis, Bill Spiller, Teddy Rhodes, and other notable black golfers fought to see that PGA tournament events were opened to everyone regardless of race. A significant event that helped open the doors and bring attention to the plight of black golfers took place in 1952 when Louis, playing as an amateur, participated in the San Diego Open. That same year the PGA relaxed its racial policies by allowing blacks to play in ten sanctioned tournaments that were not held in the South. Spiller, Rhodes, and Eural Clark all qualified to play in the Phoenix Open, the first of those ten tournaments, and while not finishing at the top of the leader board, were instrumental in furthering the cause of racial equality in the sport. Finally, in 1961 the PGA dropped the "Caucasian only" clause from its constitution. Tellingly, the PGA's decision to eliminate its "Caucasian only" clause came about largely because of the pressure exerted by California Attorney General Stanley Mosk who made clear to the organization that they would no longer be able to hold tournaments on the state's public and private courses if they continued their segregationist practices.

The PGA's decision in 1961 to drop its "Caucasian only" clause was enthusiastically received by black golfers who were now officially permitted to compete in the sport's most prestigious tournaments. This enthusiasm would slowly evolve into a more realistic understanding of the place of blacks in golf and how difficult it would be to fully integrate it. Four years would pass before Charlie Sifford became the first black playing member of the PGA and it would not be until 1975 that Lee Elder became the first African American golfer to qualify for the prestigious Masters Tournament in Augusta, Georgia. The black presence in golf, with the notable exception of Calvin Peete who would capture twelve PGA tournaments, continued to be almost nonexistent over the next couple of decades. In 1997 many observers believed that perhaps a new day had dawned in regard to minority involvement in the sport with Tiger Woods's historic victory in the Masters Tournament. There would be no "Tiger effect," however, regarding the participation levels of black golfers as many had predicted. In spite of realizing enormous success, including capturing fourteen major championships and seventy-nine official PGA tournaments, Woods's career, while extraordinarily important from a symbolic standpoint, never translated into an increasing number of blacks into the sport. The "First Tee" program and other efforts to increase minority involvement in the sport have largely proved unsuccessful.

The LPGA also experienced difficulties in attracting black golfers. Founded in 1950 by such noted golfers as Patty Berg, Louise Suggs, Betty Jameson, and Babe Didrickson Zaharias, the LPGA tournaments were white-only events through the first thirteen years of the organization's existence. In 1964 that would change when Althea Gibson, the outstanding tennis player turned golfer, began playing on the LPGA tour. Suffering from a weak short game and inconsistent putting, Gibson never played consistently on the LPGA tour and never won a LPGA-sponsored tournament during her seven years of play. In 1967 Renee Powell, a former player at Ohio State, followed Gibson into the LPGA and enjoyed twelve solid seasons, capturing the LPGA sponsored Kelly Springfield Open in Queensland, Australia, in 1973. Because of cost and access, only a very small number of black women would follow Powell into the LPGA. Progress has only been made recently in regards to black participation in the LPGA. In 2016 the LPGA, for the first time in its sixty-six year history, would have four black women—Cheyenne Woods, Mariah Stackhouse, Sadden Parks, and Ginger Howard—playing on its tour.

Amateur Sport, Resistance, and
Southern Hospitality

The struggle to integrate professional sport following Jackie Robinson's entry into MLB would be duplicated at the amateur level of competition. In fact, at many levels of amateur sport the struggle to integrate would be especially difficult because of the persistence of deep-seated racial stereotypes, southern tradition, and the apparent lack of financial incentives necessary to enlist the services of African American athletes. A classic example of the struggles encountered by African American athletes was in the sport of tennis. Like some other sports, segregation in the sport was not always rigidly enforced with black and white players sometimes competing with and against one another in exhibition matches. Examples of crossing racial lines in the sport are numerous. In 1940, L. B. Icely, president of Wilson Sporting Goods, arranged a match between the outstanding grand slam champion Don Budge and the great African American player Jimmy McDaniel at the Cosmopolitan Tennis Club. The match, won by Budge in two sets in front of approximately two thousand spectators at the famous black club in Harlem, was followed by a doubles match that pitted Budge and black player Reginald Weir against McDaniel and current ATA champion Richard Cohen. The following year, Icely organized another exhibition match at Tuskegee Institute during the Silver Jubilee between the outstanding black player Harold Mitchell and the white British champion Charles E. Hare. In 1944, the great champion Alice Marble teamed with Bob Ryland in a mixed double match against Weir and Mary Hardwick at the Cosmopolitan Tennis Club.

In spite of these interracial matches and the fact that African Americans were finding much enjoyment, realizing a sense of community, and satisfying their competitive urges through the ATA, they continued to fight to play at the very highest levels of the sport. It would not be easy to bring about as the United States Lawn Tennis Association (USLTA) resisted integration at every turn. As early as 1929, Weir, who would have an outstanding career at City College of New York and become a multiple ATA singles champion, and Gerald Norman Jr., the great black player from Howard University, would be denied entry into the USLTA Junior Indoor tournament in New York City. The NAACP made efforts to get the two players reinstated, but the USLTA refused to rescind its decision. For the next twenty-nine years, the USLTA held firm on its segregationist policies. In 1948, however, the USLTA racial policies would begin to soften. In that year, Oscar Johnson, after initially being denied the opportunity to compete, participated in the

USLTA National Junior Indoor Championships in St. Louis and Weir played in the USLTA Indoor Championships in New York. Two years later, history was made when Althea Gibson, the talented player from Harlem who had attended Florida A&M University, became the first black to participate in the US Open tournament at Forest Hills, New York. Coming about largely through secret negotiations between ATA and USLTA officials and as a result of a scathing letter published by Alice Marble in the *American Lawn Tennis Magazine* regarding the latter organization's racially discriminatory practices, Gibson lost to Wimbledon champion Louise Brough, but the match set the stage for a career marked by important victories in the most prestigious tournaments in the world. In 1956, Gibson won both the singles and doubles titles at the Paris Open and doubles championship at Wimbledon. The following year she captured the Wimbledon singles and doubles championship as well as the US Open singles title. In 1958 she repeated the feat, winning once again the Wimbledon singles and doubles championships and the US Open singles title. On her retirement from amateur tennis at the end of 1958, Gibson had captured fifty-six singles and doubles titles. Her status as the main African American player in the world would eventually be taken over by Arthur Ashe, the Richmond, Virginia, native and UCLA star who captured both the US Open and Wimbledon titles. He, in turn, would be followed into the sport by a smattering of African American players, the most successful being Venus and Serena Williams.

The struggle to integrate amateur sport was particularly problematic when national sports organizations came in conflict with their state and regional associations in the South who held fast to racist policies. This was an issue that the AAU had to face with some regularity, but it also extended to Little League Baseball. A very disheartening and poignant example of this is the story of the 1955 Cannon Street YMCA Little League team from Charleston, South Carolina. A very talented and skilled group of eleven- and twelve-year-olds, the all-black Cannon Street team suffered the indignities of their race when all the white teams in Charleston refused to play against them for the city championship. The Cannon Street team suffered the same fate at the next levels of play, with none of the sixty-one teams eligible for the state tournament willing to take the field against them and the seven state champions adopting the same position regarding the southeastern regional tournament. These boycotts were not decisions made by the white children who played with and against black children in more unorganized and informal settings. It was the parents of the white players who made the call, still reeling from the previous year's *Brown v. Board of Education* decision, which

Figure 5.2.   Althea Gibson reaching high for a shot during women's singles semifinal match against Christine Truman at Wimbledon in 1957.
Courtesy of Library of Congress Prints and Photographs Division. LC-USCZ62-79902.

they viewed as a threat to the southern way of life and prevailing social order. White and black children competing on the playing field on equal terms was just as troubling as them sharing the same classroom.

The Little League's national office responded to the boycotts by declaring the Cannon Street team the city, state, and regional champions and therefore a qualifier for the annual World Series in Williamsport, Pennsylvania. Little League officials in South Carolina and other southern states countered by establishing what would become known as Dixie Youth Baseball, an organization that would remain racially segregated until 1967. Unfortunately, the national Little League, in spite of its nondiscriminatory policies, chose to enforce its rule that no team could participate in the World Series that had advanced by forfeits. Why the national Little League made their decision is uncertain, but some have speculated that the organization feared that allowing the all-black team from Charleston to compete in the World Series would have hastened the move of southern affiliates into the newly created Dixie Youth Baseball program. Irrespective, what happened next is difficult to comprehend by present-day standards. Officials of the national Little League, apparently feeling some tinge of guilt about their decision, invited the Cannon Street team to attend the World Series in Williamsport as their guests and stay in the Lycoming College dormitories along with the eight regional champions. The parents and coaches of the Cannon Street team accepted the invitation, but did not inform the players until their arrival in Williamsport that they would only be spectators at the tournament and not participants. Distraught when finally learning of their fate, the players must have felt some degree of satisfaction when the five thousand fans in Williamsport spontaneously began chanting "Let them play" when they were allowed by Little League officials to put on their uniforms and warm-up on the field and immediately thereafter when asked by fans to sign autographs as they sat in the stands watching other teams compete for the championship.

The recent past has seen repeated attempts by Little League Baseball and others to make amends for the way the Cannon Street team was treated. In 2000, the city of Charleston unveiled a plague in honor of the team at a local park close to the field where they used to play. In 2002, Little League Baseball invited the Cannon Street team and their families back to Williamsport to throw out the ceremonial first pitch at the World Series and to receive the South Carolina State Championship banner it had been denied close to a half century earlier. On that occasion, Little League Executive Director Stephen Keener told those in attendance that, "There is no way to right the wrong perpetrated on the boys of the Cannon Street YMCA Little League team, just as there is no way to right the wrongs perpetrated throughout history on people because of their skin color."[6] In 2005, the Cannon Street team was invited back again to Williamsport to throw out the ceremonial first pitch at the World Series in commemoration of being excluded from the tournament fifty years earlier. In 2007, the Cannon Street team was inducted into the Charleston Baseball Hall of Fame and five years later were honored with a historical marker in the city they had not been allowed to represent.

The Cannon Street team's exclusion from the Little League World Series in 1955 helped lay bare the South's position on race. Although paling in comparison to the awful murder that year of fourteen-year-old black Chicago native Emmett Till in Money, Mississippi, the mistreatment of the Cannon Street team made clear that even preadolescent children were not immune from the racist views of white southerners. The eleven- and twelve-year-old members of the Cannon Street team were treated in a cruel fashion by white adults, who simply could not fathom black and white children taking the field together in the sport considered America's national pastime. Remarkably, their World Series experience had no long-term negative effects on members of the Cannon Street team as most of them went on to productive and successful professional careers and have apparently rid themselves of any bitterness regarding their exclusion from Little League Baseball's most important event.

Also making clear the racial views of white southerners was the long-standing refusal of the region's universities to integrate their athletic teams let alone their general student bodies. While the Big Eight, Missouri Valley, and Big Ten Conferences in the Midwest would drop their Jim Crow policies in football and basketball during the late 1940s and early 1950s, white institutions in the South generally took longer to integrate their athletic programs. Not unexpectedly, it was smaller independent institutions in the border-states rather than those schools in the Deep South with conference memberships that first integrated their athletic teams. As noted by historian Charles Martin, the University of Louisville was a leader in regard to the elimination of Jim Crow in southern college sport. The school, a private institution at the time and far more liberal in regard to race than the University of Kentucky, recruited four black football players in 1954. One of those players was Lenny Lyles, a defensive back who had an outstanding career at Louisville and in the NFL for twelve years. Although slower to integrate its basketball team, not having black players on its varsity hardwood squad until 1963, the inclusion of four black players on its gridiron team was an important precedent that other independent schools in the border-states would eventually emulate.

In 1956, basketball coach George McCarty of Texas Western University recruited George Brown and his nephew, Cecil, the first two black athletes to play at a predominantly white major institution in a former confederate state. Three years later, the Miner's football coach Ben Collins recruited his first black player and over the next couple of years signed several others. In 1957, Abner Haynes and Leon King, two outstanding black players from Dallas, played their first varsity football games for North Texas State College. King played two seasons before dropping out of school, while Haynes became the team's outstanding player, realizing All-American status his senior year before enjoying an outstanding career in the AFL. In 1964, the University of Houston garnered headlines by recruiting three outstanding black athletes, one in football and two in basketball. Coach Bill Yeoman pulled in the year's prized football recruit by convincing outstanding black running back Warren McVea to attend the university and coach Guy Lewis did the same for his basketball team by attracting heralded black hoopsters Elvin Hayes and Don Chaney. McVea garnered second team All-American honors his senior season and Hayes and Chaney led the Cougars to three NCAA appearances and then had distinguished careers in the NBA.

While the University of Louisville would take the lead in recruiting black athletes among independent institutions, the University of Maryland would do the same among conference schools. Maryland, which had accepted a black law student as early as 1935 and both undergraduate and graduate students in the 1950s, became the first school in what was then an eight-member Atlantic Coast Conference (ACC) to have an African American on its football team. The player, Darryl Hill, was a wide receiver from Washington, D.C., a true student-athlete who realized success on the playing field and in the classroom. His career would be deemed extraordinary for no other reason than that he became the first black to play in Carolina Stadium at the University of South Carolina and in Memorial Stadium (better known as "Death Valley") at Clemson University. Hill's pioneering role was not an easy one, of course, as the first African American to play in the ACC. He had spectators throw drinks on him, was on the receiving end of racial epithets, was denied service at restaurants, and was not allowed hotel accommodations.[7]

In 1964, Maryland once again contributed to integration in the ACC by recruiting black basketball players Billy Jones and Julius "Pete" Johnson. Jones, an outstanding guard from Towson, Maryland, and Johnson, an excellent guard from Fairmont Heights, Maryland, would make significant contributions to the Maryland basketball program. Jones would ultimately become co-captain of the team and Johnson its leading scorer. Other schools in the ACC would ultimately take Maryland's lead and integrate its football, basketball, and other sports programs. Following Maryland's Darryl Hill, along with two other black players, Ernie Torain and Alvin Lee, who had signed with the Terrapins, into ACC football were Kenneth "Butch" Henry and Robert Grant with Wake Forest University in 1965; Rickey Lanier with the University of North Carolina in 1968; Clyde Chesney with North Carolina State in 1969; Ernest Jackson and Clarence Newsome with Duke University in 1969; Jackie Brown with the University of South Carolina in 1970; Marion Francis Reeves with Clemson University in 1971; and Harrison Davis III, Kent Merritt, Stanley "Bubba" Land, and John Rainey with the University of Virginia in 1971. Following Maryland's Jones and Johnson into ACC basketball were Claudius B. Clairborne with Duke University in 1967; Norwood Todmann with Wake Forest University in 1967; Charles Scott with the University of North Carolina in 1968; Al Heartley with North Carolina State University in 1969; Craig Mobley with Clemson University in 1970; Casey Manning with the University of South Carolina in 1970; and Al Drummond with the University of Virginia in 1972. In addition to football and basketball, integration took place in several other sports among ACC institutions, most notably at North Carolina State University where as early as 1957 Irwin R. Holmes Jr. and Walter V. Holmes competed in an indoor track meet against the University of North Carolina. Holmes also played three years of varsity tennis, being selected during his senior year as co-captain, a significant event since it made him the first black captain of any sport in the ACC.

The slow rate of integration in football and basketball in the ACC would be duplicated in the Southwest Conference (SWC) and Southeastern Conference (SEC). Other than the initial entry of African Americans into SWC basketball, which resulted in limited press coverage because of the relative lack of popularity of the sport in Texas, integration of football in the SWC and integration of football and basketball in the SEC drew a great deal of attention from sportswriters and other observers of college sport. The volume of press coverage partly had to do with the quality of black athletes who were in the initial wave of integration of the two conferences, the academic and athletic prestige of member institutions, and legendary stature of the coaches involved in the desegregation of the SWC and SEC.

History was made in SWC football in 1965 when SMU coach Hayden Fry recruited running back Jerry Levias out of all-black Hebert High School in Beaumont. Fry, far more racially sensitive than many of his white colleagues in the coaching profession, pursued Levias because he was genuinely interested in breaking the color line in college football while at once trying to upgrade the quality of his team and become more competitive in the talent-laden SWC. Fry picked the right man. Although experiencing a sense of isolation and various forms of racial discrimination, as did black walk-on John Westbrook at Baylor who also started his varsity career in 1966, Levias overcame extra punishment dished out by opponents to carve out a very successful career at SMU. In his initial year of varsity play he led SMU to their first SWC title since 1948, was selected to the All-SWC team three times, and was a consensus All-American his senior year. He played six years in the NFL with the Houston Oilers and San Diego Chargers.

The success of Levias would encourage Fry to recruit more black athletes at SMU and coaches at other SWC schools to do the same thing at their institutions. In 1966, Fry would recruit Rufus Cormier, Lee McElroy, and Walter Haynes, three black athletes who would ease the sense of social isolation for Levias and contribute to the success of the SMU football program. In 1968, black JC All-American wide receiver Linzy Cole joined the Texas Christian University football team and enjoyed two solid seasons for the Horned Frogs. In 1969, black running back Danny Hardaway played the first of his two varsity seasons at Texas Tech University; Rodrigo Barnes, Stahle Vincent, and Mike Tyler made their varsity debuts at Rice University; and Hugh McElroy made the varsity squad as a walk-on at Texas A&M. In the following year, black players appeared on the gridiron for the first time for two of the most prominent football programs in the SWC. Offensive lineman Julius Whittier became the first black letterman at the University of Texas, joining a squad that had just captured the national championship, and halfback Jon Richardson played his first varsity season for the University of Arkansas Razorbacks. By 1974, there were a total of 165 black football players in the SWC, with the highest percentage (27.4 percent) of those players at SMU and lowest percentage (7.7 percent) at Texas Christian University.

The integration of SEC football followed a similar timeline as that in the SWC. The University of Kentucky led the integration process in the SEC by recruiting halfback Nat Northington and end Greg Page in 1966. Integration of the football programs at other SEC schools would follow in succession at the University of Tennessee, Auburn University, Vanderbilt University, Mississippi State University (MSU), University of Florida, and the University of Alabama. Of all the SEC schools that integrated their football programs, none of them came close to realizing the level of attention generated by the University of Alabama. The Crimson Tide, representing a state deeply divided by race and governed by George Wallace who tried in vain in 1963 to stop black students from entering the university, created a football powerhouse led by legendary coach Bear Bryant. Since his arrival at the university in 1957, Bryant recruited great players to the flagship school in Tuscaloosa that resulted in multiple national championships. The only problem was that for over a decade the only players he recruited were white. Bryant was slow to recruit black players, so much so that in the summer of 1968 the school's Afro-American Association (AAA), with assistance from the NAACP, filed a lawsuit claiming racial discrimination in the athletic department, which was code for the football team.

Evidently unbeknownst to the AAA, Bryant had made attempts to lure black athletes to Tuscaloosa prior to the federal lawsuit filed against him and certainly well before the shellacking Alabama took in 1970 at the hands of the USC that some writers have erroneously argued was the singular event that convinced him to alter his recruiting policies.

Five black players participated in spring practice in 1967, but were not offered scholarships. Following the 1968 season, Bryant offered scholarships to outstanding black high school players James Owens and Frank Dowsing, but both spurned the offers with Owens deciding instead to attend arch rival Auburn University and Frank Dowsing taking his talents to MSU. In 1969, the Crimson Tide signed its first black scholarship athlete Wilbur Jackson, an outstanding wide receiver from Ozark, Alabama. Two years later, Alabama brought in the talented black defensive end John Mitchell from Eastern Arizona Junior College and three black high school stars Mike Washington, Ralph Stokes, and Sylvester Croom. The signing of these four players provided additional talent to an already very strong football team while at once apparently convincing the AAA that Alabama was headed in the right direction since it dropped its lawsuit against the school's athletic department in 1971.

SEC schools took even longer to integrate their basketball teams. Although basketball would always be second fiddle to football in the SEC, the conference included some talented hoopsters and one of the most famous and controversial coaches in the land in Kentucky's Adolf Rupp. The first SEC school to have a black player on its basketball team was Vanderbilt University who signed Nashville's Pearl High School star center Perry Wallace to a scholarship in 1966 and the last conference school to integrate its hoop squad was MSU who signed Jerry Jenkins of Gulfport, Mississippi, and Larry Fry of Lexington, Kentucky, to scholarships in 1972. During the intervening years black players would find their way onto the hard courts at Auburn University, University of Alabama, University of Georgia, University of Kentucky, University of Tennessee, University of Florida, Louisiana State University, and University of Mississippi.

Efforts to integrate the basketball programs at SEC institutions were all complex and fraught with difficulties, but perhaps none of them were as racially charged and divisive as that at MSU. The last SEC school to accept blacks into its general student body, the MSU administration would for years not allow its basketball team to play against schools with integrated teams, let alone consider recruiting a black player for their own squad. This created a particularly sensitive situation and pitted various constituencies against one another in regards to involvement of the MSU basketball team in postseason play. On three separate occasions—1959, 1961, 1962—the MSU administration, to the chagrin of students, some fans, and coach Babe McCarthy, refused to allow the basketball team to participate in the NCAA Tournament after capturing the SEC championship. It was only in 1963, after bitter disputes over the issue of postseason play involving leaders of the Mississippi Board of Trustees, state senator F. W. "Billy" Mitts, Judge L. D. Porter, and others, did the MSU basketball team find its way to the NCAA Midwestern Regional Tournament in East Lansing, Michigan. This breakthrough, however, did nothing to speed up MSU's search and active recruitment of black basketball players. Only in 1972 did coach Kermit Davis, seeking ways to improve a faltering program that was losing regularly to other SEC schools that all now had at least one black player on their rosters, integrate the MSU basketball team by signing Larry Fry and Jerry Jenkins who would contribute significantly to the program and the signing of other black players.

As important as the integration of athletic programs at predominantly white universities were in the Deep South, there were two nationally televised college basketball championship games that overshadowed them and would become watershed events in sport history and the civil rights movement. The first was the 1963 NCAA Championship game played between Loyola University Chicago and the University of Cincinnati. The significance of the game is that seven of the ten starters in the contest were black and it was played in one of the southern hotbeds for basketball, Louisville, Kentucky. Although blacks had participated in NCAA basketball title games in the past (Cincinnati started three black players when they captured the 1962 NCAA championship), never before did such a large percentage of them start on the court, with Loyola and Cincinnati beginning the contest with four and three black players respectively. This was unprecedented since college basketball coaches had always maintained a strict racial quota as to how many blacks could be on the court at the same time. Loyola—led by All-American guard Jerry Harkness and having already played in the previously mentioned regional semifinal against segregated Mississippi State in East Lansing, Michigan—beat Cincinnati 60–58 in overtime for the NCAA title on a last-minute jump shot by forward Vic Rouse.[8]

Drawing far more attention and certainly more deeply embedded in the public consciousness, particularly now with the release of the movie *Glory Road*, was the NCAA basketball championship game played three years later at the University of Maryland. On the evening of March 9, 1966, in Maryland's Cole Field House, the heavily favored University of Kentucky Wildcats led by the legendary Adolph Rupp faced off against relatively unknown coach Don Haskins and his Texas Western University Miners for the NCAA basketball championship. Rupp, who had played for the famous Forrest "Phog" Allen at the University of Kansas and had already coached the Wildcats to four NCAA titles, had a talented squad of white players with the centerpiece being All-American forward Pat Riley. Haskins, a native of Enid, Oklahoma, who would coach the Miners for almost forty years, had a squad that included seven black players which was far more than any other program at a predominantly white university at that time.

To the surprise of most everyone, the underappreciated Miners beat the powerful Wildcats from Kentucky 72–65. The game itself was not the most exciting in college basketball history, mostly devoid of spectacular plays and key moments or suspense. What was culturally significant, however, was Haskins's decision to start the game with an all-black lineup. It was made that much more significant because the five players—which included Harry Flournoy, Orsten Artis, Willie Worsley, Bobby Joe Hill, and David Lattin—started an NCAA championship game in the South against a team that had no black players and a coach who resisted integration and regularly used racially disparaging language. Although Kentucky became the first school in the SEC to integrate its football team, Rupp, under pressure to recruit black players, only halfheartedly pursued schoolboy legends Butch Beard and Wes Unseld who would go on to great careers at the University of Louisville and in the professional ranks and would not have a black player on his team until 1970. Equally important is that the game helped dispel on a national stage during the height of the civil rights struggle the long-held myths that blacks could not perform in pressure situations and needed white leadership to achieve victory. Pat Riley, the great Kentucky All-American who was on the losing end of the game and who later became an NBA player and even more successful coach and administrator, summed up the game by calling it "The Emancipation Proclamation of 1966."[9]

CHAPTER SIX

~

Sport and the
Civil Rights Movement

The initial wave of black athletes who integrated predominantly white organized sport was very courageous, withstanding various forms of racially discriminatory practices. For the most part, however, they did not directly confront racial prejudice, choosing instead to maintain a quiet public demeanor and focus on honing their physical talents and garnering the rewards, sense of satisfaction, and adulation that all athletes desire. In the 1960s, however, black athletes began to shed their quiet public demeanor and to speak out about their mistreatment and the racial inequality in sport and America more generally. Impacted by the civil rights struggle and black power movement, black athletes at both the professional and amateur levels of sport voiced their dissatisfaction and publically protested racism at the risk of incurring the wrath of the sports establishment and jeopardizing their careers. They exerted a sense of independence, manhood, and black pride characteristic of black activists on the forefront of the civil rights movement.

The emerging willingness on the part of black athletes to protest racial inequalities and discrimination certainly became evident at the professional level of sport. Some of the most elite black professional athletes, both individually and collectively, voiced their anger and made concerted efforts to eliminate it at every turn. These men included the likes of basketball's Bill Russell, football's Jim Brown, tennis' Arthur Ashe, baseball's Curt Flood, and boxing's Muhammad Ali. Among this group, no one was more important to the civil rights struggle and made more evident the consequences of individual sacrifice than Ali, the brash and outspoken world-heavyweight

131

boxing champion who joined the Elijah Muhammad–led Nation of Islam and refused to enter the Vietnam War on account of his religious conviction. Ali suffered for his refusal to enter military service, incurring the wrath of a more conservative older generation and having his world-heavyweight title stripped. On the other hand, he realized hero status among young black and whites, especially college-educated students, for his stand against an unpopular war and insistence on staying true to his principles and not backing down from the US government.

Black athletes at the amateur levels of sport, especially those at predominantly white universities, were inspired by Ali and the outspokenness of other black professional athletes and encouraged to engage in the larger civil rights movement. The result was their involvement in a number of protests to make visible and ultimately eliminate the racially discriminatory practices in sport and the larger society. A signature event in the civil rights struggle was the proposed boycott of the 1968 Olympic Games in Mexico City led by Harry Edwards and involving a number of outstanding young black athletes. Although the boycott never materialized, the games in Mexico City was marked by a number of protests—the most famous being the black-gloved power salutes by Tommie Smith and John Carlos while on the medal stand after their first and third place finishes in the 200 meter dash—that brought international attention to the plight of black Americans and the civil rights movement. Following the 1968 Olympic Games in Mexico City, a large number of revolts (Edwards estimated that there were some thirty-seven revolts just in 1968) involving black athletes took place at some of the most prestigious predominantly white universities across the country. Often in collaboration with other students, black athletes lodged complaints against white coaches, threatened boycotts, and spoke out against racially discriminatory practices on campus and elsewhere. Black athletes did this at great risk, sometimes losing their scholarships and suffering the wrath of coaches, athletic directors, and others in the upper-level administration.

The revolts of black athletes would gradually come to a halt in the early 1970s. The women's rights movement and the desegregation resulting from the civil rights legislation of the 1960s combined with a preoccupation with unemployment and inflation took energy out of the black athletic protests like it did the larger black power movement. Although continuing to speak out against discriminatory practices, they increasingly became popular subjects of the writings and scholarly studies completed by individuals who had become fascinated by the black athlete's past and sensitized to racial issues through the very visible athletic protests. Black athletes were, like the fledgling black studies movement, now in vogue among both blacks and whites inside and outside of academia who weighed in on how they were treated and analyzing the difficulties they had to surmount in order to become full participants in American sport.

Nothing seemed to be off limits as a steady stream of publications were completed on everything from analyzing why black athletes were disproportionately represented in certain playing positions and what accounted for their overrepresentation in some sports and underrepresentation in others to studies examining if black athletes were receiving fair compensation for their athletic accomplishments and why their academic performances were judged inferior to their white counterparts.

The People's Champ Leads the Way

The initial wave of black athletes who integrated professional sport in the post–World War II era typically did not speak out about racially discriminatory practices in sport and the larger American society. Content to plying their trade at the highest levels of competition and concerned about not doing anything that might jeopardize their careers, black athletes during this period focused on honing their talents so as to achieve optimal success in their chosen sport and not engaging publically in political and social activism. That approach would begin to change in the 1960s as black athletes in professional sport began to voice their concerns about racial issues in and outside of sport. Inspired by the larger civil rights and black power movement, black athletes in professional sport, some of them the biggest stars in their respective sports, adopted a more socially conscious approach made evident in an assortment of different and important ways. Five of the most influential black athletes in this regard were basketball's Bill Russell, football's Jim Brown, baseball's Curt Flood, tennis' Arthur Ashe, and boxing's Muhammad Ali.

Russell, the great center who led the University of San Francisco to two NCAA championships and Boston Celtics to multiple NBA titles, was one of the most prominent black athletes to voice concerns about the plight of black Americans. The physically gifted and highly cerebral basketball star famous for his refusal to sign autographs, Russell made clear his belief in the importance of black pride and disdain for racial inequality in two of his autobiographies, Go Up for Glory (1966) and Second Wind: The Memoirs of an Opinionated Man (1974). He would speak out forcefully about racially discriminatory practices in public forums and in other ways. Jim Brown, the outstanding running back who retired from the Cleveland Browns as the NFL's all-time rushing leader, was even more straightforward and direct in expressing his views on the mistreatment of black Americans. This is clear in his autobiographies *Off My Chest* (1964) and *Out of Bounds* (1989) as well as in his public pronouncements and interviews. Perhaps more than any other professional black athlete of the day, Brown was figuratively on the ground in establishing organizations devoted to improving the lives of poor and underprivileged black Americans. He established, for example, the Black Economic Union in 1965 in an effort facilitated by professional athletes to create black-owned businesses and other enterprises.

Curt Flood, a gifted outfielder with the St. Louis Cardinals, changed the landscape of professional sport forever by his refusal to report to the Philadelphia Phillies in 1969 after being traded by the Cardinals and filing suit against commissioner Bowie Kuhn demanding he be granted free agency. Although Kuhn denied the request—a decision that was ultimately upheld by the Supreme Court—Flood's effort was not in vain as it would eventually help lead to the overturning of the reserve clause in 1975 when arbitrator Peter Seitz granted pitchers Andy Messersmith and Dave McNally free agency. When recalling his decision to challenge baseball's long-standing free agency policy, Flood famously noted that the change in black consciousness increased his sensitivity to all forms of injustice in American life. Arthur Ashe, the great tennis player from Richmond, Virginia, who captured three grand slam singles titles, fought for equality on a number of fronts. Although criticized by some of the more radical black activists for not speaking out more vehemently against racial injustice, Ashe was steadfast in his efforts to see that young black athletes were provided a quality education, actively opposed apartheid in South Africa, and sought better treatment of Haitian immigrants seeking asylum in the United States.

The participation of Russell, Brown, Flood, and Ashe in the civil rights struggle was noteworthy and extraordinarily important in America's sporting past. But their efforts never drew the attention or were fraught with comparable symbolism or have remained in the American consciousness like those of Muhammad Ali. The great boxer from Louisville, Kentucky, who startled experts in the fight game by beating Sonny Liston for the heavyweight championship in 1964 became the most famous man in sport, if not in the world. His early career was largely devoid of controversy, although from the very beginning he belittled his opponents, bragged about his skills, and adopted an approach in the ring inspired by professional wrestler "Gorgeous George" Wagner. Fighting under his birth name of Cassius Clay, he garnered several Golden Glove boxing titles, captured a gold medal in the light-heavyweight division at the Rome Olympics in 1960, and then won nineteen consecutive professional fights against such opponents as Henry Cooper, Jim Robinson,

Figure 6.1. Muhammad Ali standing over a fallen Sonny Liston in one of boxing's most iconic photographs.
Courtesy of Library of Congress Prints and Photographs Division. LC-USCZ62-120902.

George Logan, and Archie Moore that put him into contention for a heavy-weight title bout.

In 1964 in Miami Beach a decidedly different fighter with a decidedly different personality ascended to the throne in the most prestigious division in boxing. Heavily favored to lose, Cassius Clay stunned boxing aficionados by defeating Sonny Liston in six rounds, the man known as the "Big Bear" who had served time in prison and had close ties with the mafia. When Liston failed to answer the bell for the seventh round, Clay jumped with joy on the top ropes declaring for everyone to hear that "I am the greatest! I am the greatest! I am the greatest! I am the King of the World!"[1] Clay's declaration following the fight that he was "King of the World" was never so true when he announced he had become a member of the Nation of Islam (NOI) and changed his name to Muhammad Ali. The pronouncement that he had rid himself of his "slave name" and joined an organization that talked of white devils and had as members such controversial figures as its leader Elijah Muhammad and Malcolm X, was troubling and heavily criticized by individuals in and outside of boxing. The announcement that the new heavyweight champion renounced Christianity and associated with a supposed hate group that many considered an illegitimate religion cast Ali as an ingrate who had turned his back on America.

The criticism of Ali became even more pronounced when he refused in 1966 to enter military service on account of his membership in the NOI and the fact he viewed the Vietnam War as unjust. His refusal to fight in Vietnam, made clear in his oft-quoted comment "I ain't got no quarrel with the Vietcong," caused an outpouring of rebukes of the heavyweight champion, particularly from those of previous generations who had fought in wars in defense of America. On the other hand, much of the younger generation, especially college students opposed to the war, viewed Ali as a hero for sticking to his principles and confronting the government seemingly without fear of reprisals and impact on his boxing career. Ali's willingness to push back against authority and speak out on larger social issues spoke loudly to young blacks and whites who were involved in their own struggles against the government and desired peaceful means to end world conflict rather than war.

Ali would, unfortunately, suffer for his refusal to enter military service. He was found guilty of draft evasion, states revoked his boxing license, and his heavyweight championship was stripped. He did not fight a match between March 1967 and October 1970, a time in which he was certainly at the height of his physical powers. He finally returned to the ring on October 26, 1970, when he fought Jerry Quarry in Atlanta. A bout made possible largely through the efforts of Georgia senator Leroy R. Johnson, Ali defeated the decidedly inferior Quarry in just three rounds. Over the next decade, Ali's legend would grow as he recaptured the heavyweight championship and fought some of boxing's most memorable bouts. Besides the much written about and documented 1974 bout in Zaire against George Foreman famously known as the "Rumble in the Jungle," perhaps Ali's three most important fights were those against his nemesis Joe Frazier, the enormously powerful and hard punching boxer from Philadelphia. Their first bout on March 8, 1971, in New York's Madison Square Garden was a classic, made that much more bitter and antagonistic by Ali's prefight comments labeling Frazier "too dumb to be champ," "too ugly to be the champ," and an "Uncle Tom."[2] In a grueling fifteen-round match, Frazier won by a decision. In their second fight on January 28, 1974, also held in New York's Madison Square Garden, Ali enacted revenge by beating Frazier in a twelve-round decision. Their third fight in the capital city of the Philippines, commonly referred to as the "Thrilla in Manila," was a vicious and bloody bout that physically damaged both fighters. In sweltering heat approaching 100 degrees Fahrenheit, Ali and Frazier pummeled one another until Frazier's manager Eddie Futch refused to let him come out for the fifteenth round. It was the right decision as repeated blows to the great Philadelphia fighter's head had swollen both his eyes shut.

Ali's memorable victories in the ring, performance style, sheer beauty, bravado, quick wit, and love of people would garner him millions of new fans of all races and religions worldwide by the mid-1970s. His growing appeal and increasing popularity also resulted from changes in the NOI following the death of Elijah Muhammad, the winding down of the Vietnam War, decrease in racial turmoil, and a host of other social changes in the United States and internationally. He became a beloved figure that only seemed to become more pronounced in retirement following his bout with Trevor Berbick in 1981 and his gradual physical deterioration brought on by the advancement of age and Parkinson's disease. The recognition for his many accomplishments in and outside the ring are many and varied, including being chosen to light the flame at the opening of the 1996 Olympic Games in Atlanta and being a recipient of the Presidential Medal of Freedom in 2005.

It is impossible to assess who was most influenced by Ali. "The People's Champ" impacted the lives of a countless number of people throughout his long, storied, and sometimes tumultuous career. There is little question, however, that he served as an inspiration to other black athletes of different ages, in all sports, and at various levels of competition. He certainly inspired Bill Russell, Jim Brown, Curt Flood, Arthur Ashe, and other black professional athletes to speak out about inequality and racially discriminatory practices. He certainly must have emboldened the twenty-one black players, many of them from HBCUs, who successfully had the 1965 AFL All-Star Game moved from New Orleans to Houston because of the racial discrimination in the "Crescent City." He most certainly served as a source of inspiration for those black players in the NFL who spoke out about the racial divisiveness on their individual teams and the league more generally during the late 1960s. And without question he inspired young college-aged black athletes to speak out more forcefully about racial inequities and discrimination on their campuses and society at large during the late 1960s and early 1970s.

Harry Edwards, the Olympic Project for Human Rights, and Mexico City Olympics

Harry Edwards is a name that has long been associated with racial issues, student activism, and the serious study of sport. Born in East St. Louis in 1942, Edwards was an outstanding all-around high school athlete who competed in basketball and track and field at Fresno City College before receiving a scholarship and participating in the same two sports at San Jose State College. Always more than just an athlete, Edwards was a very capable student who earned an undergraduate degree in sociology at San Jose State in 1964 before taking his master's degree in 1966 and PhD degree in 1971 in the same field at Cornell University. Edwards, influenced heavily by the thinking of such black intellectuals and writers as W. E. B. Du Bois, Paul Robeson, and Louis Lomax, involved himself in the civil rights struggle while an undergraduate student at San Jose State and continued to do so when he returned to campus as an instructor of sociology in 1967.

The uniqueness of Edwards was that he fought for equality of opportunity and civil rights largely through the medium of sport. Recognizing early on that one of the best ways to garner attention regarding racial inequality and discrimination was to disrupt in some way the sacred institution of sport, Edwards first made visible his strategy in this regard when he, along with disgruntled black athletes and other black students on campus, forced cancellation of San Jose State's first football game of 1967 against the University of Texas at El Paso. Frustrated by the unwillingness of the upper-level administration to take seriously their concerns about discriminatory practices in the athletic department and in other areas of the campus, Edwards and the school's black athletes and other black students arranged a protest demonstration at the game that portended possible violence. Although Governor Ronald Reagan offered to bring in the National Guard to help prevent any potential mayhem, the administration decided it was in the best interests of the administration to cancel the game against the institution that just the previous year had made history by capturing the NCAA basketball championship with a starting lineup made up of all black players. Because of its decision, San Jose State forfeited the $12,000 that was agreed upon between the two institutions in case of a cancellation.

Edwards was very encouraged by what had resulted from the proposed protest demonstration involving the San Jose State and University of El Paso football game in 1967 and began to plot strategy to boycott the 1968 Olympic Games in Mexico City. The idea was not a new one. As early as 1960, black comedian, civil rights activist, and former competitive distance runner Dick Gregory had proposed an Olympic boycott to protest the treatment of black Americans. In 1964, Mal Whitfield, multiple gold medal middle-distance runner in the 1948 and 1952 Olympic Games and member of the famed Tuskegee Airmen during World War II, proposed that black athletes not participate in the Tokyo Olympics in an article in *Ebony* magazine titled "Let's Boycott the Olympics." A remarkable position to take for a number of reasons, including the fact that at the time and for many years after he worked for the State Department and US Information Service, Whitfield advocated a boycott of the games in Tokyo because he believed "it is time for American Negro athletes to join in the civil rights fight" and "time for America to live up to its promises of Liberty, Equality, and Justice for all."[3]

In the fall of 1967, Edwards, certainly aware of the earlier pleas made by Gregory and Whitfield, organized the Olympic Project for Human Rights (OPHR), a group made up largely of outstanding young black athletes expected to compete in the upcoming summer games who were frustrated by racial inequality and discrimination and anxious to do whatever they could to see that it came to an end. After much thought and consideration, Edwards and the OPHR membership announced at a carefully orchestrated news conference in New York City that black athletes would boycott the Mexico City games unless specific demands were met prior to actual competition. The demands included the appointment of another black coach to the American track and field team, elimination of the discrimination committed against blacks and Jews by the New York Athletic Club (NYAC), addition of a black man to the United States Olympic Committee (USOC), ouster of Avery Brundage as president of the International Olympic Committee

(IOC) because of his racist views, not permitting South Africa and Rhodesia to participate in Olympic competition because of their apartheid policies, and restoring the heavyweight championship to Muhammad Ali.

The radical approach taken by Edwards and the OPHR was met with much criticism and made clear the deep philosophical divide in the black community and America at large over the role and meaning of sport and its potential impact on societal changes. While Edwards and the OPHR saw the threat of protest and nonparticipation in sport as essential in bringing attention to and ultimately overcoming racial inequality, there were many others who contended that success in sport was the most effective way to combat racial discrimination and positively impact the lives of all blacks. Those taking the latter view were some prominent black athletes expected to garner medals in the Mexico City games, including sprinter Charles Greene and long jumper Ralph Boston. Others adopting this position were such legendary Olympians from the past as Jesse Owens, the four-time gold medalist from the 1936 Berlin games, and Rafer Johnson, the UCLA star who captured the gold medal in the decathlon at the 1960 games in Rome. Edwards was highly critical of those opposing the boycott movement, reserving much of his ire for Owens who he viewed as naïve and labeled an "Uncle Tom." To Edwards, Owens had no critical understanding of American culture and was wrong to believe that participation in sport would bring blacks and whites closer together and eliminate racial discrimination.

Irrespective of the philosophical differences, Edwards and the OPHR moved forward with their boycott plans. The group first exerted its influence when it led a boycott of the NYAC's one-hundredth anniversary track and field meet scheduled for the new Madison Square Garden in February 1968. Targeting the NYAC because of its exclusion of blacks and Jews, the OPHR received support from a number of important individuals and groups, including H. Rap Brown, chairman of the Student Non-Violent Coordinating Committee; Roy Innes, Associate National Director of CORE; Urban League; NAACP; and the Anti-Defamation League of B'nai B'rith. Although the meet went off as scheduled, the OPHR protest successfully deterred world-class athletes and entire teams from competing. San Jose State sprinters Tommie Smith and John Carlos, two stalwarts of the OPHR, stayed away as did other outstanding black track and field athletes such as Paul Drayton, Lee Evans, Bill Gaines, Martin McCrady, and Kirk Clayton. The track and field teams from such institutions as Rutgers University, Manhattan College, Villanova University, St. Johns University, New York University, and Morgan State University chose not to participate. The Russian national track team elected not to compete in the meet after being asked to do so by the OPHR. Besides these defections, the NYAC protest proved to be successful in that it energized and united rebellious black athletes from across the country in a common cause for the first time.

The NYAC protest boded well for the OPHR in regards to their planned boycott of the Mexico City games. But plans are never as clear or as easy to accomplish as they portend. Events in the spring of 1968 made evident that the OPHR had to think very seriously as to how to get black athletes to congeal around one common approach regarding the proposed boycott of the upcoming summer games. One particularly important event took place on April 20 when the IOC reversed course on South Africa by voting to bar that country from participation in Mexico City. Although satisfying only one of the several demands made by the OPHR in order to insure participation in the games, the IOC decision helped moderate the stance of black athletes who were seemingly already backing away from their commitment to boycott the Mexico City Olympics. It was apparent from the very beginning of the boycott movement that it would be especially difficult for black athletes in such marquee Olympic sports as track and field to stay away from Mexico City after spending years honing their talents and making sacrifices to participate in the world's most important athletic event.

The upshot was that most of the disgruntled black athletes ultimately decided to show some form of protest at the Mexico City games rather than to boycott. With the notable exception of UCLA great Lew Alcindor, his two teammates Mike Warren and Lucius Allen, and a few other world-class performers, the largest majority of black athletes elected to compete in Mexico City while expressing their disapproval of racial inequality and second-class citizenship through public demonstrations. The most famous of these was the black power salutes of Tommie Smith and John Carlos on the victory stand following their first- and third-place finishes in the 200 meter dash. The two great San Jose State sprinters startled the world and would forever have their images etched in memory by bowing their heads and raising their black-gloved fists high into the air during the playing of America's national anthem. Both men paid dearly for their actions. IOC President Avery Brundage was livid about the protest, forcing the USOC to kick Smith and Carlos out of the Olympic village and sent them back to the United States. Many members of the press castigated the two athletes for their overtly political demonstration and refusal to honor the American flag in the appropriate fashion. Smith and Carlos lost out on opportunities following the Mexico City games, never realizing the public adulation and career success that typically came the way of Olympic champions.

Figure 6.2. Tommie Smith and John Carlos (with Peter Norman of Australia on their right) giving their black-gloved power salute on the victory stand following their first and third place finishes in the 200-meter race.
Courtesy of Library of Congress Prints and Photographs Division. LC-USZ62-107184.

The legacy of the black athletic protests at the Mexico City Olympic Games, even with the perspective offered by the passage of time, is difficult to assess with any certitude. There seems little question that the boycott movement overshadowed Dick Fosbury's gold medal in the high jump using at that time his unorthodox "Fosbury Flop," Bob Beamon's world record–breaking performance in the long jump, Al Oerter's fourth consecutive gold medal in the discus, and many other great athletic accomplishments. In a revealing interview with David Leonard of *Colorlines* thirty years after the boycott movement, Harry Edwards heaped praise on the black athletes who protested at Mexico City, noting how impressed he was with their commitment to the larger civil rights struggle and the heroic stance they took on behalf of the less fortunate members of their community. They acted in an uncompromising fashion, taking the Olympic stage, which "was second only to the United Nations as an international political forum," to heroically take their place alongside other brave men involved in the broader civil rights movement. Edwards, however, did express some regrets about the OPHR and the boycott movement. He believes he made a mistake in not embracing more fully those white athletes who were sympathetic to the black boycott movement. Although recognizing that he may have alienated some in the black community, Edwards believes the movement would have benefited if he had made a more concerted effort to establish a closer connection with white athletes. In addition, Edwards freely admitted that the OPHR made a mistake by not engaging women athletes in the proposed boycott of the Mexico City games. The OPHR was, in contemporary parlance notes Edwards, a sexist organization, a claim that could be made of the entire civil rights movement.

Disgruntled Black Athletes on College Campuses

Disgruntled black athletes did not express their frustration with racial inequality simply during one Olympic competition. There were literally hundreds of various kinds of protests lodged by black athletes at predominantly white universities between approximately 1968 and 1972. Harry Edwards estimated that in 1968 alone there were some thirty-seven black athletic protests at predominantly white institutions. Often in concert with other black students and sometimes with white students, black athletes at predominantly white institutions varying widely in demographic profiles, academic programs, and geographical location, expressed a new sense of black pride through protests meant to bring attention to the civil rights struggle and overcome racial inequality. The racial protests on predominantly white university campuses often centered on confrontations with white coaches, black athletes questioning how they were being treated, revolting against authority, and, in some cases, withholding their services on behalf of larger civil rights causes. How these confrontations played out varied by campus, but all white coaches were faced with a conundrum in that they needed their increasingly assertive black athletes in order to be competitive on the playing field yet could not run the risk of having their authority questioned and team unity disrupted.

Some of the more notable black athletic protests took place at the University of Texas at El Paso, Oregon State University, Syracuse University, University of California at Berkeley, Michigan State University, University of Wyoming, University of Kansas, University of Oklahoma, San Francisco State University, Marquette University, Western Michigan University, and Princeton University. Of these black athletic protests, those at the University of Wyoming and Oregon State University provide good examples of the different kinds of issues associated with the revolts and how black athletes navigated the racial realities of predominantly white universities and society at large. In the fall of 1969, the University of Wyoming would experience one of the most famous and written about black athletic protests. On October 17 of that year, the fourteen black players on the Wyoming football team, wearing black armbands, approached coach Lloyd Eaton and told them of their plans to lodge a protest during the following day's game against Brigham Young University (BYU) because of the Mormon institution's policy that prohibited blacks from becoming members of the priesthood. Eaton, an authoritarian and disciplinary-oriented coach in the mold of Ohio State's Woody Hayes and other leaders of football teams during the era, immediately revoked the scholarships of the fourteen players and dismissed them from the team. He apparently told them, "You can get on Negro relief or colored relief and then maybe at these Morgan States and Gramblings they'll put up with this kind of stuff. You're with a bunch of black people so they might tolerate this action, but here it's not going to be tolerated."[4]

The dismissal of the fourteen players resulted in meetings involving the university president, governor, board of trustees, and other representatives of the university. Although there were some changes in university policies regarding how to deal with protests in the future, the players were not reinstated to the football team. They responded by filing, with assistance of NAACP attorney William Waterman and later leaders of the American Civil Liberties Union (ACLU), a $1.1 million dollar lawsuit against the university and Eaton in the US District Court in Cheyenne. Wyoming's attorney general countered that the players were employees of the state and any protests on the athletic field would have violated the laws of Wyoming and the US Constitution's demand for the separation of church and state. Unfortunately, US District Court Judge Ewing T. Kerr ruled in favor of the university. All but one of the players eventually left the university, with most of them going on to productive and successful professional careers. The racial protest, on the other hand, would have a deleterious effect on the Wyoming football program. Over the next ten years, black players refused to attend the school and the result was a string of losing seasons for the football team. As for BYU, the institution held fast to its racial policies until June 9, 1978, when leaders of the Mormon Church proclaimed that they had received a divine revelation granting permission to open the priesthood to blacks.

The black athletic protest at Oregon State University was sparked by the refusal to shave off facial hair rather than a condemnation of the Mormon Church's policy toward blacks. In February 1969, Fred Milton, a black linebacker from Richmond, Washington, was told by head football coach Dee Andros to cut off his mustache and Van Dyke beard or face disciplinary action. After Milton refused, Andros—a member of Bud Wilkinson's great football team at the University of Oklahoma in the 1950s and former Marine who was affectionately known as "The Great Pumpkin" because of his rotund shape and fondness for orange and black—responded immediately by kicking his black linebacker off the football team. Milton's dismissal set off a series of events that pitted black and white athletes against each other.

The tension between white and black athletes was palpable in regard to the Milton affair. Black athletes, facing the almost impossible task of being loyal to the civil rights struggle while at once not wanting to jeopardize their athletic careers and future career success, ultimately made clear that the Milton incident was merely a symptom of various grievances that had been bubbling to the surface for them and their fellow black students on the isolated campus in Corvallis. The list of grievances was quite long, including not feeling welcomed by local merchants and other businessmen, lack of black coaches, a university that included no black studies in the curriculum, inadequate housing facilities on campus, and "unwritten policy" of the athletic department that prohibited them from dating white women. White athletes on campus, with the notable exceptions of gold medal high jumper Dick Fosbury and All-American fullback Bill Enyart, would hear nothing of it, believing that the Milton affair was not a racial issue but merely the case of an athlete who received the appropriate punishment for violating team rules and disrupting team unity. Led by All-American center John Didion, some 173 athletes presented a signed petition to Oregon State President James Jenson indicating their support for Andros and his decision to dismiss Milton from the football team. Andros was only doing what was fair and equitable and in the best interests of the football team.

Equally contentious was the relationship among the athletic department, Black Student Union (BSU), NAACP, and the university. Andros, of course, adamantly defended his position, publicly stating that he had never discriminated against one of his athletes irrespective of race. Other coaches in the athletic department circled the wagons and stood up for the embattled football coach. Athletic director James Barratt told the Oregon State faculty that the Milton event had never been about racial prejudice and that the university's black students had "confused discipline for discrimination."[5] University President James Jensen did everything he could to squelch the racial antagonism on campus, including establishing a Commission on Human Rights and Responsibilities that was charged with settling disputes when decisions of coaches and other faculty personnel threatened a student's human rights. The BSU would have none of it, calling Jensen spineless, claiming the athletic department and university were racist, and encouraging black students to leave the school that practiced a plantation mentality. The Portland branch of the NAACP conducted its own investigation of the Milton affair and concluded that the grievances of black athletes and their fellow black students were legitimate and should be addressed immediately by the university administration.

Finally, in May 1969, approximately three months after Andros had dismissed Milton from the football team, the Commission on Human Rights and Responsibilities came out with its report detailing recommendations as to how to improve race relations in the athletic department specifically and university more generally. As a whole, however, the report lacked any real substance. Although claiming that Milton's human rights had been violated, the report noted that the inequitable treatment he received was not intentional and that Andros and his staff were simply not aware of the emerging needs and changes in the black community. The report satisfied no one, including Milton and Andros. Milton believed it had no teeth, lacking specific guidelines to ensure that he would be compensated in some way for the way he had been treated. Andros, for his part, was terribly disappointed that the report claimed that Milton's human rights had been violated. His disappointment, however, only seemed to embolden him as he maintained he would continue to do things his way and hold fast to the rules he had established for his football team. It is understandable that Andros took this position as he was at the height of his popularity among the followers of Oregon State football, leading the Beavers to many victories on the gridiron and mesmerizing fans with his oversized body and personality. Although having his image tarnished some by the Milton affair, he remained enormously popular and a coach eagerly sought after by other high-powered college football programs.

In the end, the Milton incident certainly sensitized Oregon State and the local community to the concerns of black students. But damage had been done, relationships had been severed, and those directly involved in the incident had their lives dramatically impacted. Six of Oregon State's seventeen black athletes chose to leave the university, including Milton who transferred to Utah State University. There were no black athletes in Andros's recruiting class the year after the Milton incident, the black community urging recruits not to play for the racially insensitive and discriminatory university in Corvallis. Racial antagonisms would continue to be evident in the school's athletic department. A prime example took place in 1972 when black outfielder Verdell Adams from Portland accused baseball coach Gene Tanselli of racial discrimination. Although found innocent of the charges, Tanselli was fired from his coaching position by athletic director James Barratt who contended that the decision was not the result of racially discriminatory practices, but because of the baseball team's poor won-loss record.

The revolts of black athletes at the University of Wyoming, Oregon State University, and other predominantly white institutions make clear that there was no coordinated response to the racial disturbances and each school handled them in their own way. Like academics and other areas of university life, each institution typically chose to deal with the various demands made by black athletes as they saw fit without seemingly much interest in seeking advice and joining forces with other schools experiencing the same issues and problems. That would change, however, in 1972 when the Big Ten appointed a joint advisory committee to identify the specific concerns expressed by black athletes in the conference and how those concerns should be addressed. The committee came about largely in response to a group of black academics led by Michigan State professor Robert L. Green who protested the treatment of black athletes in the conference in a report addressed to the Big Ten Joint Committee (faculty athletic representatives and athletic directors) titled "The Status of Blacks in the Big Ten Athletic Conference: Issues and Concerns."[6] Among the issues voiced by Green and his fellow black academics was the inadequate education provided to black athletes and racial discrimination in employment opportunities in the athletic programs of conference schools.

The joint advisory committee, which was made up of former black athletes from conference schools, concurred with many of the claims made by Green's group and made a number of suggestions to the Big Ten Joint Committee which without delay implemented changes and established programs that would benefit all student athletes and safeguard against racial inequality. Athletic-academic counseling programs were established at conference schools that were under the control of faculty athletic representatives rather than coaches or athletic directors. Seminars were implemented to improve the communication between coaches and black athletes and lists were compiled of blacks who had the skills to be employed as coaches, athletic trainers, umpires and officials, athletic administrators, and other athletic department personnel. A fifth year of financial aid was also granted to those athletes who had yet to finish their degrees and announced plans to hire a black assistant commissioner of the Big Ten Conference to help implement the aforementioned initiatives. The man eventually hired was Dr. C. D. Henry.

Black Athletes as Popular and Scholarly Subjects

The racial disturbances on predominantly white university campuses gradually came to an end. Importantly, these disturbances, along with those that took place at other levels of sport, garnered an enormous amount of attention regarding the various issues, problems, and racially discriminatory practices faced by black athletes, coaches, and administrators. This factor, combined with a rapidly growing interest in the life, history, and culture of black Americans during the 1970s and 1980s resulted in an outpouring of popular writings and scholarly studies devoted to the African American experience in sport. Also contributing to the growing literature on black athletes were a number of new professional organizations devoted to encouraging and promoting the serious study of sport, including the North American Society for the Sociology of Sport (NASSS), North American Society for Sport History (NASSH), North American Society for the Psychology of Sport and Physical Activity (NASPSPA), and The International Association for the Philosophy of Sport (IAPS). These professional organizations, through their various scholarly journals and other publishing outlets, disseminated a plethora of research studies on various aspects of the black experience in sport. The growing literature on black athletes resulted, moreover, from the changing nature of both commercial and university presses who expanded their subject base to include more books on sport. Recognizing people's fascination with the topic and certainly looking for ways to increase sales, the University of Illinois Press and then later other university presses at such institutions as Syracuse University and University of Tennessee would establish series devoted exclusively to sport. These series would produce a host of studies on black athletes and more broadly the interconnection among race, sport, and American culture.

Topics that garnered a great deal of attention from scholars and others interested in black athletes were the differences in academic performance among black and white athletes, disparity between the sport performance of black athletes and financial rewards they received, and underrepresentation and overrepresentation of black athletes in different sports and by playing position. Academicians from various disciplinary perspectives were interested in the factors that accounted for the relatively poor academic performance of black athletes—especially males—compared to their white counterparts. At the center of the discussion were Propositions 48 and 42, legislation implemented by the NCAA in 1986 and 1989 respectively to improve academic performance and erase the problem of low graduation rates of all athletes. Academicians from various disciplinary perspectives also addressed the issue regarding the lower salaries of black athletes relative to white athletes of comparable athletic skill and accomplishments. Academicians from various disciplinary perspectives, moreover, addressed the question as to why black athletes were disproportionally represented in some sports and in certain playing positions and not others. Generating much interest were the possible factors accounting for the large number of black athletes grouped into "noncentralized" as opposed to "centralized" playing positions in sport. The one playing position most closely associated with this discussion was that of quarterback, the most important "centralized" position in football traditionally closed to black athletes because of their perceived lack of intelligence and leadership skills.

Also drawing much attention was the continual debate regarding the supposed superiority of black athletes. Harking back to discussions made earlier in American history, most notably those surrounding the 1936 Olympic Games in Berlin, writer Martin Kane reignited the controversial question about the link among race, physical ability, and sport performance in a 1971 essay in *Sports Illustrated* titled "An Assessment of Black Is Best." Utilizing the various positions taken on the matter by respected medical doctors, coaches, scholars of sport, and black athletes themselves, Kane postulated that the great athletic performances of black athletes resulted from racially linked psychological, historical, and physical characteristics. Among those he quoted was famed Indiana University swimming coach James "Doc" Councilman, an interesting choice considering Councilman's involvement in a sport that was predominantly white and fraught with deep-seated racial stereotypes concerning the supposed inability of blacks to float and navigate through the water. Councilman's comments, like so many who have tried to explain the connection between race and sport performance, were convoluted and largely illogical. Although correctly noting that the relatively small numbers of black swimmers resulted from a variety of socioeconomic factors, he fed into long-standing racialist thinking by arguing that black athletes excelled in sports that required speed and power because of their larger number of white muscle fibers. Conversely, white athletes dominated sports requiring endurance because of their larger number of red muscle fibers.

The Kane article resulted in a number of heated responses. No one, however, was more publicly critical of the essay than Harry Edwards. The architect of the 1968 Olympic boycott and PhD in sociology from Cornell, Edwards dissected in great detail each of the arguments put forward in Kane's 1971 piece in *Sports Illustrated*. Like physical anthropologist Montague Cobb many years earlier, Edwards argued convincingly that it was erroneous to believe that any racial group was innately gifted physically or in any other way that would predispose them to superior performances in sport. In Edwards's view, to argue that black athletes realized their success because of innate physiological skills unique to their racial group was dismissive of the hard work, discipline, and other character traits so essential to their achievements and so admired in American culture. Edwards, though, made clear that a number of societal factors had caused black youth to devote an inordinate amount of attention to sport that resulted in the funneling of the most talented of them into selected sports at the highest levels of competition. In large part, limited opportunities in other realms of life encouraged black youth to focus their attention on the highly competitive world of sport that could potentially lead to great rewards and much adulation.

Edwards's response to Martin Kane, unfortunately, did not end the debate over race and black athletic performance. The topic would continue to hold out much interest for those who closely followed sport. The debate, however, also continued to be ahistorical in nature, chock full of racialist thinking, and ultimately a fruitless and unproductive endeavor. One of the most frequently quoted series of comments on the topic came from Jimmy "The Greek" Snyder, the famous prognosticator who worked for twelve years on the CBS show *The NFL Today*. On Martin Luther King Day in 1988 at a restaurant in Washington, D.C., Snyder told writer Edward Hotaling that the superiority of black athletes had its beginning years ago on southern plantations when "the slave owner would breed his big black with his big woman so that he could have a big black kid." He went on to claim that black athletes "jump higher and run faster because of their thigh size and big size."[1] Snyder's comments drew harsh criticisms. One cartoon in the *Boston Globe* pictured Snyder being consoled by a hooded KKK member. A *Washington Post* columnist drew a comparison between Snyder and Joseph Goebbels, Nazi Germany's sadistic Minister of Public Enlightenment and Propaganda. The public outcry was so great that CBS fired him just two days after the debacle.

The debate over the connection between race and sport performance seemingly reached its crescendo with the publication in 2000 of *Jon Entine's Taboo: Why Black Athletes Dominate Sports and Why We're Afraid to Talk About It*. Taking off from the one-hour documentary he produced on the subject with legendary television broadcaster Tom Brokaw in 1989, Entine, an author and journalist who founded and is executive director of the Genetic Literacy Project wrote a book of over three hundred pages that encapsulates many of the issues always associated with the discussion regarding race and its connection to athletic success. If anything, the book resurrected, in the most extreme cases, academic fissures pitting scientists against cultural theorists. Although claiming that his message was not meant to spread racialist thinking, careful to divorce himself from the Bell Curve that linked intelligence and ethnicity, and that he was only interested in celebrating human diversity, Entine's view of race as a biological phenomenon and insistence that science is objective and neutral laden negated a knowledgeable consideration of the cultural factors which have contributed greatly to the sports black athletes participate in and those in which they have been most successful. The most glaring example of this is his grouping of African Americans and Africans into the same category and his convoluted explanation about the differences between distance runners and sprinters resulting from variations in lung capacity, muscle mass, body size, muscle fibers, enzymes, and centers of gravity. Equally alarming are his erroneous statements about black athletes realizing success in disproportionate numbers in most sports, assertions about white athletes being marginalized, and offering no explanation as to why he places such trust in racial science while at once contending that the racist eugenics studies of the late nineteenth and early twentieth centuries that he traces in such detail in the book were ill-informed and misguided.

One of the most telling aspects of the debate regarding the link between race and sport performance was the relatively lack of attention paid to African American female athletes. Although some involved in the discussion mentioned African American women athletes, including Entine himself, the majority of the debate has seemingly centered on African American male athletes. How to explain this discrepancy? Perhaps the best explanation can be gleaned from Jennifer Bruening's analysis of African American athletes in her insightful essay "Gender and Racial Analysis in Sport: Are All the Women White and All the Blacks Men?" She persuasively argues that African American women have routinely been overlooked, either lumped into the same category as white women or black men. They have, in other words, been "defined by others," not being recognized for their unique experiences forged by a combination of class, gender, and racial differences. It follows, then, that African American women athletes have been largely invisible in sport, alternately characterized as similar to their white counterparts or far more recognizable African American male athletes.[8]

The same line of racialist thinking used to explain the outstanding performances of black athletes were also used to rationalize the dearth of black coaches and upper-level administrators. Members of the African American community had expressed for years their frustration with the very small number of black coaches and administrators at various levels of sport and it is understandable why they did so. Bill Russell did not become the first black head coach in the NBA until 1966 when he was hired as player-coach by the Boston Celtics. The first black head coach at the Division I level in college basketball did not occur until 1970 when Illinois State University hired Will Robinson. Division I college football did not have its first black head coach until 1979 when Willie Jeffries was hired at Wichita State University. The first black manager in MLB did not take place until 1975 when Frank Robinson assumed leadership of the Cleveland Indians. Finally, Art Shell would not become the first black head coach in the modern NFL (Fritz Pollard had been head coach of the Akron Pros in 1921) until 1989 when he was hired for that position by Al Davis of the Los Angeles Raiders.

While the leaders of college and professional sport were not explicit about why they were so slow to hire black coaches, it was apparent to close observers that it stemmed from long-held views by whites that blacks did not have the intelligence, decision-making skills, and leadership abilities to assume such positions. Any question as to why the leaders of sport were hesitant to hire black coaches was, for all intents and purposes, put to rest in 1987 by Al Campanis, a top executive with the Los Angeles Dodgers. In an interview with Ted Koppel on the *Nightline* television show, Campanis famously noted that the lack of African Americans in upper-level management positions in baseball resulted from their lack of abilities. "I truly believe," noted Campanis, "they may not have the necessities to be, let's say, a field manager or perhaps a general manager."[9] The public outrage over Campanis's comments would result, like that of Jimmy "The Greek" Snyder the following year for his remarks about the supposed natural abilities of black athletes, in his firing

Figure 6.3.   Frank Robinson became the first black manager in MLB when he assumed the reigns of the Cleveland Indians in 1975.
Courtesy of the National Baseball Hall of Fame and Museum.

by the Dodgers. Following the firing of Campanis, Baseball Commissioner Peter Ueberoth would hire Harry Edwards to examine the steps that should be taken to increase the number of blacks in coaching and management positions in the MLB.

The Campanis interview also led to the founding of the Black Coaches Association (BCA) in 1988. Initially organized by two separate groups of racially aware black football and basketball coaches, the BCA, under the early leadership of Executive Director Rudy Washington, battled to see that more minority coaches and administrators were hired in high school, college, and professional sport. The BCA directed much of its anger at the NCAA, boycotting the annual meeting of the National Association of Basketball Coaches in 1993 and voicing their complaints about racial inequality in sport with the congressional Black Caucus.

Tellingly, other groups, particularly at the professional level of sport, were sometimes slow to establish rules and implement legislation in an effort to hire minority coaches. It was not until 2003 that the NFL established the Rooney Rule in an attempt to see that more minorities, especially African Americans, were hired as head coaches. Named after Dan Rooney, owner of the Pittsburgh Steelers, which had a history of employing African Americans in leadership positions, the Rooney Rule came about after the 2002 firings of Dennis Green of the Minnesota Vikings and Tony Dungy, two black head coaches that had enjoyed a string of winning seasons. The rule, which requires teams to interview minority candidates for head coaching and upper-level administrative positions, seemingly had some positive effects shortly after its implementation. At the beginning of the 2006 NFL season, the overall percentage of African American coaches stood at 22 percent, some 16 percent higher than it had been prior to the passage of the Rooney Rule just three years earlier. That percentage would rise until 2012 and then dip over the next several years before rebounding very recently with the hiring of more minority coaches. Included among these hires were Vance Joseph who was brought on as head coach of the Denver Broncos and Anthony Lynn who assumed the head coaching position with the Los Angeles Chargers.

Blacks would find it just as difficult to assume jobs in sports journalism as they did coaching positions. Recent reports from various groups and organizations point out the limited opportunities for blacks and women in the positions of sports editors, assistant sports editors, columnists, reporters, and copy editors. While the high profile of such black journalists as James Brown, Bryant Gumble, and Robin Roberts could lead one to believe that the opportunities for minorities and women in sports journalism are unlimited, the data indicates otherwise. In 2012, for instance, the Institute for Diversity and Ethics in Sport at the University of Central Florida reported that white males held 90 percent of sports editor positions, and the percentages were in the 80 percent and above range for assistant sports editors, columnists, reporters, and copy editors. The one major company that is an exception to the rule in the hiring of minority and women journalists is ESPN. The sports network in Bristol, Connecticut, has a very strong diversity hiring policy, providing access and opportunities to talented minority and women journalists. It regularly features minorities and women as announcers, journalists, analysts, and hosts. The company also works closely with the National Association of Black Journalists (NABJ) Sports Task Force in an effort to attract and prepare a more diverse group of sports journalists. One of the many ways that the NABJ Sports Task Force encourages minority group involvement in sports journalism is by offering the Larry Whiteside Scholarship, named in honor of the first African American to work as a sportswriter for the Boston Globe.

Those involved in the contentious debates regarding race and sport performance and dearth of black coaches, upper-level administrators, and journalists would probably have benefited from a more thorough understanding of the information provided in the increasing number of scholarly studies being disseminated on the history of black participation in sport. Emerging out of the civil rights movement and its aftermath were a plethora of books and articles on black history, including the struggles encountered and contributions made by black athletes to America's sporting past. The person who led the way in providing a history of the African American experience in sport was Edwin Bancroft Henderson, a black physical educator, author, and civil rights activist. A multitalented and passionate man who fought tirelessly his entire life to ensure equality of opportunity for all citizens, Henderson has been referred to as the "Father of Black Sport History" for his many publications chronicling both the struggles and triumphs of black athletes in the United States.[10] In 1968, Henderson, in collaboration with the editors of *Sport* magazine and at the urging of Charles H. Wesley who had succeeded Carter G. Woodson as president of the Association for the Study of Negro Life and History (now Association for the Study of Afro-American Life and History), published the frequently cited *The Black Athlete: Emergence and Arrival.* This was nearly thirty years after the publication of his *The Negro in Sports* (1939), the first survey text written on the African American experience in sport. These two texts, while perhaps the most significant and noteworthy of Henderson's writings, were complemented by a very long list of essays on the topic that he published in a variety of influential outlets with large readerships.

Henderson's publications are all nicely written, interesting, and thought-ful. While typically not including citations, it is apparent that he used a variety of published sources in his writings, including black newspapers that usually devoted a great deal of coverage to all aspects of sport at various levels of competition. Henderson also depended to an extent on experien-tial knowledge to craft his narrative and draw his interpretations as he was actively involved in sport organizations and had coached athletes and knew personally some of the subjects he covered. What is apparent, moreover, in all of Henderson's publications is that he had a sincere belief in sport's power to bridge the racial divide, bring people of different backgrounds together, and ultimately lead to integration on and off the playing field. By recount-ing the individual accomplishments of black athletes in the face of racial discrimination, Henderson provided evidence of black progress and hoped to shatter racial stereotypes surrounding black athletes while engendering racial pride among all African Americans. In large part, his writings were used as an instrument, a tool used to alter racial beliefs and prove that blacks were just as competent as whites in sport and, with adequate support and encourage-ment, in other areas of American life. Unfortunately, what Henderson did not bargain for, or perhaps was just unwilling to admit, is that the increasing success of black athletes often seemed to delimit the sense of black identity rather than break down racial stereotypes and only confirmed white beliefs about strong black bodies and weak minds.

The influence of Henderson's work is evident in other survey texts published on the history of African American participation in sport. It is certainly true for Andrew S. "Doc" Young's 1963 book *Negro Firsts in Sports*. Young, a writer for *Ebony* magazine, *Los Angeles Sentinel*, and *Chicago Defender*, was obviously indebted to Henderson for many of the facts he provided in his more interpretive and analytical book on black athletes. Former basketball players Wally Jones and Jim Washington owe a great deal of gratitude to Henderson for the information they include in their 1972 book *Black Champions Challenge American Sports*. So does Arthur Ashe, the great tennis player, civil rights activist, and author. In 1988, Ashe published the well-known three-volume book *A Hard Road to Glory: A History of the African-American Athlete*, a work with a long shelf life that has been cited by most everyone who has examined the experience of black participation in sport. The thoughtful and intellectually engaged tennis player who always had a deep love of history, Ashe noted that the idea for a survey text on the history of black athletes came to him in 1981 when he had difficulty finding sources on the topic for a course he taught on the "Black Athlete in Contem-porary Society " at Florida Memorial College in Miami. Careful to pinpoint

Henderson's *The Negro in Sports* as major exception to the rule, the relative lack of sources on the topic of black athletes convinced Ashe to complete a book on the African American experience in sport. Armed with some financial resources and benefitting from his celebrity, Ashe assembled a team of researchers and writers to assist him with the project. The result was a book full of information about the history of the black athlete at various levels of competition and in a number of different sports. Although marred by factual errors, blurred images, lack of analysis, and an organizational structure that provides no sense of changes that took place over time, the book provides information on little known black athletes and obstacles they faced while struggling to become full participants in American sport. Ultimately, like Henderson, Ashe's intent was to showcase the exploits of African American athletes to engender racial pride and combat racist beliefs and feelings of inferiority. To a significant degree, recounting the successes of black athletes was most important to Ashe because they served as symbols of possibility.

The publication of Ashe's survey text took place during an especially important decade in regard to the historical writings on black athletes. The 1980s would witness, largely as a result of the legitimization of both sport history and black history as academic disciplines, a surge in the number of quality articles and books on the history of the African American experience in sport. Although defying easy categorization and unfortunately largely limited to males, these studies were far more sophisticated than many of the previous works completed on African American athletes, characterized by the utilization of little known sources, the connection of sport to larger societal issues, and more historical analysis and interpretations.

These path-breaking studies ranged from such celebrated works as Jules Tygiel's, *Baseball's Great Experiment: Jackie Robinson and His Legacy* (1983) and Randy Roberts, *Papa Jack: Jack Johnson and the Era of White Hopes* (1983) to William J. Baker's *Jesse Owens: An American Life* and Rob Ruck's *Sandlot Seasons: Sport in Black Pittsburgh* (1986). The last three decades have continued to see a number of works published on the history of the African American experience in sport. These works have dealt with an assortment of different topics, including the use of African American athletes on State Department tours during the Cold War period, integration of sport at predominantly white universities in the South, the pattern and role of African American women in sport, and the involvement of African American athletes in the Civil Rights movement.

CHAPTER SEVEN

~

Race, Black Athletes, and the Globalization of Sport

Recent scholarly publications make clear the complex connection among race, gender, and sport, and how black athletes have been cast as cultural heroes and global icons. In addition to the debates regarding race and sport performance and concerns about the inability of blacks to secure coaching, administrative, and sports journalism positions, blacks continue to attach a great deal of importance to careers in sport, participate in some sports in very large numbers and not others, and are faced with the challenges posed by racialist thinking and white privilege. Perhaps no group found it more difficult to find their way into sport than African American women. Although the passage of Title IX in 1972 would open up increasing opportunities for African American women in interscholastic and intercollegiate sport, their level of participation is much lower than their white counterparts and any identifiable racial or ethnic group. The number of African American women participating in soccer, lacrosse, and rowing is especially small, a significant fact considering that these are the three fastest growing sports for women at the intercollegiate level of competition.

The continuing struggle of African Americans to find their way into a larger number of sports did not preclude a select number of them from becoming global icons. The very best African American athletes have garnered worldwide appeal, realizing a level of acceptance and legitimacy that has been difficult to come by for even the most famous individuals in politics, business, and other supposedly more serious endeavors. Not unexpectedly, several black stars in basketball would realize this status, largely a result of the sport's enormous popularity in the United States and abroad. There were also, however, a small number of outstanding black athletes from sports in which their racial group was decidedly underrepresented who realized global icon status.

Reckoning with Sport and Racial Progress

African Americans have always taken seriously the role of sport and offered their views as to how or if athletic success contributes to racial progress. Since at least the late nineteenth and early part of the twentieth centuries, some blacks have voiced their belief in the symbolic power of sport, viewing the individual success of black athletes as having expressive connotations that were far more important than the successes themselves. The triumphs of black athletes, particularly when they took place against whites, were crucially important because they engendered racial pride, helped eliminate white beliefs about black inferiority, and could further the progress of the race. The belief in the representational power of sport was countered by other blacks that cautioned against an overemphasis on sport for fear it would perpetuate the stereotype of blacks as physically gifted and intellectually inferior. For some blacks, success in sport, while materially advantageous and psychologically satisfying to a few gifted black athletes would never be able to eliminate the problems of the race. It is for this reason, and many others, that many blacks stressed to young black athletes the importance of broadening their horizons and establishing more than just a sport-related identity. Although not necessarily discouraging them from participating in sport or asking them to give up their dreams of success on America's playing fields, some blacks stressed to young black athletes the importance of placing more emphasis on education and focusing more intently on preparing for life after sport.

These discussions have continued to take place unabated with individuals from seemingly every walk of life and from different racial and ethnic groups offering their views as to the impact of sport on the black community. A key event in the dialogue regarding black participation in sport and connection to racial progress was the publication of John Hoberman's 1997 book *Darwin's Athletes: How Sport Has Damaged Black America and Preserved the Myth of Race*. Hoberman, a white academician in Germanic Languages from The University of Texas at Austin, brought the topic to a never-before-seen level of public discussion. An extraordinarily controversial book, Hoberman's basic thesis was that African Americans, because of their long exclusion from many of the most prestigious professions, developed a fixation on sport that has inflicted great harm on their community. With no other heroes to celebrate, the black community lionizes great African American athletes that has led to the erroneous belief that integration has occurred while at once contributing to social divisions. The obsession with highly paid flamboyant black athletes helped foster a white belief in black intellectual inferiority and black violence, and discouraged black academic achievement.

Hoberman's arguments regarding the black community's fixation on sport drew strong rebukes from many respected and high-profile black intellectuals. Jeffrey Sammons, a historian at NYU who has written extensively about black boxers, engaged in a heated exchange with Hoberman shortly after the book was published through a "Book Forum" in the *Journal of Sport History*. Sammons spared no criticism of Hoberman's work. Although acknowledging that Hoberman had raised some important issues and concerns regarding race and sport, Sammons was highly critical of the book, claiming it was "at once marred and betrayed by a serious problem of tone—at once accusatory and superior. It is the tone of the expert observer with all the answers, the trained eye who can pass judgement and the self-righteous abstainer who can impose values."[1] Hoberman, for his part, countered by claiming that Sammons provided misleading statements regarding the book's intent and subject matter. Although acknowledging that some of Sammons's criticisms were valid, Hoberman noted unapologetically that his book was a "one-sided cultural history," intentionally detailing the negative impact of sports on blacks rather than regurgitating the arguments of other scholars who had painted an unrealistic picture of the positive effects that sport had on the African American community.[2]

The antagonism toward Hoberman's book was slow to dissipate. In 2007, ten years after the initial publication of the book, Sammons organized a symposium at NYU titled "Sport Matters: Black Intellectuals Respond to and Transcend Darwin's Athletes." Touted as a symposium to discuss black America's supposed preoccupation with sport, Sammons invited Hoberman and a number of prominent black intellectuals, many of them who had spent the majority of their careers writing about sport, to discuss the controversial topic. Hoberman declined the invitation, contending that he was being used as a scapegoat and had not been given adequate time to have a serious dialogue about the book. Sammons had better luck with the black intellectuals he invited, receiving confirmations from such noted individuals as Donald Spivey from the University of Miami, Gerald Early from Washington University, Kenneth Shropshire from the University of Pennsylvania, Arnold Rampersad of Princeton University, and Kenneth Manning of the Massachusetts Institute of Technology. These individuals, and others in attendance, took turns taking swipes at Hoberman with one participant concluding his remarks by shouting "F-John Hoberman."[3] Similar to the beliefs expressed by Sammons in his dialogue with Hoberman in the *Journal of Sport History*, the participants were uniform in their views that Hoberman's book lacked historical context and that he did not have a thorough understanding of sport and African American life. Perhaps most importantly, the participants shared the view that Hoberman was simply wrong in his assessment that lower-class blacks were obsessed with sport and that black intellectuals have done a disservice to their community by not pointing out the negative impact that sport was having on black Americans.

Irrespective of whether blacks have been more obsessed with sport than other groups in America, the data is clear that they continue to be represented in very high numbers in a select number of sports and vastly underrepresented in many others. The difference in these rates of participation has remained fairly stable over the last number of years with little discernable fluctuation in spite of concerted efforts by individuals and groups to see that minorities are furnished opportunities to engage in those sports traditionally closed to them. This reality is confirmed by what has taken place in swimming. Historically denied access to pools and suffering from deep-seated stereotypes about their inability to float, being afraid of the water, and unwillingness to get their hair wet, African Americans have found it difficult to engage in swimming at both the recreational and competitive levels of participation. In spite of programs like Black Kids Swim, which makes efforts to get more blacks involved in the sport, and notwithstanding the recent success of such outstanding black swimmers as Simone Manuel, Lia Neal, and Anthony Ervin in international competitions, swimming remains closed for most African Americans. USA Swimming, the national organization of the sport, has some 337,000 members, but only 1.3 percent of those are black. Of the 107 HBCUs, none of them have an operational fifty-meter pool and only Howard University has a competitive swimming team.

Baseball does not fare any better than swimming. African Americans are underrepresented at all levels of the sport that at one time was our national pastime and holds such symbolic importance in regard to racial integration. When the Boston Red Sox finally signed Pumpsie Greene in 1959, it brought the number of African Americans in MLB to sixty-nine, which represented 17 percent of all players. By 1975, African Americans represented their highest total ever at 27 percent, but by 2011 that percentage had fallen to just 8.5 percent. Why African American players have deserted the sport is open to speculation. One scholar has made the argument that African Americans no longer find their way into baseball because they never loved the sport to the same extent as whites and, therefore, never passed on the intricacies of the game to their children and other loved ones. There are others who lay the blame for the dearth of African American players in MLB on the limited opportunities and financial resources available to perfect the skills essential to playing at the highest levels of the sport. Still others contend that African Americans, unlike Latin Americans who make up 24.2 percent of all Major

Figure 7.1.   Hank Aaron hitting his 715th home run.
Courtesy of the National Baseball Hall of Fame and Museum.

League players, simply do not receive the family and community support necessary to achieve success in the sport. Finally, some observers of the sport contend that the lack of African Americans in baseball largely stems from the limited number of scholarships in college baseball and the changing format of the Major League draft. Quite simply, most African Americans do not have the financial wherewithal to play college baseball because of the meager scholarship money available and, therefore, fewer of them are eligible for the Major League draft that selects more college than high school players.

Finally, the long apprenticeship that players have to serve in order to get to the Major Leagues is a daunting prospect for physically gifted blacks that may deter them from seriously pursuing careers in baseball, especially when basketball and other sports typically offer quicker alternatives to fame and fortune. Even someone as talented as David Ortiz had to endure the long bus rides and years of preparation before getting the opportunity to play at the Major League level. "At seventeen, it was going to be a while before I was ready to play in the minors, never mind the majors," wrote Ortiz in his autobiography *Big Papi: My Story of Big Dreams and Big Hits*, "so the Mariners (Seattle) knew they had to take it slow with me."[4]

While the possible reasons for the small number of African Americans in MLB are interesting to contemplate, it is perhaps even more important to ascertain why officials in the league are so troubled by it. There is little question they are always concerned about having an adequate flow of talent into the league so as to maintain a high level of skill and competitive balance in order to continue to bring large numbers of fans through the turnstiles. But that seems to be taking place irrespective of the dearth of African Americans in the league. Ultimately, the concern that officials in the league have regarding the dearth of African American players seemingly has less to do with attracting black fans than it does with the fact it runs counter to their romanticized version of the past and does not adequately reflect their concern for democratic principles and freedom of opportunity. This idealized conception of the sport is why MLB sponsors and places such emphasis on events that commemorate Jackie Robinson, Negro League Baseball, and the civil rights struggle. Examples of these events would include Jackie Robinson Day, Civil Rights Game, and Negro League Weekend, among others.

The African American community certainly needs no reminder about the struggles they have faced in the sport and it is impossible to really know how much attention they pay to the commemorative events sponsored by MLB. What is obvious is that black Americans are highly represented and avid followers and observers of football and basketball at all levels of competition. The two sports resonate with them like no other. As of this writing, blacks make up some 56 percent of college football teams and 70 percent of NFL players. In basketball, blacks make up some 61 percent of college teams and 74.4 percent of NBA players. At the 2016 Olympic Games in Rio de Janeiro, seven of the twelve players on the women's basketball team were black, while all twelve members of the men's basketball team were black. Their attachment to these two sports has brought forth much discussion and speculation, especially basketball because of its extraordinarily close connection with African American life and culture. Sometimes described as the "Asphalt Gods," black athletes are synonymous with the sport that is often referred to as the "City Game" and perhaps can now lay claim as America's national pastime.[4] The stars of the game, including the likes of Michael Jordan, Kobe Bryant, Stephen Curry, Kevin Durant, and LeBron James, have had a significant global reach whose popularity extends far beyond the borders of the United States.

A number of possible reasons have been proffered in an effort to explain the love affair that African Americans have with basketball. Some have argued that basketball has been particularly attractive to impoverished young blacks that see it as a "way out of the ghetto," particularly because it is a game that requires little resources, equipment, and space to hone the skills necessary to be successful. Michael Novak, philosopher, author and theologian, contended as early as 1976 in his highly acclaimed *The Joy of Sports* that basketball is ideally suited for African Americans because it emphasizes and places a high value on improvisation and deceptions and feints that are such an important part of black culture and performance style. Now more than ever, it is a black man's game, characterized by the flow of the city with an emphasis on cool and sophisticated moves and smooth and spectacular style of play. To Novak, the sport is symbolically urban rather than rural and will "become more black with every passing year."[5]

Novak's assertion that basketball will "become more black with every passing year" now seems quite prophetic considering the increasing number of African Americans that continue to find their way into the sport. It is probably unlikely, however, that Novak could ever have predicted the very close relationship that would be forged among basketball, hip-hop, and the drug culture over the last several years. As Jeffrey Lane made clear in *Under the Boards: The Cultural Revolution in Basketball* (2007), an "incestuous relationship" developed among hip-hop, basketball, and a drug culture that is evident in an assortment of different ways.[6] It was customary for hip-hop videos to include well-known rappers decked out in NBA clothing while bragging about their drug dealing and fondness for smoking weed. During the 1990s, the celebrated rapper Tupac Shakur actually played the role of a

Georgetown recruit who struggled to realize his hoop dreams while continually being tempted by the hustling lifestyle. Some of basketball's biggest stars have made cameos in rap videos, including Tracy McGrady of the Houston Rockets appearing in Mike Jones's "Flossin" and the Los Angeles Lakers Lamar Odoms dancing in Jadakiss's "Knock Yourself Out." Allen Iverson and Chris Webber, two of the most famous and controversial NBA players who had both been arrested for marijuana possession, made their own rap albums.

Certainly one of the most notable examples of the relationship between hip-hop, basketball, and drug culture is the Entertainers Basketball Classic (EBC) played at the famed Rucker Park in New York City. Organized in the early 1980s by several rappers, the EBC is the crown jewel of the summer basketball leagues, attracting outstanding amateur and professional players from across the country. With squads sponsored through the years by such famous rappers as Jay-Z and Sean "Puffy" Combs, the EBC is played in front of wildly howling and partisan fans who come to watch the legends of the playgrounds and professional athletes perform their spin-moves, behind-the-back passes, and high-flying dunks. The prestige of the EBC is made very clear by the number of outstanding professional players who have taken time out from their schedules, risked injuries, and put their reputations on the line by taking part in the tournament at Rucker Park. Irrespective of the millions they have made and the celebrity status they have realized as NBA players, exhibiting their skills and triumphing on the court at the EBC was extraordinarily important in establishing legitimacy in the "hood" and among legendary street ballers.

The close relationship among hip-hop, basketball, and the drug culture never set well with the NBA and its corporate sponsors. Always concerned about alienating their white fanbase and portraying a wholesome public image, the NBA became increasingly troubled by the connections of its predominantly black players with rap artists and their perceived thuggish behavior and trouble with the law. In 1984, David Stern, a Columbia Law School graduate, became commissioner of the NBA, entering the league at the same time as four other giants of the game—Hakeem Olajuwon, Michael Jordan, Charles Barkley, and John Stockton. With these four stalwarts as a base, particularly Jordan, along with the great rivalry between two other legendary players Larry Bird and Magic Johnson, Stern would guide the league to unprecedented growth and popularity and profit. His tenure as commissioner, however, was also fraught with much controversy and negative publicity of the league centering to a large extent on the off-court behavior of black players and increasingly more flamboyant hip-hop culture. In 1997, Philadelphia 76ers guard Alan Iverson was charged with carrying a concealed weapon and marijuana possession after being pulled over for speeding in Virginia.

That same year Latrell Sprewell of the Golden State Warriors choked and threatened to kill his coach P. J. Carlesimo after Carlesimo had criticized him for not making crisper passes. In 2002, Iverson—who, in addition to his previous concealed weapon and marijuana charges, already had famous confrontations with his head coach Larry Brown and ran afoul of the NBA's projected image by wearing cornrows, diamond studded earrings, and highly visible tattoos—was issued fourteen felony and misdemeanor charges for a domestic dispute with his wife. In 2003 the Los Angeles Lakers' Kobe Bryant was accused of raping a nineteen-year-old girl at a mountain resort in Colorado, a circumstance that would seriously damage his clean-cut image and cost him millions in endorsements. Finally, at the beginning of the 2004 season a melee ensued when a fan hurled a beer cup at the Indiana Pacers' Ron Artest shortly after an altercation between Artest and the Detroit Pistons' Ben Wallace. Artest and teammate Stephen Jackson, and eventually other players, responded by going into the stands and exchanging blows with fans for several minutes before the police and security restored some kind of order. The Piston players involved in the skirmish were escorted out of the arena, but not before being pelted by fans throwing garbage and food and drinks at them as well as folding chairs.

These incidents, which was evidence of an obvious deep cultural divide in the league and between players and fans based on race and generational differences, were a public relations nightmare for the NBA. After realizing such enormous success and popularity during the initial stages of Stern's commissionership, the league was now faced with the dilemma as to how to simultaneously meet the needs of their beleaguered corporate sponsors, a dissatisfied television audience, and increasingly restless fanbase. One thing they did was implement a player dress code, which was "remarkably enough" agreed to by the Players Association. Obviously cosmetic rather than substantive in nature and intended to help restore the league's reputation as quickly as possible, it stipulated, among other things, that players were required to wear "business casual" clothing for all team and league functions. This meant wearing dress shoes or dress boots or "other presentable shoes" as well as collared dress shirts and turtlenecks or sweaters. Any time a player attended a game as a spectator they were required to add a sport coat to their attire. Perhaps most significantly, they were not permitted to wear such items as chains, pendants, work boots, jerseys, headbands, tennis shoes, construction boots, do-rags, baseball caps, bandanas, and sunglasses indoors. These were, of course, the very items that young black players in the NBA commonly wore and signified hip-hop culture.

The new dress code received mixed responses, with many contending that it was an attack on black culture and racially discriminatory in nature while others seemingly welcomed what they viewed as more professional attire that was crucial in maintaining a positive image of the league. David J. Leonard, a scholar of race and cultural studies at Washington State University, recently provided an assessment of the NBA dress code in *Dime Magazine* that furnishes important insights into how black athletes have dealt with it and turned it to their advantage. Accurately pointing out that the NBA had always tried to take advantage of the "economic popularity" of hip-hop while not alienating their white customers, Leonard notes that one of the more interesting responses to the dress code was the adoption of the "nerd chic" style of clothing associated with black stars such as Russell Westbrook, Kevin Durant, LeBron James, Amar'e Stoudamire, Dwight Howard, and Dwayne Wade. By donning bowties, black horn-rimmed glasses, and gingham and argyle-patterned clothing, notes Leonard, these prominent black players took a "sartorial stance" that was "clearly a challenge and a subversion to the dress code" but yet not a threat to the NBA establishment.[7] The one player who took this approach to the extreme was Westbrook who has violated all customary notions of masculine dress by wearing designer overalls, leather pants and printed shoes, and frilly three-quarter sleeve shirts. His bold fashion statements would probably have alienated players from yesteryear and called into question his sexuality.

Concerns about hip-hop culture and the alienation of white fans did not negate the enormous popularity and following that great NBA players would realize internationally. The 1992 "Dream Team," which included as starters Michael Jordan, Larry Bird, Magic Johnson, Patrick Ewing, and Charles Barkley, helped showcase and contributed to the growth of basketball that had always had deep and long ties in some locales globally. Unlike NFL players who have failed to gain much of a following internationally because of their involvement in a sport that has generated relatively little interest outside the United States, NBA stars have garnered celebrity status in Europe as evidenced by jersey sales, hawking of other sports paraphernalia, and close attention paid to league games as well as All-Star weekend and championship finals. The enormous popularity of the NBA worldwide also stems from the increasing number of foreign-born players who have found their way into the league and, in some cases, realized star status. Germany's Dirk Nowitski and China's Yao Ming are two of the most prominent among many foreign-born players who have helped spread the gospel of basketball to an international audience. Nowhere is enthusiasm for the sport more evident than in China, a country loaded with avid basketball fans who have followed intently the careers of Michael Jordan, Kobe Bryant, LeBron James, and their own hero Yao Ming.

Left Behind: Black Women Athletes

The passage of Title IX in 1972 would be extraordinarily important for women as it would eventually lead to dramatic increases in their participation in highly organized sport at various levels of competition. A law that prohibits gender discrimination in federally funded educational institutions, a wider interpretation and level of enforcement of Title IX took place with the passage in 1988 of the Civil Rights Restoration Act that accelerated even further the growth of women's sport participation. Although an increase would be seen in all women's sports on college campuses, it was the sports of rowing, golf, lacrosse, and soccer that educational institutions most frequently used to satisfy Title IX requirements. These particular sports, therefore, would witness a dramatic upsurge in the number of women participants. Evidence of this is certainly seen in soccer. In 1982, 2,743 women were participating in soccer at 103 colleges, but by 2001 the number of women competing in the sport had grown to 21,709 players at 930 colleges.

While on the surface these numbers are very encouraging and bode well for the future of women's sports, there is a more discouraging side to the story. Those four sports most frequently added by colleges to satisfy Title IX requirements are the same ones that primarily attract white rather than minority women athletes. One of the first people to point out this racial disparity in great detail was Welch Suggs of the *Chronicle of Higher Education*. In a 2001 report, Suggs noted that black women made up 35 percent of all basketball players and 25 percent of all track and field athletes, but only 2.7 percent of scholarship athletes in all the other sports at the Division I level of participation.[8] These numbers were an obvious indication that those sports added by colleges to satisfy Title IX requirements were primarily attracting white women from the suburbs and even foreign-born women rather than black women. Importantly, as small as the numbers were for black women, the participation rates for Hispanic, Asian, and Native American women athletes were even lower.

The percentages of black women participating in college sport would not dramatically change by the time of the fortieth anniversary celebration of Title IX in 2012. Although the percentage of African American women participating in basketball would actually rise to 47.9 percent and in softball to 20.5 percent since Suggs had initially provided his data, they still made up only 8.6 percent of all women athletes at the Division I, II, and III levels of college sport. As to why the percentage of African American women participating in college athletics, with the major exceptions of basketball, and track and field, would remain so relatively small was a source of discussion among many of those who came together to commemorate forty years of Title IX. Not unexpectedly, there were significant differences of opinion as to why black women athletes were not represented in greater numbers in a wider range of sports. For instance, on May 31 a public symposium was held in Washington, D.C., by the Aspen Institute Sports & Society program focusing on the theme "Title IX and Beyond: How Do We Get the Rest of Our Girls in the Game?"[9] The panel, which included as participants Anita DeFrantz, president of the LA 84 Foundation and IOC member; Benita Fitzgerald Mosley, Olympic gold medalist in track and field; Maya Moore, University of Connecticut basketball standout; and Dionne L. Koller, professor of law at the University of Baltimore and director of the Center for Sport and the Law, discussed the widening athletic participation rates between white and nonwhite women. Although a variety of opinions were expressed by the panelists and those in attendance, the general consensus expressed at the day-long symposium was that the underrepresentation of minority women in sport resulted from, in the words of New York Times sportswriter William C. Rhoden, "an intentional blind spot that could be corrected with good will."[10]

A decidedly different view regarding Title IX and inequality of opportunity for black women athletes was expressed by some at a private gathering among several prominent women a short time later at the Schomburg Center for Research in Black Culture in Harlem. Titled "What's Not Being Said about the Title IX Anniversary," the gathering included recently retired athletes, coaches, and executives of sports organizations, among others. Unlike the earlier symposium in Washington, D.C., some of those in attendance blamed the lack of opportunities for black women athletes on white power and privilege. Tina Sloan Green, first black head coach of lacrosse at Temple University and co-founder and president of the Black Women in Sport Foundation, was very pointed in her comments regarding inequitable opportunities for black women in sport. She made clear her belief that the lack of opportunities for black women in college sport resulted from matters of race rather than gender. "These white women (white administrators) don't want us to compete with them," noted Green. "They want their kids to get the scholarships. They're thinking about themselves. They give us all kinds of awards, but when it comes time to distributing the money, it's a whole other story."[11]

Irrespective of why more black women have not found their way into college sport as a result of Title IX, this pattern of participation continues to exist and it is very evident in the racial makeup of national teams representing the United States in international competitions. One sport that serves as a good example of the pattern of exclusion of African American women is soccer. During the last two decades Team USA has generated enormous enthusiasm for soccer on a national basis and inspired countless young girls to take up the sport through their multiple victories in prestigious international competitions. They captured the first World Cup in 1991 and then followed it up as bronze medalist in the second World Cup in 1995, winner and Olympic gold medalist in 1996, winner of the World Cup in 1999, Olympic silver medalist the following year, bronze medalist in the World Cup in 2003, winner and Olympic gold medalist in 2004, bronze medalist in the World Cup in 2007, and Olympic gold medalist in 2008.

The very best players on these teams realized hero status, became household names, and parlayed their success into an assortment of business deals and sponsorships. Unfortunately, almost all the players have been white. With the notable exception of Brianna Scurry, the outstanding goalkeeper who sealed her fame with a great performance in the 1999 World Cup in Los Angeles, Team USA has been almost entirely white with its most prominent players consisting of the likes of Michelle Akers, Kristine Lilly, Brandi Chastain, Julie Foudy, Joy Fawcett, Amy Wambach, Carli Lloyd, Alex Morgan, Hope Solo, and most famously Mia Hamm. Like other sports in which they have been underrepresented, a variety of social, cultural, and economic factors have accounted for the dearth of African American women on Team USA and soccer more generally. Among these factors would be the high cost of select travel teams, tradition, and lack of role models in the sport. There does seem to be some glimmer of hope, however, based on the racial makeup of the currently constituted 2017 US women's national team that includes such outstanding black players as Crystal Dunn, Jessica McDonald, Brianna Pinto, and Casey Short. Not surprisingly, three of these players have ties to the University of North Carolina at Chapel Hill, the institution with the most dominant soccer program in the United States. McDonald and especially Dunn enjoyed outstanding careers at North Carolina and Pinto has recently committed to the Tar Heels.

While black women have struggled to find their way into soccer, they have continued to participate in large numbers and distinguish themselves in track and field in international competitions. Although typically not enjoying the plaudits of their male counterparts, African American women, first with Alice Coachman and then later Wilma Rudolph and her Tennessee State Tigerbelles, have established a great tradition in track and field, realizing enormous success in Olympic competitions and world championships.

Gold medalists, world recordholders, and great competitors, black women have distinguished themselves in a sport that has never garnered a consistent following in the United States, but resonates internationally and has always held center stage every four years at the summer Olympic festival. Among the most accomplished black women track and field athletes since the days of Rudolph were Wyomia Tyus, Evelyn Ashford, Gail Devers, Valerie Brisco-Hooks, Gwen Torrance, Florence Griffith Joyner, Jackie Joyner-Kersee, and Allyson Felix. Two of the most prominent of these black women track and field athletes are Joyner and her sister-in-law Joyner-Kersee.

Florence Griffith Joyner would become one of the most decorated sprinters in Olympic history. Born in Los Angeles in 1959, "Flo-Jo" as she became known, began her college track and field career at California State University, Northridge and then, after taking time off from college to help support her family, transferred to UCLA where she continued to run under the tutelage of Bob Kersee who had been her coach at Northridge. She realized her first success in international competition by taking the silver medal in the 200 meter dash at the 1984 Olympic games in Los Angeles. Three years later she won the silver medal in the 200 meter and gold medal in the 4x100 meter relay at the World Championships in Rome. In 1988, Griffith Joyner startled the world at the Seoul Olympic Games by capturing a silver medal in the 4x400 meter relay and gold medals in the 100 meter, 200 meter, and 4x100 meter relay.

Griffith Joyner's great performance in Seoul brought her immediate fame. Very few women athletes had ever shown such extraordinary displays of speed and power in track and field's marquee events and in the world's most prestigious sporting event. It was not, however, just her accomplishments on the track that brought her fame. She was notably different than many of her competitors in that she flaunted her sexuality and outwardly defied the masculine image in which African American women athletes had so often been portrayed through her unique performance style, dress, and appearance. She captivated people with her long flowing hair, long and multiple-colored painted fingernails, and perfectly applied makeup. Her sleek and finely tuned body was magnified and made that much more sensual by the running attire she designed and so proudly wore on the track. Her brightly colored outfits sometimes included only one pant leg and were obviously designed primarily for aesthetic purposes rather than to maximize performance. This was certainly true for Griffith Joyner's famous white-laced bodysuit that she referred to, as historian Jennifer Lansbury reminds us, as an "athletic negligee."[12]

As much as Griffith Joyner mesmerized track and field fans and the larger sporting public, she was dogged by continual questions about her great athletic accomplishments. She had shown remarkable advancements on the track in a relatively short period of time. In a sport where records are not easily toppled and when they are it is usually by the smallest of margins, Griffith Joyner's rapid improvement in sprint times was remarkable and truly astounding. In the semifinals of the 100 meters at the Olympic trials in Indianapolis, Griffith Joyner shocked track aficionados by shattering Evelyn Ashford's world record with a time of 10.49 seconds, which bettered her previous best time by .4 seconds. This astounding improvement in time, which proved not to be wind aided, resulted in allegations—allegations that would persist until her untimely death at the age of thirty-eight—that Griffith Joyner's successes on the track came about because of performance-enhancing drugs. Brazilian middle-distance runner Joaquim Cruz, for one, noted how feminine Griffith Joyner appeared in her first Olympic Games in 1984, but just four years later "looks more like a man than a woman."[13] In spite of Cruz's allegations and those of others, which came at a time when accusations and rumors were swirling about athletes in track and field and other sports taking performance-enhancing drugs, Griffith Joyner never failed a drug test during her running career. If she had, it certainly would have cut into the some $3 million in endorsement deals that Griffith Joyner's agent Gordon Baskin had secured for her following the Seoul Olympic Games.

Allegations regarding the use of performance enhancing drugs would also be leveled at Griffith Joyner's sister-in-law Jackie Joyner-Kersee. Like Griffith Joyner, however, Joyner-Kersee would never fail a drug test during her long and storied career. The East St. Louis–born woman who would star in both basketball and track and field at UCLA, withstood the continual allegations to become an outstanding long jumper and perhaps the greatest heptathlete the world has ever known. Under the training of husband-coach Bob Kersee, Joyner-Kersee captured gold medals in the long jump and Heptathlon at the 1987 World Championships in Rome, gold medal in the long jump at the 1991 World Championships in Tokyo, gold medal in the heptathlon at the 1993 World Championships in Stuttgart, gold medal in the long jump at the 1987 Pan American Games in Indianapolis, gold medals in the long jump and heptathlon at the 1988 Olympic Games in Seoul, gold medal in the heptathlon at the 1992 Olympic Games in Barcelona, silver medal in the heptathlon at the 1984 Olympic Games in Los Angeles, bronze medal in the long jump at the 1992 Olympic Games in Barcelona, and bronze medal in the long jump at the 1996 Olympic Games in Atlanta. The world record of 7,291 she set in the heptathlon at the 1988 Olympic Games in Seoul still stands. Following her retirement from the sport in 1998, Joyner-Kersee joined with several other great athletes to form Athletes for

Hope, an organization that assists professional athletes and ordinary citizens in becoming more involved in charitable work and volunteerism. She also founded the Jackie Joyner-Kersee Foundation that has as its mission, among other things, to provide children with quality after-school programs and safe recreational spaces.

The high participation rates and success of African American women in track and field at the international level of competition has been duplicated in Olympic basketball and in the Women's National Basketball Association (WNBA). In 1976, the United States fielded its first Olympic basketball team. Coached by Billie Moore from California State University, Fullerton, the team was racially integrated and made up of highly talented and motivated college players rather than athletes from the AAU which had made up US national teams in the past. Reasons for the change in team composition stemmed from the fact that there were a steadily increasing number of outstanding players in women's college basketball and the USOC had taken over control of the team from the AAU that would now focus primarily on youth sports. Included on the roster were such legendary players as Ann Meyers (Drysdale) from UCLA, Nancy Lieberman from Old Dominion University, and Pat Head (Summitt) from the University of Tennessee as well as four lesser known African American players who contributed prominently to the team and deserve to be remembered for their contributions to women's basketball. The four players were Patricia Roberts, a University of Tennessee product who would go on to play professionally and become a college coach; Gail Marquis, a Queens College product who would become a Wall Street executive following her basketball career; Luisa Harris, a Delta State University product who would go on to play professionally, have the distinction in 1977 of being drafted by the New Orleans Jazz of the NBA, and eventually be selected to the National Basketball Hall of Fame; and Charlotte Lewis, an Illinois State University product who would go on to play professionally.

In spite of its talent level and intense preparation prior to the games, the 1976 US women's Olympic basketball team was no match for the powerful and vastly more experienced Soviet Union squad and had to settle for a silver medal. The team's involvement, however, in the first basketball competition in Olympic history for women was an important event and set the stage for the following decade that would prove to be a turning point in US women's basketball. Although the women's game continued to face challenges, not least of which was the continuing struggle with Title IX legislation, there were some significant changes taking place in women's basketball during the 1980s that would have a lasting impact on the sport. One of the most significant of those changes, as noted by Pamela Grundy and Susan Shackelford in

Shattering the Glass, were the increasing number of African American women who were finding their way into the college game during this time period.[14] Evidence of this change was perhaps most noticeable at USC, which would become a powerhouse in women's college basketball largely on the backs of great African American players. In 1980, USC pulled off a recruiting coup when it convinced Pam and Paula McGee, extraordinarily talented twin sisters from Flint, Michigan, who had become legendary high school players, to attend the private institution in Los Angeles known for its outstanding athletic program. Over the next couple of years the school would add African American players Cynthia Cooper, a highly skilled athlete from Locke High in California; Rhonda Windham, an outstanding point guard from New York City; and Cheryl Miller, the extraordinarily gifted forward from Pasadena, California, who brought women's basketball to another level with beautifully executed jump shots, eye-popping dunks, and a smooth and highly energized style of play that brought her an enormous following and much admiration. These athletes would lead USC to its first national championship in 1984 in a closely contested game against a very talented team from Louisiana Tech.

A steady flow of other outstanding African American players would matriculate at predominantly white universities over the next couple of decades following the great success of Miller and her mates at USC, including such outstanding athletes as Lynette Woodard of the University of Kansas, Teresa Edwards of the University of Georgia, Clarissa Davis of the University of Texas, Dawn Staley of the University of Virginia, Teresa Witherspoon of Louisiana Tech University, Carolyn Jones of Louisiana Auburn University, Katrina McClain of the University of Georgia, Sheryle Swoopes of Texas Tech University, Nikki McCray of the University of Tennessee, Janice Braxton of Louisiana Tech University, Carla McGhee of the University of Tennessee, Chamique Holdsclaw of the University of Tennessee, and Lisa Leslie of USC. These athletes would form the nucleus of some outstanding US women's Olympic basketball teams during the 1980s and 1990s.

The US women's basketball team captured the gold medal at the Los Angeles Olympic Games in 1984 behind the great play of Miller and a supporting cast that included such outstanding players as Anne Donovan, Lynette Woodard, Pam McGee, Teresa Edwards, and Denise Curry. Led by famed Tennessee coach Pat Summitt, the US women beat South Korea by a score of 85–55 in the gold medal game with Miller scoring sixteen points and adding eleven rebounds. In 1988, the US women would repeat as gold medalists at the Seoul Olympics with a 77–70 victory over Yugoslavia in the title game. The team would be led by University of Georgia All-American Katrina McClain who averaged 17.6 points over five games, University of

Figure 7.2. Cheryl Miller, the great star from USC, grabbing a rebound in the 1984 Olympic Games.
Courtesy of the LA84 Foundation. Copyright LA84 Foundation.

Georgia great Teresa Edwards who averaged 16.6 points over five games and led the team in assists with seventeen and steals with twenty-three, and USC's outstanding guard Cynthia Cooper who averaged 14.2 over the same number of games. The 1992 Olympic Games in Barcelona was a bitter disappointment for the US women's basketball team as they had to settle for a bronze medal after losing to the Unified Team in the semifinals 73–79.

The 1996 US women's basketball team was extremely important for a number of reasons. Intent on spreading the women's game to a larger audience, and undoubtedly trying to improve on their bronze medal performance from four years earlier in Barcelona, the NBA, several corporate sponsors, and the USOC provided large sums of money for the US women's basketball team so that it could engage in a full year of practice and play a series of exhibitions prior to the actual games in Atlanta. The team, which included nine African American women on a twelve-person roster, was loaded with talented players whose names still resonate with fans of women's basketball. Among those players were such great black athletic performers as Dawn Staley, the highly competitive and aggressive five-foot, six-inch guard who was equally adept and committed to playing well at both ends of the court; Lisa Leslie, the silky smooth and talented six-foot, five-inch center from USC by way of Inglewood, California, who dazzled fans on the court with her uncanny shooting touch and off it with her good looks and gracefulness; Katrina McClain, the talented six-foot, two-inch shooting forward from the University of Georgia who would play on three Olympic teams; Ruthie Bolton, the extraordinarily quick five-foot, eight-inch ball-hawking guard from Auburn University; and the fabulously talented six-foot forward Sheryl Swoopes from Texas Tech University who mesmerized fans with her shot-making and was part of a historic first in women's sport when Nike came out with their "Air Swoopes" shoes.[15]

These players, along with other great hoopsters like the University of Georgia's Teresa Edwards, the University of Connecticut's Rebecca Lobo, Stanford University's Jennifer Azzi, and the University of Tennessee's Nikki McCray, sailed through eight opponents on their way to the gold medal. Expertly coached by Stanford's Tara VanDerveer, the team beat Cuba in their opening contest 101–84 and then ran off victories against Ukraine, Zaire, Australia, South Korea, Japan, and Australia again before demolishing Brazil in the final 111–87. The victory in 1996, reflective of rapidly growing and increasingly important intercollegiate basketball programs and largely attributable to the growing financial support for the US Women's National Team, would set the stage for gold medals in all subsequent Olympic competitions to date. Perhaps most important, the victory in 1996 would help make possible a resurrection in women's professional basketball.

In 1996, a women's American Basketball League (ABL) was formed in San Jose, California, but was forced to declare bankruptcy after just three years of operation. In 1997, the NBA-sponsored WNBA began play with teams in Sacramento, Los Angeles, Salt Lake City, Houston, Cleveland, Charlotte, Phoenix, and New York. Although facing some initial difficulties, including being in direct competition for a time with the ABL, the WNBA has become the world's most important professional league for women with great players coming from top college programs and an increasing number being lured from foreign countries. One of the distinguishing features of the WNBA is that it continues to exceed other professional sports leagues overall in regard to gender and racial hiring. The latest data from Richard Lapchick's annual *Racial and Gender Report Card* (2016) indicates that 68.5 percent of players in the league are African American, 24.5 percent are white, 3.5 percent are Latina, and 2.8 percent are designated as "other."[16] The league president is Lisa Borders, an African American; 26.1 percent of the league's professional office staff are people of color; two of the league's CEOs/presidents and two of the league's general managers are African American; and three of the league's head coaches are African American. Nothing exemplified more the diversity of the league than the 2016 WNBA champion Los Angeles Sparks whose owner Earvin "Magic" Johnson, president and CEO Christine Simmons, and general manager Penny Toler are all African American.

As much attention as African American women athletes received from their participation in college basketball, the Olympic Games, and in the WNBA, it pales in comparison to the headlines and media coverage garnered by tennis greats Venus and Serena Williams. The two black tennis stars, taking a decidedly different route into the upper echelons of the sport than most of the top players by initially honing their skills on the public courts of crime-ridden Compton, California, rather than in a country club or tennis academy, carved out marvelous careers that mixed a large number of victories in the most prestigious tournaments with controversy, family drama, and racism. The two sisters learned the game first from their father Richard, a complex and controversial man who was at once a coach, advisor, promoter, and marketer who was quick to anger and constantly at war with the media. In 1991 Richard moved his family to Florida where Venus and Serena began to train under the tutelage of professional instructors. Unlike many parents of talented tennis players, Richard eventually withdrew his two daughters from the junior tournaments they had dominated as preadolescents so they could concentrate on school and hone their skills through long and intensive practices prior to becoming professionals.

Whatever his parenting methods and philosophy in nurturing the skills of athletic prodigies, Richard's two daughters became strong, independent, confident, innovative, self-assured, and spirited women who have realized great success in their sport. Venus, the oldest and more reserved of the two sisters, began her professional career at the age of fourteen, but only played, at the insistence of her father, a few events during her first few years on the tour. Her career started slow, with the lack of competitive play against quality opponents on the junior circuit very evident to those who watched her play. In 1997, however, she began to realize her enormous potential with several quality performances against some of the world's best players, including a loss in two sets in the US Open final to the number one ranked player, Martina Hingis. In 2000 she emerged as one of the game's great players by capturing the singles titles at the US Open and Wimbledon, repeated the feat at the two prestigious tournaments the following year, and then captured three more singles championships at Wimbledon in 2005, 2007, and 2008. Serena, far more outgoing than her older sister and someone who wears her feelings on her sleeve, has far surpassed Venus in regards to career singles titles and number of major championships. As predicted by her father, Serena has realized a far greater number of singles titles than Venus, winning a total of seventy-two singles titles to Venus's forty-nine and capturing twenty-three Grand Slam singles titles to Venus's seven. Her powerful serve and ground game, mental toughness, and sheer determination have allowed her to come just one tournament shy of tying Margaret Court's all-time record for number of Grand Slam singles titles. Her Grand Slam singles titles include seven Wimbledon (2002, 2003, 2009, 2010, 2012, 2015, 2016), seven Australian (2003, 2005, 2007, 2009, 2010, 2015, 2017), six US Open (1999, 2002, 2008, 2012, 2013, 2014), and three French Open (2002, 2013, 2015) championships.

Matches that were eagerly anticipated by tennis fans and the media were those between Venus and Serena. While the sisters themselves, and the entire Williams family, undoubtedly had mixed emotions each time these matches took place, they were perfect theater because of the relationship between Venus and Serena and the fact that the two African American women were two of the best and most exciting players in the world. The two sisters have met twenty-eight times as of this writing, with Serena victorious in seventeen of those matches, the latest being a two-set win in the 2017 Australian Open. Tellingly, the intense rivalry between Venus and Serena did nothing to negatively affect the close friendship between the two sisters. Whether it was the early bond they established coping with the demands of their father or their shared experiences as black women trying to navigate the racial realities of American culture and the predominantly white sport of tennis, the two sisters are incredibly close, share a mutual respect, and are very supportive of one another. A testament to their close bond was their commitment to playing doubles. Irrespective of how either one of them performed in singles in any given tournament, Venus and Serena loved being partners and it showed on the court as they captured multiple doubles titles. They have won three

Figure 7.3. Serena Williams, the outstanding tennis champion who captured twenty-three major singles titles.
Courtesy of National Portrait Gallery, Smithsonian Institution.

Olympic (2000, 2008, 2012), six Wimbledon (2000, 2002, 2008, 2009, 2012, 2016), four Australian (2001, 2003, 2009, 2010), two French Open (1999, 2010), and two US Open (1999, 2009) doubles titles.

Venus and Serena, while different in personality, appearance, and demeanor on the court, both confronted hostility from opponents and fans alike as well as various forms of racialist thinking and insensitivity during their careers. Over time, however, their popularity has seemingly increased among tennis fans with both women realizing more appreciation and respect for their accomplishments. Part of the reason for this is that their father had faded into the background and no longer had the same influence over his daughters. In addition, the increasingly confident and self-assured sisters

gradually modified their public images, as evidenced by their warmer relationships with other players, openness in which they dealt with the public,
and more trusting relationship they established with the press. This transformation was accompanied by a plethora of interests the sisters continued to
pursue off the court and the busy schedules they kept as part of their many
sponsorship deals. Venus, who has garnered $34.4 million in prize money
and 4.5 million followers on social media, has both a clothing line and de-
sign company and endorsement deals with Wilson, Kraft, Tide, and Ralph
Lauren. Serena, now arguably the most famous female athlete in the world as
evidenced by her 17.8 million followers on social media, has a clothing line
and endorsement deals with Nike, Wilson, Beats by Dre Headphones, IBM,
and Delta Airlines. She also has a net worth of $81.7 million and owns stake
in the Miami Dolphins.

This does not mean, however, that the specter of gender and race does
not continue to impact both sisters on and off the court. Although both
have made millions in endorsement deals, they pale in comparison to the
sponsorship money garnered by other men and women athletes who have
accomplished far less in their athletic careers. Writer Marc Bain points out in

**Figure 7.4. Tiger Woods, the winner of fourteen major championships and seventy-nine
official tour events.**
Courtesy of Shutterstock.

an August 31, 2015, essay in *The Atlantic* that Serena Williams ranks forty-seventh on the *Forbes's* list of the highest-paid athletes. Among the seven tennis players on the list, she ranks last in endorsement money, making some $45 million less than Roger Federer, $10 million less than Maria Sharapova, and $2 million less than the men's fourth-ranked player Kei Nishikori. Bain correctly notes that the "only logical explanation" for the large differences in the amount of endorsement deals has to do with "long-held prejudices regarding female sports stars and how people feel they should look." Williams, in spite of the fact she has won multiple grand slam titles and accumulated one of the best win-loss ratios in tennis history, will never realize the endorsements her talent level and accomplishments deserve because she is a black woman "with prominent, athletic muscles" and not a "willowy, white, and blonde" woman that sponsors covet and fans supposedly prefer.[17]

Global Heroes with a Conscience

The attention lavished on Venus and Serena Williams and their rise to stardom globally has been realized by a number of other great contemporary African American athletes. Certainly three of the most notable of these are Tiger Woods, Michael Jordan, and LeBron James. Born to Earl and Kultida Woods in Cypress, California, in 1975, Woods showed prodigious golfing talent at a very early age. When just two, he engaged in a putting contest with comedian Bob Hope on the *Mike Douglas Show*, a famous episode that has been shown countless times since its initial airing in 1978. Unlike many talented young athletes who are never able to realize their potential and reach the pinnacle of their respective sports, Woods's abilities continued to blossom as he got older and he would go on to one of the most successful and remarkable careers in the history of golf. He has captured fourteen major titles, including being a four-time winner of the Masters Tournament, four-time winner of the PGA Tournament, three-time winner of the Open Championship, and three-time winner of the US Open. His many championships have garnered him golf's most prestigious awards and resulted in endorsement contracts with Nike, General Motors, American Express, Titleist, Accenture, and Buick, among others. His career earnings are over one billion dollars.

Jordan, the fourth of five children born in Brooklyn, New York, to James Jordan and Deloris Peoples, did not show prodigious athletic talents at an early age like Woods. In fact, an oft-told and true story about Jordan is that he was cut from the varsity basketball team at Emsley A. Laney High School in Wilmington, North Carolina, his sophomore year. He would realize, however, a dramatic growth spurt and become an outstanding high school player who was sought after by some of the top college basketball programs in the country. He ultimately elected to play for the legendary Dean Smith at the University of North Carolina where he led the Tar Heels to the NCAA championship in 1982 and twice was selected Player of the Year. Forgoing his senior year at North Carolina, Jordan joined the Chicago Bulls in 1984 and would lead them to six NBA championships, play in fourteen NBA All-Star Games, and garner five NBA Most Valuable Player awards. He complemented his great NBA career by playing on the 1984 United States Olympic gold medal–winning basketball team and being perhaps the biggest attraction on the famous "Dream Team" in Barcelona in 1992. Jordan's great accomplishments on the hardwood, combined with a dynamic and engaging personality, would result in his becoming one of the most famous and recognizable and richest people in the world. "Air Jordan," the name of the Nike-endorsed shoe in which he become synonymous, became a global celebrity who seemingly transcended race in his own country and other white-dominated societies.

LeBron James, born and raised by a single mother in Akron, Ohio, displayed his enormous physical talents on the basketball court at a very early age. As a freshman on the varsity basketball team at Dayton's St. Vincent-St. Mary's High School, James averaged twenty-one points and six rebounds per game. He would go on to a great high school career in which he was named Mr. Basketball in Ohio three times, Mr. Basketball in the United States twice, and Naismith Prep Player of the Year during his senior season. His talents were so special that he skipped college and went directly into the NBA where he has garnered the most prestigious honors and rewards as well as multiple championships. He was named NBA Rookie of the Year in 2004, has been selected ten times to the All-NBA first team, named four times as NBA Most Valuable Player, and has been a member of three NBA championship teams. He was named Sports Illustrated Sportsperson of the Year in 2012 and 2016 as well as the Associated Press Athlete of the Year in 2013 and 2016. In addition to his NBA career, James has represented the United States in Olympic basketball competition, being a member of the bronze medal–winning team in Athens in 2004, gold medal–winning team in Beijing in 2008, and gold medal–winning team in London in 2012. James, like many other great athletes of the day, has been able to take advantage of his success and international acclaim to carve out a multifaceted business empire that has enhanced his influence and fame and increased his already extraordinary wealth. He is also a philanthropist who is an active supporter of many charities and causes.

Tiger Woods, Michael Jordan, and LeBron James, like a host of other outstanding black athletes through the years, served as important examples

Figure 7.5. LeBron James, the great Cleveland Cavaliers star, has been one of the highest profile African American athletes to speak out about racial injustice and discrimination.
Courtesy of National Portrait Gallery, Smithsonian Institution.

of achievement and symbols of possibility in the African American community. They were also expected—to the chagrin of basketball's Charles Barkley who famously noted that it was not his responsibility—to serve as positive role models for African American youth. They were, moreover, always expected and frequently pressured by other African Americans to become more involved in the civil rights struggle by speaking out more forcefully against racial inequality in both sport and the larger society. Not unexpectedly, black athletes have responded in different ways to the call to become more active participants in the civil rights movement. Family background, educational attainment, religious beliefs, financial status, personal value schemes, social context, and a host of other factors have influenced the approach taken by black athletes with some always hesitant to speak out on racial matters, others seemingly taking a more middle ground on racial issues, and still others adopting a more public and aggressive stand against racial inequities and civil rights concerns. To say that black athletes have been burdened by expectations that they become more involved in the civil rights struggle would be an understatement since they always had to weigh the costs that speaking out on racial issues would have on their individual careers, the African American community, and the integration process more generally.

Examples of the divergent ways black athletes have dealt with the expectations that they become active participants in the civil rights struggle are many and make clear the pressure they faced as black men and women participating in an institution that is supposedly apolitical and in a society that makes them feel as if they should be grateful for having the opportunity to realize fame and fortune. One early example of a black athlete who struggled with the expectation to be more vocal and speak out on racial issues was Althea Gibson, the great tennis star who captured ten straight ATA championships before winning the French Open in 1956 and Wimbledon and the USLTA in both 1957 and 1958. In oft-repeated passages from her autobiography *I Always Wanted to Be Somebody*, Gibson expressed her frustration with the black press who were constantly pressuring her to become involved in the civil rights struggle. Confirming the assessment of one observer who claimed she was decidedly different then Jackie Robinson who "thrived on his role as a Negro battling for equality," Gibson explained that she was "not a racially conscious person" and did not fashion herself "as a champion of the Negro race." She expressed the view of many other black athletes, both those who preceded her and those that came after, by noting that she could do more for her race through her accomplishments on the tennis court than through "militant crusading."[18]

Equally troubled by the pressure he received to become more active in the civil rights struggle and speak out more forcefully about racial inequality was Arthur Ashe, the great tennis star from Richmond, Virginia, who captured, among other titles, the US Open, Australian Open, and Wimbledon during his playing career. Ashe, a highly intelligent and thoughtful man as well as an outstanding tennis player, always struggled with how to navigate the racial divide in the United States. In large measure, Ashe's struggles in this regard calls forth W. E. B. Du Bois's famous notion of double-consciousness in that he constantly had to reconcile being both black and an American. This was made abundantly clear in his notable 1975 essay "Don't Tell Me How to Think" in which he pointed out to his critics that he was a free man who would conduct himself according to his own principles irrespective of the expectations heaped upon him. As we now know, Ashe would evolve, perhaps partly as a result of having his consciousness pricked by those critics he condemned, into a man who spoke out valiantly against the inadequate education of black children, actively protested apartheid policies in South Africa, and publicly disapproved of the treatment of Haitians seeking asylum in the United States. As was his style, Ashe did all of this in a highly disciplined and dignified manner rather than through the angry rhetoric and bombast employed by many radicals involved in the civil rights movement.

Perhaps no single event made more visible the pressure exerted on black athletes to become more active in the civil rights struggle and the deep philosophical differences regarding the role of sport in overcoming racial inequities than the Harry Edwards–led boycott of the 1968 Olympic Games in Mexico City. As part of the proposed boycott, Edwards tried to drum up support for his plan, publicly demonstrate racial solidarity, and map goals and strategy through the creation of the OPHR. Although he received immediate support from many younger black athletes expected to participate in the Mexico City games, others expressed their opposition to the boycott, contending, as did outstanding Tennessee State University long jumper Ralph Boston, that "Negroes can do more good for themselves and their race by going to the Olympics and doing well than they can by staying home." Legendary black track and field performers such as 1960 Olympic decathlon champion Rafer Johnson and 1936 Olympic hero Jesse Owens took similar positions, arguing that sport had been one institution in the United States that had provided blacks equal opportunities and why deny prospective black Olympians the chance to participate in the most prestigious athletic event in the world after they had spent years training and honing their talents.

The dissenting voices of such black athletic heroes as Johnson and Owens did not sit well with Edwards and his loyal followers in the OPHR. In fact, Edwards leveled a barrage of criticisms and insults at Johnson, Owens, and anyone else who opposed the boycott movement. The person who received the brunt of Edwards's ire, however, was Owens. In his well-known 1969 book *The Revolt of the Black Athlete*, a must-read for anyone interested in firsthand information about the boycott movement and racial disturbances on predominantly white university campuses, Edwards was unmerciful in his attacks on the man who had startled the world by capturing four gold medals in a country that would commit the worst forms of atrocities resulting from a belief in Aryan racial superiority. Edwards labeled Owens an "Uncle Tom," a man who naively believed that sport was devoid of racial discrimination and contributed to a greater understanding between blacks and whites. Owens, like Johnson and many other black athletes of the past, had been duped in thinking that his accomplishments brought about racial harmony when, in fact, his successes had been exploited by the white establishment to "hinder the liberation efforts of black people."[19] It was difficult to understand how Owens could hold firm to his belief in the sanctity of sport and its power to bridge the racial divide when he himself experienced racism after his return from Berlin.

Edwards's criticism of Owens did not result in any changes in the great track stars belief in the power of sport to bring blacks and whites together and contribute to racial equality in America. If anything, Owens became more obstinate in his belief that it was counterproductive for black athletes to withhold their services in an institution that had always been open to them and that their nonparticipation would impede rather than improve race relations. He also expressed disdain for Edwards and other black militants such as H. Rap Brown and Stokely Carmichael for the divisiveness they had caused in a country that was making racial progress. Evidence of this was made clear in Owens's 1970 book *Blackthink: My Life as Black Man and White Man*, one of five autobiographies penned with ghostwriter Paul G. Neimark. The 1968 Olympic "incidents damaged the image of the Negro athlete in America," stated Owens, "and sports are important, so important. Because more than anything else to the kid who starts off poor or underfoot, sports represent the American dream." Edwards and other blackthinkers who spew "pro-negro, anti-white bigotry" enact a militancy that "is in an almost exact proportion to their lust for revenge and, beneath that, to their own hidden feelings of self-disgust about themselves." They "are the real Uncle Toms."[20]

Owens's hostility toward Edwards and other militants as well as some naïve and controversial views he expressed on race in *Blackthink* did not sit well with many blacks and weighed heavily on the Olympic hero. He had, as noted by his biographer William J. Baker, "second thoughts about his fiery rhetoric, his broad-brush denunciation of the motives of all black militants, and his insistence that any black American could succeed by trying hard enough."[21] As a result, Owens published in 1972 yet another autobiography with Paul E. Neimark, *I Have Changed*, in which he backpedaled on previous positions, confirming the right of people to protest racial discrimination and inequality, acknowledging the urban blight and inferior education provided to blacks, and pointing out the lack of blacks in upper-level administrative positions in sport and other fields. In spite of his self-styled transformation, however, it was apparent that Owens, through his actions and words, was still a very conservative man who could not understand the new generation of blacks who were threatening violence and taking to the streets to angrily protest racial inequality. Young black athletes knew this full well, realizing that the legendary track and field star had not changed and, for all his cliché-filled oratory, pleasant demeanor, and apparent sincerity, could not be trusted.

A prime example of the continued mistrust of Owens on the part of younger black athletes can be gleaned from the story told by track athlete Vince Matthews in his provocative, but underutilized 1974 autobiography with Neil Amdur, My Race Be Won. In the 1972 Olympic Games in Munich, Matthews and his teammate Wayne Collett took a page out of the book of Tommie Smith and John Carlos from four years earlier by turning their backs on the American flag and standing casually with hands on hips during the playing of the national anthem while receiving their gold and silver medals for the 400 meter run. Receiving little publicity at the time and largely forgotten partly because of the overwhelming coverage given to other events in Munich, including the tragic murder of eleven Israel athletes by Palestinian terrorists, Matthews and Collett caused the ire of Olympic officials who immediately began to discuss what actions should be taken against the two stubbornly defiant black athletes. Owens, who acted as an intermediary as he had done on other occasions with usually limited effect, tried to get Matthews and Collett to apologize for their behavior, insinuating that they ran the risk of losing out on high-paying corporate jobs waiting for them after the Olympics. Matthews responded by stating: "That all sounds nice but how come you never came to us before? None of your so-called large companies stepped forward for all the other black athletes after other Olympic Games."[22]

The protests lodged by black athletes would begin to diminish by the early 1970s as increased integration along with the rise of the black middle class, dismantling of Jim Crow, women's movement, economic recession, and other factors would combine to take some of the steam out of the civil rights movement. Although there would be instances over the following decades in which black athletes, particularly those with lower profiles, protested inequality and mistreatment of African Americans and other minorities, the largest majority would refrain from speaking out on these matters and taking an activist role on any political and social issues. Fearful of jeopardizing multimillion dollar contracts and endorsement deals, black athletes were seemingly more interested in minutes played, individual statistics, and their public image than protesting controversial issues both within and outside of sport.

The reluctance of black athletes to become involved in sensitive social causes would result in a rash of criticism leveled against them by segments of the African American community. Although none of the great black athletes were immune from the criticism, a favorite target of the detractors was

Michael Jordan, the great Chicago Bulls star and sports icon who was one the most famous and wealthy celebrities in the world. He received a constant barrage of criticism from a variety of people who were deeply troubled by Jordan's refusal to use his vaulted status to speak out about larger social and political issues. One of those people was Jordan's own Chicago Bulls teammate Craig Hodges, a ten-year NBA player who once delivered a handwritten letter to President George H. W. Bush criticizing the administration for their treatment of the poor and minorities. Always highly critical of the league's African American players for their refusal to use their influential positions to bring attention to the plight of the poor and disenfranchised, Hodges saved some of his more biting comments for Jordan who he believed had not adequately used his wealth to help combat poverty, racial inequality, and other societal issues. Unfortunately, following his release by the Bulls in 1992, Hodges was unable to secure an offer from another NBA team, in spite of being only thirty-two years of age and physically capable of playing at a high level. He ultimately filed a $40 million lawsuit against the NBA, claiming he had been blackballed by the league for his association with the controversial NOI leader Louis Farrakhan and criticism he had leveled toward Jordan and other African American players.

Hodges's criticism of Jordan was mild compared to those lodged against the Bulls star by black sportswriters Shaun Powell and William Rhoden. Powell, a veteran columnist who has worked at the *Miami Herald*, *Newsday*, and a number of other publications, wrote in obvious reference to Tommie Smith and John Carlos's victory stand protest in 1968 when he noted that: "Jordan's method of activism wasn't with a clenched fist in the air but with a clenched fist full of money."[23] In Powell's view, Jordan, while deserving of credit for the large sums of money he has given to charity, had squandered his status and popularity in mainstream culture by not giving voice and taking stands on serious issues and great causes. With the one possible exception of his public stance in the labor dispute between players and owners during the 1998–1999 season, Jordan had not, wrote Powell, lent his name and reputation to fight causes larger than himself. For the great Chicago Bulls player, it was more about keeping "his mouth shut," protecting his financial assets, and "serving as a slave to the swoosh."[24]

William Rhoden, a former columnist with the *New York Times*, was perhaps even harsher than Powell in his criticism of Jordan. He argued that Jordan had remained "publically neutral" on political and racial issues, showing at every stage of his career an obsession with "wealth and image." He was only interested in making money, hawking products, and maintaining silence on an assortment of controversial issues while at once crafting a carefully designed public persona that appealed to the American mainstream. While "becoming an important symbol of black prowess, he could have been so much more." He refused to publicly endorse black Democrat Harvey Gant in his 1996 senate seat battle against former segregationist Jesse Helms of North Carolina and expressed no public condemnation when it was determined that Nike was using Asian sweatshops to make some of its products. This approach, writes Rhoden, was "merely a microcosm of the dilemma facing today's black community" that has been splintered by increased integration. Unlike African American athletes of the past, Jordan and other black athletes of his generation did not necessarily identify and feel connected to the black community, which partly accounted for their indifference toward racial matters and apparently little interest in fighting for justice and equality of opportunity. In truth, "black athletes like Jordan have abdicated their responsibility to the community with an apathy that borders on treason."[25]

The criticisms of Jordan are interesting to consider when juxtaposed with the very recent show of activism by black athletes. There seems to be a new movement afloat in which black athletes are speaking out through social media and a host of other forums about contentious and controversial social and political issues. Taking a page from protesting black athletes of the civil rights era, they have demonstrated a renewed racial consciousness spurred by, among other things, the mistreatment of ordinary black citizens, the Black Lives Matter movement, and the fact the Oval Office was occupied by a black man for eight years.

A watershed event that stimulated an increased level of activism on the part of black athletes was the tragic death of Trayvon Martin in 2012. A racially divisive event that caused much anger in the black community when George Michael Zimmerman was acquitted of second-degree murder in the death of Martin, it also marked the beginning of a flurry of activism on the part of black athletes that had not been evident for decades. Setting in motion the renewed level of activism was, on the surface, one of the most unlikely of people. Actress Gabrielle Union, at the time friend and now wife of Miami Heat star Dwayne Wade, contacted Martin family advisor Michael Skolnik to discuss with him ways to bring attention to the Trayvon Martin story. The two decided that the best way to bring it about was to involve in some way both Wade and his even more famous teammate LeBron James. They approached Wade and James and the two stars ultimately decided to have a picture taken with their teammates wearing official Miami Heat hoodies up the way Martin had done when killed. James posted the picture on Twitter and almost overnight, because of the celebrity status of the Miami

Heat star and the power of sport, the Martin event became front-page news in the press and the top story on major television networks. Skolnik, while perhaps engaging in a bit of hyperbole, poignantly noted that the "picture was John Carlos and Tommie Smith of our generation."[26]

Black athletes on other NBA teams followed the lead of the Miami Heat and protested the controversial death of Martin by posting similar photographs with hoodies up or actually wearing them to games. Over the next several years black NBA players would lodge complaints on social media and protest public events that had taken place in and outside of basketball. In 2014, many of the league's black players voiced criticism and exhibited their disdain for Los Angeles Clippers owner Donald Sterling after audio had been posted of him making racist remarks about blacks. In protest of Sterling's racially offensive comments, Clippers' players wore their warmup shirts inside-out so as to hide the team logo. Two days later, Sterling would be banned from the league for life. Later that year several NBA players, including James and Chicago Bulls star Derrick Rose, wore shirts on the court imprinted with "I Can't Breathe" in recognition of the quote from Eric Garner who died at the hands of the police in Staten Island. Ariyana Smith, a basketball player at Knox College, laid on the court for four minutes and thirty seconds in recognition of the amount of time Michael Brown laid on the street after being killed in Ferguson, Missouri. Five members of the NFL's St. Louis Cardinals paid their respects to Brown by walking onto the field together holding each other's hands high in the air.

The increased activism of black athletes was partly a result, no doubt, of having for eight years a sports-loving black man with a particular fondness for basketball in the White House. Barack Obama, when not engaged in negotiations, meeting with political leaders, and dealing with another world crisis, could be found playing basketball or watching sports or welcoming athletes and honoring championship teams at the White House. When afforded an audience with the president, black athletes would promote their causes and seek support from the president. When honored at the White House in 2016 for their NBA championship, several members of the Cleveland Cavaliers, including James, expressed their concerns about police brutality in a closed-door session with the president. Obama, especially in his second term as president, sought the support of black athletes on controversial issues. Most prominent among those was the president's much-debated Affordable Care Act.

Two other events in 2016 make clear the renewed activism of black athletes. In July of that year, James, Dwayne Wade, Carmelo Anthony, and Chris Paul encouraged their fellow athletes to speak out about police brutality and racial injustice in a joint opening statement at ESPN's annual ESPY awards. Following on the heels of the high-profile killings of Alton Sterling and Philando Castile by police officers in Baton Rouge, Louisiana, and St. Paul, Minnesota, respectively and the killing of five police officers and injuries to seven others at a Black Lives Matter rally in Dallas, Texas, the individual statements by the four black NBA superstars were poignant and heartfelt and memorable. "I know tonight we're honoring Muhammad Ali, the GOAT," said James, "but to do his legacy any justice, let's use this moment as call to action for all professional athletes to educate ourselves, explore these issues, speak up, use our influence and renounce all violence."[27]

Just six weeks after James and his fellow NBA all-stars made headlines at the ESPYs, an even more visible and controversial protest of racial inequality and police brutality was made when San Francisco 49ers quarterback Colin Kaepernick began taking a knee (he initially took a seat on the bench, but it was suggested to him by retired Green Beret and former NFL player Nate Boyer that it would be more respectful to protest by taking a knee) rather than standing for the national anthem. Although Denver Nuggets guard Mahmoud Abdul-Rauf made news in 1996 when he refused to stand for the national anthem, which resulted in his suspension from the NBA, Kaepernick's disruption of America's song brought far more attention since it took place in a popular national pastime fraught with patriotic symbolism and largely followed by a white and conservative fanbase. Not unexpectedly, Kaepernick was heavily criticized for his actions, pummeled with a barrage of negative press and vitriolic denouncements from a variety of people. Supreme Court justice Ruth Bader Ginsburg called Kaepernick's protest "dumb and disrespectful" prior to issuing an apology to the San Francisco 49ers quarterback.[28] Former Arkansas Governor Mike Huckabee asserted that Kaepernick was un-American and "an arrogant fool." US Representative Steve King of Iowa contended that Kaepernick was undermining patriotism and that his activism was no different than ISIS sympathizing.[29]

Kaepernick also had his supporters, one of them being not surprisingly Harry Edwards, the architect of the proposed boycott of the 1968 Mexico City Olympic Games. Although some of his fellow footballers disagreed with his message and his approach and were concerned about possible negative repercussions resulting from participation in protests, Kaepernick's actions helped spark individual and collective activism in an assortment of different ways on the part of black and white athletes, coaches, and others. The examples are many and varied. For instance, on September 1, 2016, Jeremy Lane of the Seattle Seahawks became the first NFL player not associated with the San Francisco 49ers to show support for Kaepernick when he sat during the playing of the national anthem in an exhibition game against the Oakland Raiders. Three days later, Megan Rapinoe, a well-known player on the Seattle Reign of the National Women's Soccer League, knelt during the national anthem prior to a game against the Chicago Red Stars to lend her support for Kaepernick. The eleven- and twelve-year-old players on the Beaumont Bulls youth football team, along with coach Rah-Rah Barber and his assistants, followed the lead of Kaepernick by kneeling during the playing of the national anthem prior to a game on September 10. On September 23, players from Oakland's Castlemont High School lay on their backs with their arms raised in the air during the playing of the national anthem against Kings Academy while Kaepernick, who had spoken to the team in their locker room prior to the game, kneeled on the sideline.

That Kaepernick helped contribute to a national dialogue on race was not just evident in the replication of his national anthem protests, but also in a number of personal statements by black and white athletes, collective action by teams and organizations, town hall meetings, and conversations with governmental leaders about racial inequality and police brutality. As for Kaepernick himself, the protests he launched landed him on the cover of *Time* magazine, resulted in his jersey number seven becoming the biggest seller in the NFL, and increased his followers on social media at one point by some eighteen thousand per day. All the attention he received and the controversy surrounding his refusal to stand for the national anthem should not blind us to the fact that Kaepernick was deeply committed to the cause of racial equality and the elimination of discrimination. He is a man who immersed himself in black history, was cognizant of the civil rights struggles of Malcolm X and other black activists, held "Know Your Rights Camps" for young children, and donated thousands of dollars to organizations devoted to social justice. As to his future in football, it is as of this writing open to question. Kaepernick is a free agent who has not received overtures from any NFL teams, with speculation that the lack of interest in him stems from team's concerns about his vegan diet and having to deal with the media attention and controversy that will always accompany him. Time will tell, but all the excuses for not signing Kaepernick is probably nothing more than code for blackballed.

CHAPTER EIGHT

~

An Altered Athletic Landscape

The inability of Colin Kaepernick to catch on with an NFL team thus far should not come as a surprise to close followers of sport. Anyone who tries to disrupt in some way the sacred institution of sport, especially its time-honored traditions and symbolic gestures, have often been ostracized and shunned. At times, the negative off-field behavior of athletes, including those of a criminal nature, seem to be of less concern to the leaders of sport than protests and boycotts. Sportswriter Christine Brennan makes this point very well in a recent essay in *US Today* regarding the 2017 NFL draft. She questioned the priorities of the NFL and whether it has a moral compass by astutely noting that several players who had either been accused of rape or physical assault of women were drafted, while Kaepernick was apparently not being welcomed back into the league because of his refusal to stand for the national anthem. "Is Kaepernick a less-desirable member of an NFL team or community," wrote Brennan, "than, say, Oakland Raiders first-round draft pick Gareon Conley, who is being investigated by the Cleveland police on a rape allegation, or Cincinnati Bengals second-round pick Joe Mixon, who was caught on videotape knocking out a woman with a devastating punch?"[1]

Irrespective of whether he ever finds himself back in the league, it is important to note that Kaepernick's protests and the discussions that followed, resurrected a national conversation about race. Not to be forgotten, however, is that while much of the discussion regarding race centered on police brutality and the deaths of black men, there was an upsurge in the number of racial incidents in sport immediately before and following Kaepernick's

Figure 8.1. Colin Kaepernick caused a great deal of controversy for his refusal to stand for the national anthem as a member of San Francisco 49ers. He now finds himself out of the NFL as a result.
Courtesy of Shutterstock.

protests regarding the national anthem. Richard Lapchick, well-known civil rights activist and director of the University of Central Florida's Institute for Diversity and Ethics in Sport, pointed out that there were eleven racial incidents in sport in the United States in 2015, but the number had risen to thirty-one in 2016. All told, 104 incidents of racist incidents in international sport would be reported for 2016. This dramatic increase, which perhaps can partly be accounted for by people feeling emboldened to engage in racist acts because of President Donald Trump's campaign rhetoric regarding immigrant groups and minorities, makes clear that sport is not immune from racial prejudice and the worst forms of discriminatory behavior. Among the incidents in 2016 were the lewd text messages sent by Columbia University's wrestling team and Amherst College's cross country team that included misogynistic, racist, and homophobic language. For their actions, the two schools suspended both teams. In the NFL, a man dressed in a gorilla suit and wearing a T-shirt that read "All Lives Matter" and "Put the Guns Down" ran onto the field during a Chicago Bears and Detroit Lions game. Nikita Whitlock, a player with the New York Giants, had his house robbed and the perpetrators spray-painted a swastika on the walls, the letters KKK, and a note that said "Go Back to Africa." In one of the most hideous cases, a Serena Williams fan dressed up in blackface during the Australian Open.[2]

The following year witnessed more racial incidents in sport. The most publicized of these incidents involved the Baltimore Orioles outstanding centerfielder Adam Jones. In the May 1, 2017, game against the Boston Red Sox at Fenway Park, Jones was called the N-word on several occasions by Red Sox fans, with one of them throwing a bag of peanuts onto the field. Jones, not one to back down from any skirmish, responded almost immediately to the racial taunts, telling a room full of reporters after the game that it was not unusual for fans to unleash racial epithets at him, but the sheer volume hurled by the Red Sox faithful during the game forced him to speak out. "I thought we moved past that a long time ago," noted Jones in a measured yet exasperated tone, "but obviously what's going on in the real world, things like this, people are outraged and speaking up at an alarming rate. It's unfortunate I had to be involved in it."[3]

The local press jumped on the story immediately, rehashing the terrible history of Boston in regard to race relations and sport. Both Massachusetts Governor Charlie Baker and Boston Mayor Marty Walsh apologized for and condemned the behavior of Red Sox fans. Red Sox owner John Henry and club President Sam Kennedy apologized to Jones and Baltimore Orioles manager Buck Showalter for the fan's behavior and vowed to make changes so that it would never happen again. They noted that they were sickened by what happened to Jones and that they adhered to a zero policy for this type of fan behavior. Baseball Commissioner Rob Manfred Jr. issued a statement the day after the incident making clear that, "The racist words and actions directed at Adam Jones at Fenway Park last night are completely unacceptable and will not be tolerated at any of our ballparks."[4] The day after the incident, Red Sox fans, apparently at the urging of Red Sox outfielder Mookie Betts, gave Jones a standing ovation. That same day, the Red Sox ejected and permanently banned a fan that shouted racial epitaphs at another fan.

The Jones incident, and the increasing number of other racial conflicts that took place in sport in 2016 and 2017, are alarming on a number of different levels. But the responses to these racial incidents, including the stands taken by LeBron James, Colin Kaepernick, and other contemporary African American athletes should be a cause for hope. In contrast to Europe and many other parts of the world where racist taunts, songs, and slogans are prevalent at different sport venues, this is not the case in the United States where overt racism in sport is now taboo. Each time an individual openly utters a racial epitaph or spews comments that are tinged with racialist thinking regarding African American involvement in sport, the offender is typically censured and punished in some way. The public backlash to this type of behavior is a far cry from the way black athletes were treated for much of American history. Although much still needs to be done to ensure racial equality in sport, significant progress has been made since black athletes first participated in sport during slavery at the behest of their masters. Unlike those who went before them, African American athletes of today do not have to worry about being forced to use separate travel accommodations, do not have to suffer the humiliation of being required to use black-only water fountains and restrooms, do not have to be overly concerned about being restricted to certain playing positions, and do not have to guard against white athletes intentionally trying to injure them on the field of play. In short, black athletes of today do not have to navigate the blatant forms of racial discrimination encountered by Tom Molineaux, Isaac Murphy, Jack Johnson, Fritz Pollard, Jesse Owens, Joe Louis, Jackie Robinson, Althea Gibson, Bill Russell, Jim Brown, and the other great African American athletes of the past.

Black athletes of today can hone their talents and strive for success in their chosen sports while trusting that like their white counterparts they will ultimately be judged by their physical skills rather than by the color of their skin. Perhaps the greatest challenge to the continued success of African American athletes is the privatization of youth sports. As sport studies scholars have noted, the privatization of youth sport potentially has the most deleterious impact on athletes from lower socioeconomic classes, in which African Americans are highly represented, because of the high cost for coaching, entry fees, travel costs, hotel accommodations, and other expenses that are incurred when searching out and competing against the best individuals and teams at that level of competition. Although young African American athletes with the means to do so can prosper in this system, those from families who occupy the lowest rung on the socioeconomic ladder can only hope for well-meaning benefactors who can provide the financial assistance necessary to develop the physical skills required for athletic success. Of course, as history has made clear, it is the very "best of the best" (a common phrase used by Andrei S. Markovits and Lars Rensmann in their well-known *Gaming the World: How Sports Are Reshaping Global Politics and Culture*) African American athletes who, by virtue of their talent, sheer luck, and supporters as well as patrons, rose to the top of the sporting world both nationally and internationally.

Whether those successes have altered racialist thinking or diminished racial discrimination or brought whites and blacks closer together is difficult to say with any degree of certainty. What is apparent is that the success of African American athletes have always been viewed by the black community as symbols of possibility and examples of achievement in a society rife with racial antagonism and inequality. Always sensitive to placing too much emphasis on sport for fear it would lend credence to the long-held notion that blacks were uniquely gifted physically but intellectually inferior, the black community nonetheless saw triumphs in sport as a means to racial uplift and an indication that they were capable of achieving success in other areas of life. In no way did this mean that black athletes would not on occasion threaten to withhold their services or black fans would not boycott segregated sporting events to protest and ultimately eliminate racially discriminatory practices. The black community understood full well how deeply sport resonated with Americans and that it could be used in an assortment of different ways in the larger fight for racial justice.

One major hurdle that needs to be overcome is the overall participation rates of African American women in sport. Although a large number of them compete in interscholastic and intercollegiate basketball and track and field, they are decidedly underrepresented in most other sports at all levels of competition. How those numbers are reversed will not be easily accomplished, but no doubt it will only be accomplished through the cooperative efforts of blacks and whites and substantive structural changes in sport and society at large. Another major hurdle involves securing more positions for African Americans in coaching, managerial, upper-level administrative, and ownership positions in sport. Although some progress has been made on this front, most notably in professional basketball, far more needs to be done in sport in making sure that African Americans are provided access to positions of power and influence. Once this is accomplished, we can legitimately claim that in regards to sport, African Americans have come closer to reaching, to quote Bill Rhoden, the "Promised Land."[5]

~

Notes

Chapter One

1. Thomas L. Webber, *Deep Like the Rivers: Education in the Slave Quarter Community, 1831–1865* (New York: W. W. Norton, 1978), 180–84.

2. Bernard Mergen, *Play and Playthings: A Reference Guide* (Westport, CT: Greenwood Press, 1982), 43.

3. George P. Rawick, ed., *The American Slave: A Composite Autobiography*, 19 vols. (Westport, CT: Greenwood Press, 1972). These 19 volumes are a compilation of the slave narratives completed by the Federal Writers Project of the Works Project Administration between 1936 and 1938. For an overview of slave recreations, see David K. Wiggins, "Recreation, Slave" in *Dictionary of Afro-American Slavery*, ed. Randall M. Miller and John David Smith (Westport, CT: Greenwood Press, 1988), 622–24.

4. Mary V. Thompson, "The Private Life of George Washington's Slaves," Excerpted from Virginia Cavalcade 48 (Autumn 1999), 178–90. Retrieved July 30, 2017, at www.pbs.org/wgbh/pages/frontline/shows/Jefferson/video/lives.html.

5. Wilma King, *Stolen Childhood: Slave Youth in Nineteenth-Century America* (Bloomington: Indiana University Press, 1995), 48.

6. David K. Wiggins, "The Play of Slave Children in the Plantation Communities of the Old South, 1820–1860," *Journal of Sport History* 7 (Summer 1980): 31.

7. Quoted in David K. Wiggins and Patrick B. Miller, *The Unlevel Playing Field: A Documentary History of the African American Experience in Sport* (Urbana: University of Illinois Press, 2003), 16.

8. Roger D. Abrahams, *Singing the Master: The Emergence of African American Culture in the Plantation South* (New York: Pantheon Books, 1992), see especially, 83–106.

9. David K. Wiggins, "Sport and Popular Pastimes: Shadow of the Slavequarter," *Canadian Journal of History of Sport and Physical Education* 11 (May 1980): 74.

10. Wiggins, "Sport and Popular Pastimes," 74.

11. Ibid.

12. Edward Hotaling, *The Great Black Jockeys: The Lives and Times of the Men Who Dominated America's First National Sport* (Rocklin, CA: Forum, 1999), 30.

13. Katherine C. Mooney, *Race Horse Men: How Slavery and Freedom Were Made at the Race Track* (Cambridge, MA: Harvard University Press, 2014), 1–17.

Chapter Two

1. Louis Moore, "Fit for Citizenship: Black Sparring Masters, Gymnasium Owners, and the White Body, 1825–1886," *Journal of African American History* 96 (Fall 2011): 453–55.

2. Jules Tygiel, *Baseball's Great Experiment: Jackie Robinson and His Legacy* (New York: Oxford University Press, 1983), 10.

3. Andrew Ritchie, *Major Taylor: The Extraordinary Career of a Champion Bicycle Racer* (San Francisco: Bicycle Books, 1988), 173.

4. Andrew M. Kaye, *The Pussycat of Prizefighting: Tiger Flowers and the Politics of Black Celebrity* (Athens: University of Georgia Press, 2004), 8.

5. Kaye, *The Pussycat of Prizefighting*, 29.

6. Geoffrey C. Ward, *Unforgivable Blackness: The Rise and Fall of Jack Johnson* (New York: Alfred A. Knopf, 2004), 15.

7. Barak Y. Orbach, "The Johnson-Jeffries Fight and Censorship of Black Supremacy," *New York Journal of Law and Liberty* 5 (2010): 290. Retrieved July 12, 2017, at www.law.nyu.edu/sites/default/files/ECM_PRO_066938.pdf.

8. Randy Roberts, *Papa Jack: Jack Johnson and the Era of White Hopes* (New York: Free Press, 1983), 105.

9. Denise C. Morgan, "Jack Johnson: Reluctant Hero of the Black Community," *Akron Law Journal* 32 (1999): 9. Retrieved July 14, 2017, at https://uakron.edu/dotasset/726868.pdf.

10. W. E. B. Du Bois, "The Prizefighter," *Crisis* (August 1914): 181.

11. Horace Nash, "Town and Sword: Black Boxers at Columbus, New Mexico, 1916–1922," in Michael B. Ballard and Mark R. Cheathem, eds., *Of Times and Race: Essays Inspired by John F. Marszalek* (Oxford: University Press of Mississippi, 2012), p. 96.

12. Werner Sollars et al., *Blacks at Harvard: A Documentary History of African-American Experience at Harvard and Radcliffe* (New York: New York University Press, 1993), 74.

13. David K. Wiggins and Patrick B. Miller, *The Unlevel Playing Field: A Documentary History of the African American Experience in Sport* (Urbana: University of Illinois Press, 2003), 173.

Chapter Three

1. J. B. Watson, "Football in Southern Negro Colleges," *Voice of the Negro* 4 (1907): 169.

2. Charles H. Williams, "Twenty Years Work of the C.I.A.A.," *Southern Workman* 61 (1932): 75.

3. David K. Wiggins and Chris Elzey, "Creating Order in Black College Sport: The Lasting Legacy of the Colored Intercollegiate Athletic Association," in *Separate Games: African American Sport behind the Walls of Segregation*, David K. Wiggins and Ryan A. Swanson, eds. (Fayetteville: The University of Arkansas Press, 2016), 158.

4. Edwin B. Henderson, *The Negro in Sports* (Washington, DC: Associated Publishers, 1939), 218.

5. David K. Wiggins and Patrick B. Miller, *The Unlevel Playing Field: A Documentary History of the African American Experience in Sport* (Urbana: University of Illinois Press, 2003), 265.

6. Carroll Van West, "The Tennessee State Tigerbelles: Cold Warriors of the Track" in *Separate Games: African American Sport Behind the Walls of Segregation*, David K. Wiggins and Ryan A. Swanson, eds. (Fayetteville: The University of Arkansas Press, 2016), 71.

7. Todd Gould, "Gold and Glory Sweepstakes: An African American Racing Experience," in *Separate Games: African American Sport behind the Walls of Segregation*, David K. Wiggins and Ryan A. Swanson, eds. (Fayetteville: The University of Arkansas Press, 2016), 120.

8. Donald Spivey, *"If You Were Only White": The Life of Leroy "Satchel" Paige* (Columbia: University of Missouri Press, 2012), xix.

9. Donn Rogosin, *Invisible Men: Life in Baseball's Negro Leagues* (New York: Atheneum, 1987), 184.

10. Rob Ruck, "The East West Classic: Black America's Baseball's Fiesta," in *Separate Games: African American Sport Behind the Walls of Segregation*, David K. Wiggins and Ryan A. Swanson, eds. (Fayetteville: The University of Arkansas Press, 2016), 129–41.

11. Ruck, "The East West Classic," 135.

12. Gerald Early, *A Level Playing Field: African American Athletes and the Republic of Sports* (Cambridge, MA: Harvard University Press, 2011), 178–80.

Chapter Four

1. Charles H. Martin, *Benching Jim Crow: The Rise and Fall of the Color Line in Southern College Sports, 1890–1980* (Urbana: University of Illinois Press, 2010), 25.

2. Martin, *Benching Jim Crow*, 42.

3. David K. Wiggins, *Glory Bound: Black Athletes in a White America* (Syracuse, NY: Syracuse University Press, 1997), 67.

4. David K. Wiggins and Patrick B. Miller, *The Unlevel Playing Field: A Documentary History of the African American Experience in Sport* (Urbana: University of Illinois Press, 2003), 164–65.

5. John Gleaves and Mark Dyreson, "The 'Black Auxiliaries' in American Memories: Sport, Race and Politics in the Construction of Modern Legacies," *The International Journal of the History of Sport* 27 (December 2010): 2. Retrieved July 17, 2017, at http://www.tandfonline.com/doi/full/10.1080/09523367.2010.5 08278.

6. William J. Baker, *Jesse Owens: An American Life* (New York: Free Press, 1986), 3–4.

7. David K. Wiggins, "'Great Speed but Little Stamina':" The Historical Debate Over Black Athletic Superiority," *Journal of Sport History* 16 (Summer 1989): 161.

8. W. Montague Cobb, "Race and Runners," *Journal of Health and Physical Education* 7 (January 1936): 56.

9. Adolph Abrahams, "Race and Athletics," *The Eugenics Review*, 44 (October 1952), 144.

10. G. P. Meade, "The Negro in Track Athletics," *Scientific Monthly*, 75 (December 1952), 370.

11. Maya Angelou, *I Know Why the Caged Bird Sings* (New York: Ballantine Books, 2009), 136.

12. David Margolick, *Beyond Glory: Joe Louis vs. Max Schmeling, and a World on the Brink* (New York: Alfred A. Knopf, 2005), 98.

13. Wiggins and Miller, *The Unlevel Playing Field*, 172.

14. Chris Mead, *Champion Joe Louis: Black-Hero in White America* (New York: Charles Scribner's Sons, 1985), 259.

Chapter Five

1. David K. Wiggins and Patrick B. Miller, *The Unlevel Playing Field: A Documentary History of the African American Experience in Sport* (Urbana: University of Illinois Press, 2003), 137.

2. Jules Tygiel, *Baseball's Great Experiment: Jackie Robinson and His Legacy* (New York: Oxford University Press, 1983), 206.

3. William Gildea, "Integrating the Redskins: George Preston Marshall vs. the U.S. Government," *Washington Post*, June 5, 2002. Retrieved June 30, 2017, at https://www.washingtonpost.com/archive/politics/2002/06/05integrating-the-red skins-george-preston-marshall-vs-the-us-government/68682386.

4. Ira Berkow, "Shirley Povich Dies at 92," *New York Times*, June 7, 1998. Retrieved July 11, 2017.

5. Thomas G. Smith, *Showdown: JFK and the Integration of the Washington Redskins* (Boston: Beacon Press, 2011), 150.

6. Little League Baseball, "1955 Little League Team from Charleston, S.C., to be Honored at Little League Baseball World Series." Retrieved June 30, 2017, at www. LittleLeague.org.

7. No one has examined in more detail the integration of college sport in the South than Charles Martin. See his *Benching Jim Crow: The Rise and Fall of the Color Line in Southern College Sports, 1890–1980* (Urbana: University of Illinois Press, 2010).

8. Hill's mother was initially denied entrance to Memorial Stadium. See Martin, *Jim Crow*, 121.

9. For insights into the Alabama and USC game of 1971, see Martin, *Benching Jim Crow*, 277.

10. Information on the 1963 Loyola University–Chicago basketball team can be gleaned from Michael Lenehan, Ramblers: Loyola Chicago 1963: *The Team that Changed the Color of College Basketball* (Chicago: Midway, 2013).

11. Frank Fitzpatrick, *And the Walls Came Tumbling Down: Kentucky, Texas Western, and the Game that Changed American Sports* (New York: Simon & Schuster, 1999), 25.

Chapter Six

1. Thomas Hauser, *Muhammad Ali: His Life and Times* (New York: Simon & Schuster, 1991), 78.

2. Hauser, *Muhammad Ali*, 220–21.

3. Mel Whitfield, "Let's Boycott the Olympics," *Ebony* (March 1964): 95–96.

4. Lane Demas, *Integrating the Gridiron: Black Civil Rights and American College Football* (New Brunswick, NJ: Rutgers University Press, 2010), 116.

5. David K. Wiggins, "'The Future of College Athletics Is at Stake': Racial Turmoil on Three Predominantly White University Campuses, 1968–1972," *Journal of Sport History* 15 (Winter 1988): 322.

6. David K. Wiggins, "Prized Performers, but Frequently Overlooked Students: The Involvement of Black Athletes in Intercollegiate Sports on Predominantly White University Campuses, 1890–1972," *Research Quarterly for Exercise and Sport* 62 (June 1991): 174.

7. David K. Wiggins, "'Great Speed but Little Stamina': The Historical Debate Over Black Athletic Superiority," *Journal of Sport History* 16 (Summer 1989): 179.

8. Jennifer E. Bruening, "Gender and Racial Analysis in Sport: Are All the Women White and All the Blacks Men," *Quest*, 57 (2012), 331.

9. Graham L. Jones, "Dodgers Fire Campanis over Racial Remarks," *Los Angeles Times*, April 9, 1987. Retrieved July 28, 2017, at http://articles.latimes.com/1987–04–09/news/mn-366_1_black-leaders.

10. David K. Wiggins, "Edwin Bancroft Henderson: Physical Educator, Civil Rights Activist, and Chronicler of African American Athletes," *Research Quarterly for Exercise and Sport* 70 (June 1999): 91–112.

Chapter Seven

1. Jeffrey T. Sammons, "A Proportionate and Measured Response to the Provocation That Is Darwin's Athletes," *Journal of Sport History* 24 (Fall 1997): 381.

2. John Hoberman, "How Not to Misread Darwin's Athletes: A Response to Jeffrey T. Sammons," *Journal of Sport History* 24 (Fall 1997): 389.

3. Ronald Roach, "Black Scholars on Sports: Controversial Book Brings Black Intellectuals Together to Discuss Whether African Americans Are Preoccupied with Sports—John Hoberman, 'Darwin's Athletes: How Sport Has Damaged Black America and Preserved the Myth of Race,'" *Diverse Issues in Higher Education*, July 13, 2007. Retrieved July 30, 2017, at diverseeducation.com/article/8474.

4. David Ortiz with Tony Massarotti, *Big Papi: My Story of Big Dreams and Big Hits* (New York: St. Martin's Press, 2007), 57.

5. Vincent M. Mallozzi, *Asphalt Gods: An Oral History of the Rucker Tournament* (New York: Doubleday, 2003); Pete Axthelm, *The City Game* (New York: Harper and Row, 1970).

6. Michael Novak, *The Joy of Sports: End Zones, Bases, Baskets, Balls, and the Consecration of the American Spirit* (New York: Basic Books, 1976), 108.

7. Jeffrey Lane, *Under the Boards: The Cultural Revolution in Basketball* (Lincoln, NE: Bison Books, 2007), 3.

8. Jack Moore, "How NBA Stars Took a Discriminatory Dress Code and Used It to Their Advantage," *Dime Magazine*, November 17, 2016. Retrieved June 30, 2017, at uproxx.com/dimemag/nba-dress-code-history.

9. David K. Wiggins and Patrick B. Miller, *The Unlevel Playing Field: A Documentary History of the African American Experience in Sport* (Urbana: University of Illinois Press, 2003), 388–89.

10. The Aspen Institute, "Title IX and Beyond: How Do We Get the Rest of Our Girls in the Game?" Retrieved June 30, 2017, at aspeninstitute.org.

11. William C. Rhoden, "Black and White Women Far from Equal under Title IX," *New York Times*, June 10, 2012. Retrieved June 30, 2017, at nytimes.com.

12. Rhoden, "Black and White Women Far from Equal."

13. Quoted in Jennifer H. Lansbury, *A Spectacular Leap: Black Women Athletes in Twentieth-Century America* (Fayetteville: The University of Arkansas Press, 2014), 214.

14. Lansbury, *A Spectacular Leap*, 223.

15. Pamela Grundy and Susan Shackelford, *Shattering the Glass: The Remarkable History of Women's Basketball* (New York: New Press, 2005), 195.

16. Nike, "Nike Air Swoopes." Retrieved June 30, 2017, at news.nike.com.

17. ESPN, "WNBA Scores High on Racial and Gender Report Card," November 2, 2016. Retrieved June 30, 2017, at cdn.espn.go.com.

18. Marc Bain, "Why Doesn't Serena Williams Have More Sponsorship Deals?" *The Atlantic*, August 31, 2015. Retrieved July 14, 2017, at https://www.theatlantic.com/entertainment/archive/2015/2015/08.

19. Althea Gibson, *I Always Wanted to Be Somebody* (New York: Harper and Brothers, 1958), 157–59.

20. Harry Edwards, *The Revolt of the Black Athlete* (New York: Free Press, 1969), 60.

21. Jesse Owens with Paul G. Neimark, *Blackthink: My Life as a Black Man and White Man* (New York: William Morrow, 1970), 80, 121.

22. William J. Baker, *Jesse Owens: An American Life* (New York: Free Press, 1986), 214.

23. Baker, *Jesse Owens*, 216.

24. Shaun Powell, *Souled Out? How Blacks Are Winning and Losing in Sports* (Champaign, IL: Human Kinetics, 2008), 34.

25. Powell, *Souled Out?*, 34.

26. Quoted in William C. Rhoden, *Forty Million Dollar Slaves: The Rise, Fall, and Redemption of the Black Athlete* (New York: Crown Publishers, 2006), 200.

27. Reeves Wiedeman, "As American as Refusing to Stand for the National Anthem: Patriots Shun the White House. Sports Stars Turn ESPN into MSNBC. And Brands Smell the Commercial Potential in Political Rage." *New York Magazine*, February 20–March 5, 2017, 36.

28. Melissa Chan, "Read LeBron James and Carmelo Anthony's Speech on Race at the ESPY Awards," *Time*, July 14, 2014. Retrieved July 28, 2017, at time.com/4406289/LeBron-james-carmelo-anthony-espy-awards-transcript.

29. Wiedeman, "As American as Refusing to Stand," 40.

30. Ross Initiative in Sports for Equality, "From Protest to Progress: Athlete Activism in 2016." Retrieved July 28, 2017, at www.RisetoWin.org.

Chapter Eight

1. Christine Brennan, "With Kaepernick, Priorities Amiss: Teams Draft Alleged Abusers as QB Remains Jobless," *USA Today*, May 4, 2017, 1C.

2. Ross Initiative in Sports for Equality, "From Protest to Progress: Athletic Activism in 2016." Retrieved June 30, 2017, at www.RisetoWin.org.

3. Bob Nightengale, "By Boldly Speaking Out, Jones Inspirers Others to Speak Up Take Action," *USA Today*, May 3, 2017, 4C.

4. Craig Calcaterra, "The Adam Jones-Boston Incident." Retrieved July 28, 2017, at http://mlb.nbcsports.com/2017/05/02/major-league-baseball-issues-a-statement-on-the-adam-jones-boston-incident/.

5. William C. Rhoden, *Forty Million Dollar Slaves: The Rise, Fall, and Redemption of the Black Athlete* (New York: Crown Publishers, 2006), 267.

~

Chronology

1810	Tom Molineaux fights the first of two bouts against Tom Crib for the world boxing championship.
1853	Anthony Bowen establishes the Twelve Street YMCA in Washington, D.C.
1866	Founding of Pythian Baseball Club of Philadelphia.
1884	Moses "Fleetwood" Walker plays with the Toledo Mudhens of the American Association.
	Isaac Murphy captures the first of three Kentucky Derbies.
1885	Founding of Cuban Giants baseball team at the Argyle Hotel in Babylon, Long Island.
1890	George "Little Chocolate" Dixon captures world bantamweight boxing championship.
1908	Jack Johnson captures world heavyweight boxing championship.
	John Baxter Taylor wins gold medal in the 4x400 relay at the Olympic Games in London.
1912	Founding of the Colored Intercollegiate Athletic Association (later Central Intercollegiate Athletic Association).
1916	Founding of the American Tennis Association.
1920	Rube Foster creates the Negro National Baseball League.
1921	Fritz Pollard becomes head coach of professional football's Akron Pros.
1923	Robert L. Douglas establishes the Renaissance Five basketball team.

1924   DeHart Hubbard captures gold medal in the long jump at the Olympic Games in Paris.
        Founding of the Colored Speedway Association.
1926   Founding of the United Golfers Association.
1927   Abe Saperstein establishes the Harlem Globetrotters basketball team.
1929   Founding of the National Interscholastic Basketball Tournament.
1936   Jesse Owens captures four gold medals at the Olympic Games in Berlin.
1938   Joe Louis defeats German fighter Max Schmeling in a much anticipated rematch.
1939   Edwin B. Henderson publishes the first edition of his *Negro in Sports*.
        Founding of National Negro Bowling Association.
1946   Kenny Washington and Woody Strode reintegrate the National Football League by signing with the Los Angeles Rams.
1947   Jackie Robinson of the Brooklyn Dodgers integrates modern Major League Baseball.
1950   Earl Lloyd, Nat "Sweetwater" Clifton, and Chuck Cooper integrate the National Basketball Association.
1955   Cannon Street YMCA Little League team denied the opportunity to compete in Williamsport, Pennsylvania, for the Little League World Series championship.
1957   Althea Gibson captures her first Wimbledon and US Lawn Tennis Association championships.
1958   Willie O'Ree begins his career in the National Hockey League with the Boston Bruins.
1960   Wilma Rudolph captures three gold medals in the Olympic Games in Rome.
1961   Wendell Scott starts his first NASCAR race.
        Syracuse running back Ernie Davis wins Heisman Trophy.
1962   Charlie Sifford becomes Professional Golf Association tour member.
1964   Cassius Clay (later Muhammad Ali) captures the World Heavyweight Championship by defeating Sonny Liston.
1966   Bill Russell becomes head coach of the Boston Celtics of the National Basketball Association.
1967   Emmlen Tunnell is inducted into the National Football League Hall of Fame.
1968   Tommie Smith and John Carlos stage their black-gloved power salute at the Olympic Games in Mexico City.
1974   Hank Aaron hits his 715th homerun to become the all-time Major League leader in that category.

1975   Lee Elder plays in the Master's golf tournament in Augusta, Georgia.
        Arthur Ashe wins the Wimbledon tennis championship.
        Frank Robinson becomes manager of the Cleveland Indians.

1984   Carl Lewis duplicates Jesse Owens's performance in Berlin by cap-
        turing four gold medals in the Olympic Games in Los Angeles.

1988   Doug Williams quarterbacks the Washington Redskins to the Super
        Bowl title by defeating the Denver Broncos.
        Black Coaches Association is founded.
        Florence Griffith Joyner captures three gold medals and one silver
        medal at the Olympic Games in Seoul, Korea.

1989   Art Shell becomes head coach of the Los Angeles Raiders of the
        National Football League.

1995   Sheryl Swoopes signs athletic shoe deal with Nike.

1997   Tiger Woods wins his first Master's golf tournament.

2002   Ozzie Newsome becomes general manager of the Baltimore Ravens
        of the National Football League.

2004   Robert L. Johnson becomes the principal owner of the Charlotte
        Bobcats of the National Basketball Association.

2012   Gabby Douglas captures the gold medal in the individual all-around
        competition at the Olympic Games in London.

2016   Simone Biles wins four gold medals and one bronze medal in gym-
        nastics at the Olympic Games in Rio de Janeiro.
        LeBron James, Dwayne Wade, Chris Paul, and Carmelo Anthony
        speak out about gun violence at the ESPY Awards.

~

Bibliographic Essay

General Secondary Sources

The first general survey on African American participation in sport is Edwin B. Henderson, *The Negro in Sports* (Washington, DC: Associated Publishers, 1939, 1949). Written at the request of historian Carter G. Woodson, the book provides important information about the lives and careers of early black athletes at both the amateur and professional levels of competition. Subsequent survey texts include such works as Andrew S. "Doc" Young, *Negro Firsts in Sports* (Chicago: Johnson Publishing, 1963); Wally Jones and Jim Washington, *Black Champions Challenge American Sports* (New York: David McKay, 1972); Arthur Ashe, *A Hard Road to Glory: A History of the African American Athlete*, 3 vols. (New York: Warner Books, 1988); and Russell Wigginton, *The Strange Career of the Black Athlete* (Westport, CT: Praeger, 2006).

In addition to general survey texts, there are a number of works, including anthologies and compilations of primary documents that provide insights into the history of African American participation in sport as well as contemporary issues regarding the interconnection among race, sport, and American culture. David K. Wiggins furnishes insights into African American participation in sport since the late nineteenth century in his *Glory Bound: Black Athletes in a White America* (Syracuse, NY: Syracuse University Press, 1997) and along with Patrick B. Miller provides primary materials on the topic in *The Unlevel Playing Field: A Documentary History of the African American Experience in Sport* (Urbana: University of Illinois Press, 2003). Thoughtful and engaging information on different aspects of the African

American experience in sport can be found in John Hoberman, *Darwin's Athletes: How Sport Has Damaged Black America and Preserved the Myth of Race* (Boston: Houghton Mifflin, 1997); William C. Rhoden, *Forty Million Dollar Slaves: The Rise, Fall, and Redemption of the Black Athlete* (New York: Crown Publishers, 2006); Shaun Powell, *Sold Out? How Blacks Are Winning and Losing in Sports* (Champaign, IL: Human Kinetics Publishers, 2007); Thabiti Lewis, *Ballers of the New School: Race and Sports in America* (Chicago: Third World Press, 2010); and Earl Smith, *Race, Sport, and the American Dream* (Durham, NC: Carolina Academic Press, 2013).

Chapter 1:
Establishing the Boundaries of Sport:
Slavery's Lasting Legacy

There is relatively limited information on sport and recreation in the plantation community. Information on the topic, however, can be gleaned from the many articles published by David K. Wiggins from his doctoral dissertation "Sport and Popular Pastimes: Shadow of the Slavequarter" (unpublished doctoral dissertation, University of Maryland, 1979) and from Wilma King, *Stolen Childhood: Slave Youth in Nineteenth Century America* (Bloomington: Indiana University Press, 2011). Insightful information on slaves who served their planters as trainers, groomers, and jockeys can be gleaned from Katherine C. Mooney, *Race Horse Men: How Slavery and Freedom Were Made at the Race Track* (Cambridge, MA: Harvard University Press, 2014). The lives and careers of Bill Richmond and Tom Molineaux have fascinated writers interested in race and boxing. One important book that includes good information on both fighters is Dennis Brailsford, *Bareknuckles: A Social History of Prize-Fighting* (Cambridge, MA: Lutterworth Press, 1988).

The well-known writer George MacDonald penned a historical novel based on Molineaux's life and career titled *Black Ajax* (New York: Carroll & Graf, 1999). Elliott J. Gorn, in his insightful *The Manly Art: Bare-Knuckle Prize Fighting in America*, also discusses both fighters.

Chapter 2:
Freedom to Participate on an Unlevel Playing Field

There are number of excellent works on African American athletes who distinguished themselves in predominantly white organized sport at the amateur and professional levels of competition during the latter stages of the nineteenth and early stages of the twentieth centuries. Receiving a great deal of attention were boxers and many of them are discussed in such works as Louis Moore, *I Fight for a Living: Boxing and the Battle for Black Manhood, 1880–1915* (Urbana: University of Illinois Press, 2017) and Jeffrey T. Sammons, *Beyond the Ring: The Role of Boxing in American Society* (Urbana: University of Illinois Press, 1988). Not unexpectedly, the boxer who has received a great deal of attention from scholars is Jack Johnson, the controversial fighter who held the heavyweight championship from 1908 to 1915. Among the best studies on Johnson are: Randy Roberts, *Papa Jack: Jack Johnson and the Era of White Hopes* (New York: Free Press, 1983); Al-Tony Gilmore, *Bad Nigger! The National Impact of Jack Johnson* (Washington, NY: Kennikat Press, 1975); Geoffrey C. Ward, *Unforgivable Blackness: The Rise and Fall of Jack Johnson* (New York: Vintage, 2004); and Theresa Runstedtler, *Jack Johnson, Rebel Sojourner: Boxing in the Shadow of the Global Color Line* (Berkeley: University of California Press, 2013).

Other African American athletes who realized success in predominantly white organized sport during this period have also had biographers. Among the most well-known are David W. Zang, *Fleet Walker's Divided Heart: The Life of Baseball's First Black Major Leaguer* (Lincoln: University of Nebraska Press, 1995); Andrew Ritchie, *Major Taylor: The Extraordinary Career of a Champion Bicycle Racer* (San Francisco: Bicycle Books, 1988); Pellom Mc-Daniels III, *The Prince of Jockeys: The Life of Isaac Burns Murphy* (Lexington: University Press of Kentucky, 2013); and Ed Hotaling, *Wink: The Incredible Life and Epic Journey of Jimmy Winkfield* (New York: McGraw-Hill, 2005). For a very good source on the early involvement of African Americans in baseball, see Ryan A. Swanson, *When Baseball Went White: Reconstruction, Reconciliation, and Dreams of a National Pastime* (Lincoln: University of Nebraska Press, 2014). The secondary sources dealing with the early involvement of African Americans in predominantly white college sport is very slim, but some good information on the subject can be found in John M. Carroll, *Fritz Pollard: Pioneer in Racial Advancement* (Urbana: University of Illinois Press, 1992) and Michael Oriard, *Reading Football: How the Popular Press Created an American Spectacle* (Chapel Hill: University of North Carolina Press, 1993).

Chapter 3:
Sport behind the Walls of Segregation

The number of scholarly publications on the separate sports teams, leagues, and organizations that were created by African Americans during the days of racial segregation are still relatively small in number. The notable exception to this is Negro League Baseball, which has drawn much attention from academicians and popular writers alike. Some of the most engaging and important works completed on Negro League Baseball are: Donn Rogosin, *Invisible Men: Life in Baseball's Negro Leagues* (New York: Athenaeum, 1987); Rob Ruck, *Sandlot Seasons: Sport in Black Pittsburgh* (Urbana: University of Illinois Press, 1987); Neil Lanctot, *Negro League Baseball: The Rise and Ruin of a Black Institution* (Philadelphia: University of Pennsylvania Press, 2004); Janet Bruce, *The Kansas City Monarchs: Champions of Black Baseball* (Lawrence: University Press of Kansas, 1985); Donald Spivey, *If You Were Only White: The Life of Leroy "Satchel" Paige* (Columbia: University of Missouri Press, 2013); Larry Lester, *Black Baseball's National Showcase: The East-West All-Star Game* (Lincoln: University of Nebraska Press, 2002); Bob Luke, *The Baltimore Elite Giants: Sport and Society in the Age of Negro League Baseball* (Baltimore: Johns Hopkins University Press, 2009); Michael Lomax, *Black Baseball Entrepreneurs, 1860–1901: Operating by Any Means Necessary* (Syracuse, NY: Syracuse University Press, 2003) and *Black Baseball Entrepreneurs, 1902–1931: The Negro National and Eastern Colored Leagues* (Syracuse, NY: Syracuse University Press, 2014).

While few in number, there are some excellent works that deal with black parallel institutions in other sports. Todd Gould, for instance, provides a very interesting account of the all-black Gold and Glory Sweepstakes car race in Indiana during the 1920s and 1930s in his *For Gold and Glory: Charlie Wiggins and the African-American Racing Circuit* (Bloomington: Indiana University Press, 2007). Randy Roberts provides an interesting look at the all-black Crispus Attucks high school basketball team in his *But They Can't Beat Us!: Oscar Robertson and the Crispus Attucks Tigers* (Indianapolis: Indiana Historical Society, 1999). Damion Thomas furnishes an insightful analysis of the interconnection between the Harlem Globetrotters and the State Department in his *Globetrotting: African American Athletes and Cold War Politics* (Urbana: University of Illinois Press, 2012). Jennifer H. Lansbury discusses in detail the outstanding women's track and field teams at Tuskegee Institute and Tennessee State University in her *A Spectacular Leap: Black Women Athletes in Twentieth Century America* (Fayetteville: The University of Arkansas Press, 2014). David K. Wiggins and Ryan A. Swanson provide important insights into various all-black sports institutions at various levels of competition in their edited *Separate Games: African American Sport behind the Walls of Segregation* (Fayetteville: The University of Arkansas Press, 2016). Included are chapters on such influential organizations as the CIAA, ATA, UGA, and NNBA, among others.

Chapter 4: Striving to Be Full Participants in America's Pastimes

Charles H. Martin covers in great detail and with much insight the integration of predominantly white college sport in the South in his *Benching Jim Crow: The Rise and Fall of the Color Line in Southern College Sport* (Urbana: University of Illinois Press, 2012). Other works that include very good information on various aspects of the pattern of African American participation in predominantly white college sport, including efforts at integration, are: Patrick B. Miller, ed., *The Sporting World of the Modern South* (Urbana: University of Illinois Press, 2002); Jaime Schultz, *Moments of Impact: Injury, Racialized Memory, and Reconciliation in College Football* (Lincoln: University of Nebraska Press, 2015); Gregory J. Kaliss, *Men's College Athletics and the Politics of Racial Equality: Five Pioneer Stories of Black Manliness, White Citizenship, and American Democracy* (Philadelphia: Temple University Press, 2012); Michael Oriard, *King Football: Sport and Spectacle in the Golden Age of Radio and Newsreels, Movies and Magazines, the Weekly and the Daily Press* (Chapel Hill: University of North Carolina Press, 2001); and John Sayle Watterson, *College Football: History, Spectacle, Controversy* (Baltimore, MD: Johns Hopkins University Press, 2000).

The lives and careers of Jesse Owens and Joe Louis have been covered in great detail, both in the context of general histories of boxing and the 1936 Olympic Games and in individual biographies. An excellent biography of Owens is William J. Baker, *Jesse Owens: An American Life* (New York: Free Press, 1986), while those with an interest in Louis would be well served to read Randy Roberts, *Hard Times Man* (New Haven, CT: Yale University Press, 2010); Chris Mead, *Champion: Joe Louis, Black Hero in White America* (New York: Scribner's, 1985); Thomas R. Hietala, *The Fight of the Century: Jack Johnson, Joe Louis, and the Struggle for Racial Equality* (New York: M.E. Sharpe, 2002); and Richard Bak, *Joe Louis: The Great Black Hope* (New York: Taylor, 1996). For a good dual biography of the two men, see Donald McRae, *Heroes without a Country: America's Betrayal of Joe Louis and Jesse Owens* (New York: HarperCollins, 2002). See also David Clay Large, *Nazi Games: The Olympics of 1936* (New York: W.W. Norton, 2007); Jeffrey T. Sammons, *Beyond the Ring: The Role of Boxing in American Society* (Urbana: University of Illinois Press, 1988); and Gerald R. Gems, *Boxing: A Concise History* (Lanham, MD: Rowman & Littlefield, 2014).

Chapter 5:
Reintegration of Sport and Its Aftermath

The reintegration of predominantly white organized sport has received much attention in the scholarly literature. Not unexpectedly, dominating the literature has been the story of Jackie Robinson and the reintegration of modern MLB. The following provide important details about the story: Jules Tygiel, *Baseball's Great Experiment: Jackie Robinson and His Legacy* (New York: Oxford University Press, 1983); Arnold Rampersad, *Jackie Robinson: A Biography* (New York: Knopf, 1997); Joseph Dorinson and Joram Warmund, eds., *Jackie Robinson: Race, Sports, and the American Dream* (New York: M.E. Sharpe, 2002); David Falkner, *Great Time Coming: The Life of Jackie Robinson from Baseball to Birmingham* (New York: Simon & Schuster, 1995); J. Christofer Schultz, *Jackie Robinson: An Integrated Life* (Lanham, MD: Rowman & Littlefield, 2016).

The integration of the American League by Larry Doby as well as other sports at both the amateur and professional levels of sport have received far less attention than Robinson's historic signing. There are very good scholarly works, however, that address these topics. For the Doby story, see Joseph T. Moore, *Pride against Prejudice: The Biography of Larry Doby* (Westport, CT: Greenwood Press, 1988) and Douglas M. Branson, *Greatness in the Shadows: Larry Doby and the Integration of the American League* (Lincoln: University of Nebraska Press, 2016). For the reintegration of the NFL, see Charles K. Ross, *Outside the Lines: African Americans and the Integration of the National Football League* (New York: New York University Press, 1999); Craig R. Coenan, *From Sandlots to the Super Bowl: The National Football League* (Knoxville: University of Tennessee Press, 2005); and Thomas G. Smith, *Showdown: JFK and the Integration of the Washington Redskins* (Boston, MA: Beacon Press, 2011). For the integration of the NBA, see Charles Salzberg, *From Set Shot to Slam Dunk: The Glory Days of Basketball in the Words of Those Who Played It* (New York: Dutton, 1987); David George Surdam, *The Rise of the National Basketball Association* (Urbana: University of Illinois Press, 2012); and Ron Thomas, *They Cleared the Lane: The NBA's Black Pioneers* (Lincoln, NE: Bison Books, 2004). For the integration of golf, see Robert J. Robertson, *Fair Ways: How Six Black Golfers Won Civil Rights in Beaumont, Texas* (College Station: Texas A&M University Press, 2015) and Pete McDaniel, *Uneven Lies: The Heroic Story of African-Americans in Golf* (Greenwich, CT: American Golfer, 2000). For the integration of predominantly white college sport, see the previous citation for Charles H. Martin, along with Richard Pennington, *Breaking the Ice: The Racial Integration of Southwest Conference Football* (Jefferson, NC: McFarland, 1987) and Frank Fitzpatrick, *And the*

Walls Came Tumbling Down: Kentucky, Texas Western, and the Game That Changed American Sports (New York: Simon & Schuster, 1999).

Chapter 6: Sport and the Civil Rights Movement

The scholarly literature is replete with books about Muhammad Ali. Among the best of these books are: David Remnick, *King of the World: Muhammad Ali and the Rise of a Hero* (New York: Random House, 1998); Elliott J. Gorn, ed., *Muhammad Ali: The People's Champ* (Urbana: University of Illinois Press, 1995); Gerald Early, *The Muhammad Ali Reader* (New York: Ecco Press, 1994); and Randy Roberts and Johnny Smith, *Blood Brothers: The Fatal Friendship between Muhammad Ali and Malcolm X* (New York: Basic Books, 2016). The other black professional athletes who became involved in the civil rights struggle certainly have not received the attention of Ali, but academicians have written about some of them with great skill. See for example: Aram Goudsouzian, *King of the Court: Bill Russell and the Basketball Revolution* (Berkeley: University of California Press, 2010); Brad Snyder, *A Well-Paid Slave: Curt Flood's Fight for Free Agency in Professional Sports* (New York: Penguin Group, 2006); Eric Allen Hall, *Arthur Ashe: Tennis and Justice in the Civil Rights Era* (Baltimore, MD: Johns Hopkins University Press, 2014); and Mike Freeman, *Jim Brown: The Fierce Life of an American Hero* (New York: William Morrow, 2016).

There has been a fascination with the Harry Edwards–led boycott of the Mexico City Olympic Games and the black athletic activism of the late 1960s and early 1970s. This fascination is reflected in the voluminous amount of literature on the topic. For examples of this literature, see David K. Wiggins, *Glory Bound: Black Athletes in a White America* (Syracuse, NY: Syracuse University Press, 1997); Louis Moore, *We Will Win the Day: The Civil Rights Movement, the Black Athlete, and the Quest for Racial Equality* (Santa Barbara, CA: Praeger, 2017); Kevin B. Witherspoon, *Before the Eyes of the World: Mexico and the 1968 Olympic Games* (DeKalb: Northern Illinois University Press, 2008); Amy Bass, *Not the Triumph but the Struggle: The 1968 Olympics and the Making of the Black Athlete* (Minneapolis: University of Minnesota Press, 2002); Simon Henderson, *Sidelined: How American Sports Challenged the Black Freedom Struggle* (Lexington: University Press of Kentucky, 2013). The personal accounts of black athletic activism during this period offer important insights. These include such works as Harry Edwards, *The Revolt of the Black Athlete* (Urbana: University of Illinois Press, 2017); Vincent Matthews with Neil Amdur, *My Race Be Won* (New York: Charterhouse, 1974); Tommie Smith, *Silent Gesture: The Autobiography of Tommie Smith* (Philadelphia: Temple University Press,

2007); John Carlos, *The John Carlos Story: The Sport Moment That Changed the World* (Chicago: Haymarket Books, 2011); Bill Russell, as told to William McSweeney, *Go Up for Glory* (New York: Conrad-McCann, 1966); Jim Brown, with Myron Cope, *Off My Chest* (New York: Doubleday, 1964); and Kareem Abdul-Jabbar and Peter Knobler, *Giant Steps: The Autobiography of Kareem Abdul-Jabbar* (New York: Bantam, 1985).

The debate over black athletic performance has largely played out in the press and in articles. The major book on the topic is John Entine, *Taboo: Why Black Athletes Dominate Sports and Why We Are Afraid to Talk about It* (New York: Public Affairs Press, 2000). A very controversial book, Entine comes down on the side of scientific racism when trying to explain the outstanding performances of black athletes. Information on Edwin B. Henderson as well as the historiography on African American athletes can be found in the previously mentioned *Glory Bound: Black Athletes in a White America* and *The Unlevel Playing Field: A Documentary History of the African American Experience in Sport.*

Chapter 7: Race, Black Athletes, and the Globalization of Sport

The role of African American athletes in contemporary culture and their increasing importance as global icons can be understood more clearly through the readings of such previously mentioned works as *Darwin's Athletes: How Sport Has Damaged Black America and Preserved the Myth of Race*; *Forty Million Dollar Slaves: The Rise, Fall, and Redemption of the Black Athlete*; *Sold Out? How Blacks Are Winning and Losing in Sports*; *Ballers of the New School: Race and Sports in America*; and *Race, Sport and the American Dream*. Other excellent works that can be consulted are: Ben Carrington, *Race, Sport and Politics: The Sporting Black Diaspora* (Thousand Oaks, CA: Sage Publications, 2010) and Andrei S. Markovits and Lars Rensmann, *Gaming the World: How Sports Are Reshaping Global Politics and Culture* (Princeton, NJ: Princeton University Press, 2010).

Chapter 8: An Altered Athletic Landscape

Much of the information on the recent activism and status of African American athletics can be gleamed from newspapers and popular magazines. One scholarly book that discusses the more contemporary role of African American athletics is Louis Moore, *We Will Win the Day: The Civil Rights Movement, the Black Athlete, and the Quest for Racial Equality* (Santa Barbara, CA: Praeger, 2017).

~

Documents

Document 1: "A Corn Shucking"

*Corn shuckings were extraordinarily important events for both slaves and planta-
tion owners in the old South. Part work and part play, they were a significant
cultural activity for slaves who eased the burden and heightened the enjoyment of
the shuckings by instilling friendly competition into the activity. The shuckings were
also meaningful to the slaves in that it provided them an opportunity to socialize
with slaves from neighboring plantations and eat and drink and dance to their own
music in an uninhibited fashion. Francis Fedric, a man who spent some fifty years
as a slave in Virginia and Kentucky, provided one of the most detailed and colorful
descriptions of a shucking in his published narrative from 1863.*

In the autumn, about the 1st of November, the slaves commence gathering
the Indian corn, pulling it off the stalk, and throwing it into heaps. Then it
is carted home, and thrown into heaps sixty or seventy yards long, seven or
eight feet high, and about six or seven feet wide. Some of the masters make
their slaves shuck the corn. All the slaves stand on one side of the heap, and
throw the ears over, which are then cribbed. This is the time when the whole
country far and wide resounds with the corn-songs. When they commence
shucking the corn, the master will say, "Ain't you going to sing any tonight?"
The slaves say, "Yers, sir," one slave will begin:

"Fare you well, Miss Lucy.

ALL: John come down de hollow." The next song will be:

"Fare you well, fare you well.

ALL: Weell ho. Weell ho.

CAPTAIN: Fare you well, young ladies all.

ALL: Weell ho. Weell ho.

CAPTAIN: Fare you well, I'm going away.

ALL: Weell ho. Weell ho.

CAPTAIN: I'm going away to Canada.

ALL: Weell ho. Weell ho."

One night Mr. Taylor, a large planter, had a corn shucking, a Bee it is called. The corn pile was 180 yards long. He sent his slaves on horseback with letters to the other planters around to ask them to allow their slaves to come and help. On a Thursday night, about 8 o'clock, the slaves were heard coming, the corn-songs ringing through the plantations. "Oh, they are coming, they are coming!" exclaimed Mr. Taylor, who had been anxiously listening some time for the songs. The slaves marched up in companies, headed by captains, who had in the crowns of their hats a short stick, with feathers tied to it, like a cockade. I myself was in one of the companies. Mr. Taylor shook hands with each captain as the companies arrived, and said the men were to have some brandy if they wished, a large jug of which was ready for them. Mr. Taylor ordered the corn-pile to be divided into two by a large pole laid across. Two men were chosen as captains; and the men, to the number of 300 or 400, were told off to each captain. One of the captains got Mr. Taylor on his side, who said he should not like his party to be beaten. "Don't throw the corn too far. Let some of it drop just over, and we'll shingle some, and get done first. I can make my slaves shuck what we shingle tomorrow," said Mr. Taylor, "for I hate to be beaten."

The corn-songs now rang out merrily; all working willingly and gaily. Just before they had finished the heaps, Mr. Taylor went away into the house; then the slaves, on Mr. Taylor's side, by shingling, beat the other side; and his Captain, and all his men, rallied around the others, and took their hats in their hands, and cried out, "Oh, oh! fie! for shame!"

It was two o'clock in the morning now, and they marched to Mr. Taylor's house; the Captain hollowing out, "Oh, where's Mr. Taylor? Oh, where's Mr. Taylor? all the men answering, "Oh, oh, oh!"

Mr. Taylor walked, with all his family, on the verandah; and the Captain sang, "I've just come to let you know.

MEN: Oh, oh!

CAPTAIN : The upper end has beat.

MEN: Oh, oh!

CAPTAIN: But isn't they sorry fellows?

MEN: Oh, oh, oh!

CAPTAIN: But isn't they sorry fellows?

MEN: Oh, oh, oh!

CAPTAIN: But I'm going back again.

MEN: Oh, oh, oh!

CAPTAIN: But I'm going back again.

MEN: Oh, oh, oh!

CAPTAIN: And where's Mr. Taylor?

MEN: Oh, oh, oh!

CAPTAIN: And where's Mr. Taylor?

MEN: Oh, oh, oh!

CAPTAIN: And where's Mr. Taylor?

MEN: Oh, oh, oh!

CAPTAIN: I'll bid you, fare you well,

MEN: Oh, oh, oh!

CAPTAIN: For I'm going back again.

MEN: Oh, oh, oh!

CAPTAIN: I'll bid you, fare you well.

And a long fare you well.

MEN: Oh, oh, oh!"

They marched back, and finished the pile. All then went to enjoy a good supper, provided by Mr. Taylor; it being usual to kill an ox, on such an occasion; Mr., Mrs., and the Misses Taylor, waiting upon the slaves, at supper. What I have written cannot convey a tenth part of the spirit, humour, and mirth of the company, all joyous—singing, coming and going. But, within one short fort-night, at least thirty of this happy band were sold, many of them down South, to unutterable horrors, soon to be used up. Reuben, the merry Captain of the band, a fine, spirited fellow, who sang, "Where's Mr. Taylor?" was one of those, dragged from his family. My heart is full when I think of his sad lot.

Document 2: W. E. B. Du Bois
Philosophizes on Recreation and Amusement

W. E. B. Du Bois, the great black intellectual and civil rights activist, was a prolific writer who provided his views on a wide range of topics throughout his long and storied public career. One of those topics he weighed in on was the importance of the church to the African American community. In the following essay published in the Southern Workman *(1897), Du Bois notes that the black church had tradition-ally denounced amusements that would relieve the stress of black workers in the North, but that now, particularly because of the growth of cities and the problems associated with that growth, the church should encourage healthy amusements and organize them when possible. Echoing the philosophy of leaders of the playground movement and other critical thinkers during the Progressive Era, Du Bois strongly promoted rational recreations alongside the more traditional moral and religious teachings offered by the church in an effort to raise healthy black children.*

I wish to discuss with you somewhat superficially a phase of development in the organized life of American Negroes which has hitherto received scant notice. It is the question of the amusements of Negroes—what their attitude toward them is, what institutions among them conduct the recreations, and what the tendency of indulgence is in amusements of various sorts. I do not pretend that this is one of the more pressing of the Negro problems, but nevertheless it is destined as time goes on to become more and more so; and at all times and in all places, the manner, method, and extent of a people's recreation is of vast importance to their welfare.

I have been in this case especially spurred to take under consideration this particular one of the many problems affecting the Negroes in cities and in the country because I have long noted with silent apprehension a distinct ten-dency among us, to depreciate and belittle and sneer at means of recreation, to consider amusement as the peculiar property of the devil, and to look upon even its legitimate pursuit as time wasted and energy misspent. . . . When now a young man has grown up feeling the trammels of precept, religion, or custom too irksome for him, and then at the most impressionable and reckless age of life, is suddenly transplanted to an atmosphere of excess, the result is apt to be disastrous. In the case of young colored men or women, it is disastrous, and the story is daily repeated in every great city of our land, of young men and women who have been reared in an atmosphere of restricted amusement, throwing off when they enter city life, not one restriction, not some restrictions, but almost all, and plunging into dissipation and vice. This tendency is rendered stronger by two circumstances peculiar to the condition of the American Negro: the first is his express or tacit exclusion from the public amusements of most great cities; and second, the little thought of fact that the chief purveyor of amusement to the colored people is the Negro church, which in theory is opposed to most modern amusements. Let me make this second point clear, for much of the past and future development of the race is misunderstood from ignorance of certain fundamental historic facts. Among most people the primitive sociological group was the family or at least the clan. Not so among American Negroes: every vestige of primitive organization among the Negro slaves was destroyed by the slave ship; in this country the first distinct voluntary organization of Negroes was the Negro church. The Negro church came before the Negro home, it antedates their social life, and in every respect it stands to-day as the fullest, broadest expression of organized Negro life. . . .We are so familiar with churches, and church work is so near to us, that we have scarce time to view it in perspective and to realize that in origin and functions the Negro church is a broader, deeper, and more comprehensive social organism than the churches of white Americans. The Negro church is not simply an organism for the propagation of religion; it is the centre of the social, intellectual, and religious life of an organized group of individuals. It provides social intercourse, it provides amusements of various kinds, it serves as a newspaper and intelligence bureau, if supplants the theatre, it directs the picnic and excursion, it furnishes the music, it introduces the stranger to the community, it serves as lyceum, library, and lecture bureau—it is, in fine, the central organ of the organized life of the American Negro for amusement, relaxation, instruction, and religion. To maintain its preeminence the Negro church has been forced to compete with the dance hall, the theatre, and the home as an amusement-giving agency; aided by color proscription in public amusements, aided by the fact mentioned before, that the church among us is older than the home, the church has been peculiarly successful, so that of the ten thousand Philadelphia Negroes whom I asked, "Where do you get your amusements?" fully three-fourths could only answer, "From the churches." . . . Under such circumstances two questions immediately arise: first, Is this growing demand for amusement legitimate? And, can the church continue to be the centre of amusements? Let us consider the first question; and ask, What is amusement? All life is rhythm-the right swing of the pendulum makes the pointer go around, but the left swing must follow it; the down stroke of the hammer welds the iron, and yet the hammer must be lifted between each blow; the heart must beat and yet between each beat comes a pause; the day is the period of fulfilling the functions of life and yet the prelude and end of day is night. Thus throughout nature, from the restless beating of yonder waves to the rhythm of the seasons and the whirl of comments, we see one mighty law of work and rest, of activity and relaxation, of inspiration and amusement. We might imagine a short sighted philosopher arguing strongly against the loss of time involved in the intermittent activities of the world—arguing against the time spent by the hammer in raising itself for the second blow, against the unnecessary alternate swing of the pendulum, against sleep that knits up the ravelled sleeve of care, against amusements that reinvigorate and recreate and divert. With such a philosophy the world has never agreed, the whole world today is organized for work and recreation. Where the balance between the two is best maintained we have the best civilization, the best culture; and that civilization declines toward barbarism where, on the one hand, work and drudgery so predominate as to destroy the very vigor, which stands behind them, or on the other hand, where relaxation and amusement become dissipation instead of recreation.

I dwell on these simple facts because I hear that even a proverbially joyous people like the American Negroes are forgetting to recognize for their children the God-given right to play; to recognize that there is a perfectly natural and legitimate demand for amusement on the part of the young people, and that no people can afford to laugh at, sneer at, or forcibly repress the natural joyousness and pleasure-seeking propensity of young womanhood and young manhood. Go into a great city today and see how thoroughly and wonderfully organized its avenues of amusements are; its parks and play grounds, its theatres and galleries, its music and dancing, its excursions and trolley rides represent an enormous proportion of the expenditure of every great municipality. That the matter of amusement may often be overdone in such centres is too true, but of all the agencies that contribute to its overdoing none are more potent than undue repression. Proper amusement must always be a matter of careful reasoning and ceaseless investigation, of nice adjustment between repression and excess; there is not a single means of amusement from church socials to public balls, or from checkers to horse racing that may not be carried to harmful excess; on the other hand it would be difficult to name a single amusement which if properly limited and directed would not be a positive gain to any society; take, for instance, in our modern American society, the game of billiards; I suppose, taken in itself, a more innocent, interesting, and gentlemanly game of skill could scarcely be thought of, and yet, because it is today coupled with gambling, excessive drinking, lewd companionship, and late hour, you can hear it damned from every pulpit from San Francisco to New York as the straight road to perdition; so far as present conditions are concerned the pulpit may be right, but the social reformer must ask himself: Are these conditions necessary? Was it not far sighted prudence for the University of Pennsylvania to put billiard tables in its students' club room? Is there any valid reason why the YMCA at Norfolk should not have a billiard table among its amusements? In other words, is it wise policy to surrender a charming amusement wholly to the devil and then call it devilish? . . .

But in . . . truth, properly conceived, properly enunciated, there is nothing incompatible with wholesome amusement, with true recreation—for what is true amusement, true diversion, but the re-creation of energy which we may sacrifice to noble ends, to higher ideals, while without proper amusement we waste or dissipate our mightiest powers? If the Negro church could have the time and the opportunity to announce this spiritual message clearly and truly; if it could concentrate its energy and emphasis on an encouragement of proper amusement instead of on its wholesale denunciation; if it could cease to dissipate and cheapen religion by incessant semireligious activity then we would, starting with a sound religious foundation, be able to approach the real question of proper amusement. For believe me, my hearers, the great danger of the best class of Negro youth today is not that they will hesitate to sacrifice their lives, their money, and their energy on the altar of their race, but the danger is lest under continuous and persistent proscription, under the thousand little annoyances and petty insults and disappointments of a caste system, they lose the divine faith of their fathers in the fruitfulness of sacrifice; for surely no son of the nineteenth century has heard more plainly the mocking words of "Sorrow, cruel fellowship!"

Document 3: Booker T. Washington, Black Respectability, and the Heavyweight Champion

Booker T. Washington, the famous president of Tuskegee Institute and spokesman for black America, rarely commented on sport. Although his school began to field strong athletic programs prior to the turn of the twentieth century and apparently was an occasional spectator at sporting events held on Tuskegee's campus, Washington showed no genuine interest in sport and following the exploits of black athletes. One black athlete, however, who attracted his attention, was Jack Johnson, the first black heavyweight champion of the world. Washington was deeply troubled by Johnson's lifestyle and it is evident in the following telegram sent to the United Press Association. Prepared by his personal secretary Emmett J. Scott and sent amid the hearings regarding Johnson's indictment for violating the Mann Act, Washington made clear that respectability and proper behavior should guide the actions of the heavyweight champion if he was to be an appropriate representative of the race. His attitude toward Johnson fit neatly into Washington's philosophy of self-help and disapproval of anything that brought discredit to the race in the eyes of White America.

[Tuskegee, Ala.] October 23, 1912

Please Rush!

Replying to your telegram, please publish the following statement exactly as submitted:

Jack Johnson's case will be settled in due time in the courts. Until the court has spoken, I do not care to either defend or condemn him. I can only say at this time, that this is another illustration of the almost irreparable injury that a wrong action on the part of a single individual may do to a whole race. It shows the folly of those persons who think that they alone will be held responsible for the evil that they do. Especially is this true in the case of the Negro in the United States today. No one can do so much injury to the Negro race as the Negro himself. This will seem to many persons unjust, but no one can doubt that it is true.

What makes the situation seem a little worse in this case, is the fact it was the white man, not the black man who has given Jack Johnson the kind of prominence that he has enjoyed up to now. And put him, in other words, in a position where he has been able to bring humiliation upon the whole race of which he is a member.

I do not believe it is necessary for me to say that the honest, sober element of the Negro people of the United States is as severe in condemnation of the kind of immorality with which Jack Johnson is at present charged as any other portion of the community.

In making this statement, I do not mean to, as I have said at the beginning, say how far Jack Johnson is or is not guilty of the charges that have been made against him. This is a question for the court to decide.

Booker T. Washington

Document 4: James Weldon Johnson Recounting Black Athletic Exploits

James Weldon Johnson was, by any measure, a renaissance man. He was an educator, civil rights activist, poet, journalist, and songwriter. Particularly well known for composing "Lift Every Voice and Sing," completed with his brother

John Rosamond Johnson and commonly known as the "Negro national hymn," Johnson proudly recounted in an assortment of different ways the achievements of African Americans in various fields in his efforts to promote race pride. One example of this is Johnson's chronicling in his book Black Manhattan *(1930) the exploits of famous black athletes who had traveled through or deeply touched the lives of those associated with the Harlem Renaissance. Here he proudly recounts the achievements of great African American athletes in the sports of baseball, horse racing, and boxing, carefully situating them alongside the actors, writers, singers, and other intellectuals who had carved out their own space in one of America's most important and powerful cities.*

I have indicated that during the fourth quarter of the last century there was a pause in the racial activities of the Negroes in the North. It would be more strictly true to say that there was a change in activities. In New York the Negro now began to function and express himself on a different plane, in a different sphere; and in a different way he effectively impressed himself upon the city and the country. Within this period, roughly speaking, the Negro in the North emerged and gained national notice in three great professional sports: horse-racing, baseball, and prize-fighting. He also made a beginning and headway on the theatrical stage. And New York, the New York of the upper Twenties and lower Thirties west of Sixth Avenue, became the nucleus of these changed activities.

Horse-racing as an American sport reached development first in the South. The Southern landowners and aristocrats had taken up from the English gentry both riding to hounds and racing early in the last century. By the middle of the century there was local racing on tracks at New Orleans, Mobile, Charleston, Richmond, Nashville, Lexington (Kentucky), and Louisville. . . . The Southern horse-owners, naturally—in fact, of necessity—made use of Negro jockeys, trainers, and stable-boys; so there grew up a class of Negro horsemen unequaled by any in the land. When the first Kentucky Derby was run, out of the fourteen jockeys who rode in the race thirteen were coloured.

Therefore when the centre of horse-racing was shifted to the East and became, somewhat in the English sense, a national sport, Negro jockeys constituted the very first ranks of the profession. When racing shifted to the East and became also a profitable business venture, with the book-maker as a recognized factor, the great jockeys jumped into national popularity. In the hey-day of racing the name of the winner of the Futurity, the Suburban, the Realization, the Brooklyn Handicap, the Metropolitan Handicap, or the Saratoga Cup was as widely heralded and almost as widely known as the name of the winner of a present-day championship prize-fight. In the days when jockeys were popular idols, none were more popular than the best of the coloured ones. No American jockey was ever more popular than Isaac Murphy. . . . Other famous Negro jockeys were: Pike Barnes, Andy Hamilton, Jimmie Winkfield, Willie Simms, Johnny Stoval, "Tiny" Williams, the two Clayton brothers, "Soup" Perkins, "Monk" Overton, Linc Jones, Bob Isom, Emanuel Morris, Felix Carr, and Jimmie Lee. . . . Willie Simms was one of the best jockeys of all time. In a great degree the success of the Dwyer stables was due to his horsemanship. Riding abroad under the Croker-Dwyer colours, he was the first non-English jockey to win a race on an English track. . . .

The record of the Negro in professional baseball makes not so full a page. He did not have so much of a chance in baseball as he had in racing and pugilism. He never gets so fair a chance in those forms of sport or athletics where he must be a member of a team as in those where he may stand upon his own ability as an individual. . . .

The Negro player could not front the forces against him in organized baseball; . . . [therefore] he was compelled to organize for himself. The first professional Negro team to be formed was the Gorhams of New York. From the Gorhams came the famous Cuban Giants. Following the success of the Cuban Giants, coloured professional and semiprofessional clubs called Giants of some kind were organized in a dozen or more cities. These professional clubs have become better organized and now play a regularly scheduled series of games. They play very good ball and are quite popular, especially when they are pitted against white teams and they are quite frequently in New York. . . .

The Negro's fairest chance in the professional sports came in the prize-ring. Here was brought into play more fully than in any other sport the advantageous factor of sole dependence upon his own individual skill and stamina. The prize-fighter had an advantage over even the jockey, who might be handicapped by hopeless mounts. The Negro prize-fighter, of course, often ran up against the hostility of the crowd, an intangible but, nevertheless, very real handicap. This very antagonism, however, according to the stout-heartedness of the fighter, might serve as a spur to victory. This is what actually happened when George Dixon defended his title of featherweight champion of the world and defeated Jack Skelly at New Orleans in 1892. This was more truly the case when Jack Johnson held his title of heavyweight champion of the world by knocking out Jim Jeffries at Reno, July 4, 1910. Johnson has said that not only did he have to fight Jeffries, but that psychologically he also had to fight the majority of the thousands of spectators, many of whom were howling and praying for Jeffries to "kill the nigger." In truth, Johnson had to do more; on that day he had to fight psychologically the majority of the population of the United States. Jeffries had been brought forth as "the hope of the white race." Indeed, during Johnson's term of championship and up to his defeat by Willard at Havana in 1915, every white fighter who was being groomed as a heavyweight contender was known as a "white hope." A good part of the press and some literary fellows were industrious in fomenting the sentiment that the security of white civilization and white supremacy depended upon the defeat of Jack Johnson. One of these writers assumed the role of both prophet and comforter and before the Reno battle wrote in the red-blooded style of the day that Jeffries was bound to win because, while he had Runnymede and Agincourt behind him, the Negro would be licked the moment the white man looked him in the eye.

This psychic manifestation of white superiority did not materialize, but that sort of thing did help to create a tenseness of feeling that constituted something real for Jack Johnson to contend with, and, furthermore, immediately after the fight, expended itself in the beating up of numerous individual Negroes in various parts of the country as a sort of vicarious obliteration of the blot of Jeffries' defeat, and in a manner not at all in accordance with the Marquis of Queensberry rules. In fact, the reaction was so great that pressure was brought which forced Congress to pass a law prohibiting the inter-state exhibition of moving pictures of prize-fights—a law which still stands to plague and limit the magnates of pugilism and of the movies. . . .

The story of the Negro in the prize-ring goes back much further than one would think; and, curiously, the beginning of the story is laid in New York City. The earliest acknowledgment of any man as champion of America was made about 1809; and that man was Thomas Molineaux (sometimes written Molyneaux). Tom Molineaux was born in 1784, a black slave belonging to a Molineaux (or Molyneaux) family of Virginia. When he was about twenty years old, he came to New York as a freeman and got a job as porter in the old Catherine Street market. The precise manner in which he procured his freedom does not seem to be known, but it appears that it was not by running away. Catherine market was headquarters for Negro boxers, and the newcomer soon proved himself the best of them all. . . .

Molineaux, after he had beaten every worthwhile fighter in America, both Negroes and the whites belonging to the crews of British vessels in port—white Americans had not yet taken up pugilism as a profession—was persuaded by the captain of one of the foreign vessels in port to go to England and seek a fight with the famed Tom Cribb, champion of England and of the world. He did go and, through the assistance of Bill Richmond, got the match. The fight between Cribb and Molineaux, which took place on December 18, 1810, at Capthall Common, Sussex, is one of the greatest prize-ring battles of England. Compared with the theatrical performances and business-like transactions of today, it takes on titanic proportions. A reading of the contemporary accounts of the fight gives the impression of an ancient gladiatorial struggle to the death. The records of the time and later English authorities on boxing admit that, technically, Molineaux won the fight and consequently the championship of the world. He lost the decision through a bit of trickery on the part of Cribb's seconds. . . . In that age, even as today, there were excuses or "alibis"; and it was asserted that Molineaux lost because up to the time of the fight he had to go barnstorming about the country in order to make a living, while Cribb underwent the best of training at Captain Barclay's estate in Scotland and was in the finest condition. It is to Molineaux's credit that this excuse was not offered by him. Molineaux fought and won a great many fights in England, Scotland, and Ireland. He lost two to Cribb, but the courage and stamina he displayed in both fights with the champion won for him the admiration of the fancy and the British public. He remains today one of the great figures in the history of the English prize-ring. . . . Within the United States the Negro has made a high record of pugilism. In every important division of the sport since its organized establishment a Negro has held the championship of the world. In the bantamweight, George Dixon; featherweight, George Dixon; lightweight, Joe Gans; welterweight, Joe Walcott; middleweight, Tiger Flowers; light heavyweight, Battling Siki (won in France); heavyweight, Jack Johnson. In addition to these champions, there is a long list of noble Negro pugilists. . . . Peter Jackson was the first example in the United States of a man acting upon the assumption that he could be a prize-fighter and at the same time a cultured gentleman. His chivalry in the ring was so great that sportswriters down to today apply to him the doubtful compliment, "a white coloured man." He was very popular in New York. If Jack Johnson had been in demeanor a Peter Jackson, the subsequent story of the Negro in the prize-ring would have been somewhat different. Nevertheless, it should be said for Johnson that, whatever he may have lacked in behavior and good sense, he was a first-class fighting man, rated, in fact, the best defensive fighter the American ring has ever seen. During the first decade of the century there was a trio of formidable Negro heavyweights: Sam Langford, Sam McVey, and Joe Jeanette. One of the most sensational fighters in the ring today is Kid Chocolate (Eligio Sardinas), the black Cuban bantamweight.

New York, the New York of the upper Twenties and the lower Thirties, was the business and social centre of most of the coloured men engaged in these professional sports, as it was also of the genuine black-face minstrels, the forerunners of the later coloured performers; wherever their work might take them, they homed to New York. And because these men earned and spent large sums of money, there grew up in New York a flourishing black Bohemia.

Document 5: Walter White Implores Jesse Owens Not to Go

Prior to the 1936 Olympic Games in Berlin, a worldwide debate ensued among countries as to whether they should send their athletes to Germany because of the apparent atrocities committed by the Nazi regime. Nowhere was the debate more intense than in the United States where different individuals and groups offered their views on the impact of participating or not participating in the most important mega sporting event in a country espousing a belief in Aryan racial superiority. Not unexpectedly, members of the African American community weighed in on the debate with no apparent uniform position on the issue. One influential African American who opposed the participation of black athletes in Berlin was Walter White, executive secretary of the NAACP. In the following letter written to Jesse Owens, White implores the great track star not to go Berlin, contending that the best way to combat racial bigotry and prick the conscious of people was best accomplished by boycotting the games rather than through participation.

December 4, 1935

My dear Mr. Owens:

Will you permit me to say that it was with deep regret that I read in the New York press today a statement attributed to you saying that you would participate in the 1936 Olympic games even if they are held in Germany under the Hitler regime. I trust that you will not think me unduly officious in expressing the hope that this report is erroneous.

I fully realize how great a sacrifice it will be for you to give up the trip to Europe and to forgo the acclaim, which your athletic prowess will unquestionably bring you. I realize equally well how hypocritical it is for certain Americans to point the finger of scorn at any other country for racial or any other kind of bigotry.

On the other hand, it is my first conviction that the issue of participation in the 1936 Olympics, if held in Germany under the present regime, transcends all other issues. Participation by American athletes, and especially those of our own race, which has suffered more than any other from American race hatred, would, I firmly believe, do irreparable harm. I take the liberty of sending you a copy of the remarks, which I made at a meeting here in New York, at Mecca Temple, last evening. This sorry world of ours is apparently coming in a fumbling way to realize what prejudice against any minority group does not only to other minorities but to the group which is in power. The very preeminence of American Negro athletes gives them an unparalleled opportunity to strike a blow at racial bigotry and to make other minority groups conscious of the sameness of their problems with ours and puts them under the moral obligation to think more clearly and to fight more vigorously against the wrongs from which we Negroes suffer.

But the moral issue involved is, in my opinion, far greater than the immediate or future benefit to the Negro as a race. If the Hitlers and Mussolinis of the world are successful it is inevitable that dictatorships based upon prejudice will spread through out the world, as indeed they are now spreading. Defeat of dictators before they become too firmly entrenched would, on the other hand, deter nations, which through fear or other unworthy emotions are tending towards dictatorships. Let me make this quite concrete. Anti-Semitic, anti-Catholic and anti-Negro prejudices are growing alarmingly throughout the United States. Should efforts toward recovery fail, there is no telling where America will go. There are some people who believe that a proletarian dictatorship will come. I do not believe this will happen and the course of history clearly indicates that it is not likely to happen. Instead, it is more probable that we would have a fascist dictatorship.

It is also historically true that such reactionary dictatorship pick out the most vulnerable group as its first victims. In the United States it would be the Negro who would be the chief and first suffered, just as the Jews have been made the scapegoats of Hitlerism in Nazi Germany. Sinclair Lewis, in his last novel, IT CAN'T HAPPEN HERE, has written what seems to me to be a very sound picture of what may happen. I have written at greater length than I had intended at the outset. I hope, however, that you will not take offense at my writing you thus frankly with the hope that you will take the high stand that we should rise above personal benefit and help strike a blow at intolerance. I am sure that your stand will be applauded by many people in all parts of the world, as your participation under the present situation in Germany would alienate many high-minded people who are awakening to the dangers of intolerance wherever it raises its head.

Very Sincerely Walter White

Secretary
NAACP

Mr. Jesse Owens
Ohio State University
Columbus, Ohio

Document 6: Maya Angelou Celebrates Joe Louis

Joe Louis was one of the greatest and most legendary boxers in history. The "Brown Bombers'" ring triumphs have been celebrated through poems and prose and songs created by musicians from the worlds of jazz, gospel, and the blues. The black fighter's historic bouts with Max Schmeling, fascinated the prominent black writer, Richard Wright. Another writer intrigued by Louis was Maya Angelou, the author of seven autobiographical books and a plethora of works of poetry. In the following excerpt from perhaps her most famous work I Know Why the Caged Bird Sings *(1969), Angelou makes clear the excitement expressed by family and friends at the local store in her town after Louis's defeat of Primo Carnera in 1935. What is readily apparent from her account is the representational impact of Louis's victory, a triumph of symbolic importance that lifted the spirit and increased the racial pride of all black Americans.*

The last inch of space was filled, yet people continued to wedge themselves along the walls of the Store. Uncle Willie turned the radio up to its last notch so that youngsters on the porch wouldn't miss a word.

Women sat on kitchen chairs, dining-room chairs, stools and upturned wooden boxes. Small children and babies perched on every lap available and men leaned on the shelves or on each other.

The apprehensive mood was shot through with shafts of gaiety, as a black sky is streaked with lightning.

"I ain't worried 'bout this fight. Joe's gonna whip that cracker like it's open season."

"He gone whip him till that white boy call him Momma."

At last the talking was finished and the string-along songs about razor blades were over and the fight began. "A quick jab to the head." In the Store the crowd grunted. "A left to the head and a right and another left." One of the listeners cackled like a hen and was quieted.

"They're in a clench, Louis is trying to fight his way out."

Some bitter comedian on the porch said, "That white man don't mind hugging that niggah now, I betcha."

"The referee is moving in to break them up, but Louis finally pushed the contender away and it's an uppercut to the chin. The contender is hanging on, now he's backing away. Louis catches him with a short left to the jaw."

A tide of murmuring assent poured out the doors and into the yard.

"Another left and another left. Louis is saving that mighty right. The mutter in the Store had grown into a baby roar and it was pierced by the clang of a bell and the announcer's. That's the bell for round three, ladies and gentlemen."

As I pushed my way into the Store I wondered if the announcer gave any thought to the fact that he was addressing as "ladies and gentlemen" all the Negroes around the world who sat sweating and praying, glued to their "master's voice."

There were only a few calls for R. C. Colas, Dr. Peppers, and Hire's root beer. The real festivities would begin after the fight. Then even the old Christian ladies who taught their children and tried themselves to practice turning the other cheek would buy soft drinks, and if the Brown Bomber's victory was a particularly bloody one they would order peanut patties and Baby Ruths also.

Bailey [Angelou's brother] and I lay the coins on top of the cash register. Uncle Willie didn't allow us to ring up sales during the fight. It was too noisy and might shake up the atmosphere.

When the gong rang for the next round we pushed through the nearsacred quiet to the herd of children outside.

"He's got Louis against the ropes and now it's a left to the body and a right to the ribs. Another right to the body, it looks like it was low. . . . Yes, ladies and gentlemen, the referee is signaling but the contender keeps raining the blows on Louis."

"It's another to the body, and it looks like Louis is going down."

My race groaned. It was our people falling. It was another lynching, yet another Black man hanging on a tree. One more woman ambushed and raped. A Black boy whipped and maimed. It was hounds on the trail of a man running through slimy, swamps. It was a white woman slapping her maid for being forgetful.

The men in the Store stood away from the walls and at attention. Women greedily clutched the babes on their laps while on the porch the shufflings and smiles, flirtings and pinching of a few minutes before were gone. This might be the end of the world. If Joe lost we were back in slavery and beyond help. It would all be true, the accusations that we were lower types of human beings. Only a little higher than the apes.

True that we were stupid and ugly and lazy and dirty and, unlucky and worst of all, that God Himself hated us and ordained us to be hewers of wood and drawers of water, forever and ever, world without end.

We didn't breathe. . . . We didn't hope. We waited.

"He's off the ropes, ladies and gentlemen. He's moving toward the center of the ring." There was no time to be relieved. The worst might still happen.

"And now it looks like Joe is mad. He's caught Carnera with a left hook to the head and a right to the head. It's a left jab to the body and another left to the head. There's a left cross and a right to the head. The contender's right eye is bleeding and he can't seem to keep his block up. Louis is penetrating every block. The referee is moving in, but Louis sends a left to the body and it's the uppercut to the chin and the contender is dropping. He's on the canvas, ladies and gentlemen."

Babies slid to the floor as women stood up and men leaned toward the radio.

"Here's the referee. He's counting. One, two, three, four, five, six, seven. Is the contender trying to get up again?"

All the men in the store shouted, "NO."

"—eight, nine, ten." There were a few sounds from the audience, but they seemed to be holding themselves in against tremendous pressure.

"The fight is over, ladies and gentlemen. Let's get the microphone over to the referee.

"Here he is. He's got the Brown Bomber's hand, he's holding it up. Here he is."

Then the voice, husky and familiar, came to wash over us—"The winnah, and still heavyweight champion of the world . . . Joe Louis."

Some Black mother's son. He was the strongest man in the world. People drank Coca-Colas like ambrosia and ate candy bars like Christmas. Some of the men went behind the Store and poured white lightning in their soft-drink bottles, and a few of the bigger boys followed them. Those who were not chased away came back blowing their breath in front of themselves like proud smokers.

It would take an hour or more before the people would leave the Store and head for home. Those who lived too far had made arrangements to stay in town. It wouldn't do for a Black man and his family to be caught on a lonely country road on a night when Joe Louis had proved that we were the strongest people in the world.

Document 7: Mixing of Race and Sport in the Crescent City

The AAU was similar to many other national organizations within and outside of sport in that it regularly had to confront the racial realities of the South when sponsoring events in that part of the country. The national AAU always faced a conundrum when its local southern chapters refused to allow African American athletes to compete in sporting events. In many instances, the national AAU acquiesced to southern racial mores and refused to come to the defense of black athletes who were eliminated from sporting events merely because of their skin color. One of those times that the national AAU stood firmly in support of black athletes, however, was in 1927 when its national track and field meet was scheduled for New Orleans. When the request by local officials to ban black athletes from competition was denied by the national AAU, New Orleans made the decision not to hold the meet and it was relocated to New York City. In the following column from the Pittsburgh Courier, *readers are reminded of the continuing racial discrimination in the South and provided details on the series of events that eventually lead to the track and field meet being moved to a more welcoming environment.*

In the midst of all the talk about the New South, little incidents arise to demonstrate the fact that much of the spirit of the old South still remains below the celebrated line of Messrs. Mason and Dixon. The Southern gentlemen of Nordic extraction remain obdurate on the question of color discrimination. Receptive to the inroads of the mechanical age and modern business methods, they continue to nourish the prejudices and narrow views in regard to people of color. And they continue to do this, even to the extent of losing much money and prestige. When it comes to deciding between coin and color, the latter is usually awarded the palm. The recent decision of the civic body of New Orleans not to accept the annual track meet of the Amateur Athletic Union is considered a great credit and advantage. Cities in all parts of the country vie for it. New Orleans was among the number who strove for the 1927 national track meet. It strove so mightily that it won the meet. But there was a fly in the ointment.

About a half dozen noted Negro athletes were scheduled to take part in the contests. Naturally they were to compete against white athletes. It was probable that some of these black athletes would win first and second places. Was New Orleans to run the risk of having Negroes competing on terms of equality with whites? Were the old traditions of the South to be disregarded and ignored? Were members of the superior race to be vanquished by inferior Negroes in the plain sight of thousands of descendants of Confederates who had fought for four bloody years to keep the blacks in bondage? A thousand times No, said the good fathers of the Crescent City. Send us floods, plagues, tornadoes, earthquakes, or what have you, said they, but spare us this black invasion.

In accordance with the celebrated Southern spirit of chivalry and fair play, pressure was brought to bear upon the Amateur Athletic Union to bar Negroes from the national track meet, lest the Civil War have to be fought over again. The spirits of "Stonewall" Jackson, Robert E. Lee and Jeff Davis were invoked and the Stars and Bars were unfurled and flung to the breeze. The Daughters of the Confederacy were shaken by shivers and gentlemen who winked at social intimacy with the blacks at night, frowned upon the prospect of athletic intimacy to Mr. Fred W. Rubien, secretary of the Amateur Athletic Union, beseeching him to spare them from the black invasion on terms of equality. Mr. Rubien could not see the point. An irresistible force had met an immovable object. The result: the Paris of America loses the track meet; the metropolis of the world gets it. Reluctant tears in New Orleans: resounding cheers in New York. It may be perfectly all right to cut off one's nose to spite one's face, but the loss hardly adds to one's attractiveness. Some day even New Orleans will learn that.

Document 8: Withheld from Participating at the Hands of a Southern Institution

There were a plethora of black athletes from northern colleges who were kept out of games against southern institutions during the first half of the twentieth century. It was customary in virtually all sports for northern institutions to bench their black players in games against segregated southern institutions because of those institutions racially exclusionary policies. One example of a northern institution that acquiesced to southern racial mores was the University of Michigan who kept their outstanding black running back Willis Ward out of a gridiron contest in 1934 against Georgia Tech because of that school's refusal to compete against integrated teams. In the following document from the October 27, 1934, issue of the Pittsburgh Courier, *sportswriter Dewey R. Jones provides insights into the treatment of Willis and how controversial Michigan's decision was to many people in the university community and beyond.*

The University of Michigan won its football game with Georgia Tech on Ferry Field Saturday, but it was an empty victory. The great "Champion of the West" and exponent of democratic principles and traditions had groveled at the feet of Jefferson Davis and the Confederate flag.

The score was 9-2 but that is unimportant. What is important is that Messrs.' Yost, Ruthven, Kipke, and Aigler, four gentleman responsible for the athletic conduct of the University of Michigan agreed upon the cowardly plan to bar from the game Willis Ward, admittedly one of the best football players in the country, simply because he happened not to be white and Georgia is not accustomed to playing football with any one who is not of Nordic extraction.

Not only was Ward not allowed to play but he was even asked not to don the uniform of the University of Michigan during the game. Instead, a seat was provided for him in the press box and he was urged to sit there and watch the game if he decided to watch it at all. To his credit, let it be said, that he chose not to watch the game. Contrary to statements over the radio and sent out by sports scribes to their newspapers, Willis Ward remained in his room at his fraternity house throughout the entire game. You can take this statement from your correspondent who was in the press stands and who knows Willis Ward when he sees him.

Students Objected

Let it also be said here to the credit of many students at the University of Michigan that the treatment of Ward did not meet with universal approval. I arrived in Ann Arbor too late to attend a meeting which was held in the auditorium of the Natural Science building Friday night but the echoes of that meeting were still resounding around the campus when I did arrive there. The meeting was attended by more than fifteen hundred students, which is no small number in anybody's language.

The meeting, according to all the rumors, was scheduled as one of protest on the eve of the game. It was an effort of an interested student body to determine whether all of the traditions for which the school had stood were to be trampled in the dust. Several members of the faculty also attended this meeting and voiced their disapproval of the plan to bar Ward from the game against Georgia Tech. Coach Kipke, athletic director Yost, and president Ruthven were invited to attend the meeting and express themselves, but they were conspicuous by their absence. During the course of the evening's activities, a statement was read from coach Alexander of the Georgia team in which he declared that Georgia did not care how many Ward's were on the team—that the "Yellow Jackets" would play to win and that the composition of Michigan's team would be left entirely to the Michigan coach.

Among the Speakers

Others who addressed the meeting included a Rev. Marley, white Unitarian minister; John R. Cottin, professor of Romance languages at Fisk now on leave as a graduate student at Michigan; Prof. McFarlan of Michigan, and several other persons of distinction on the campus. They declared in no uncertain terms that the university was embarking upon a program which was contrary to all the traditions of the school, and they called upon the authorities to check the discrimination before it was too late.

But Saturday's game gave no indication that the authorities were interested in the principles of justice and fair play. The fact that Willis Ward had been good enough to win honors for Michigan on track and football teams for two years and that he had been courageous enough to risk injury in the two previous games had no bearing on this case. He was a black man first and a Michigan man second, according to the authorities, and therefore he could not even appear in the colors of Michigan during the game with Georgia.

This fact was made more significant when it was revealed that Georgia Tech had brought to Ann Arbor a black man as a water boy. And every time either side took time out during the game, this individual, wearing a sweater in Georgia Tech colors, trotted on the field serving his white masters with water. It showed that Georgia didn't give a whoop what Michigan thought of her—this black man was a member of the Georgia squad (as a water bot to be sure) and he was to perform his function wherever the team went. But Ward, a player, couldn't even get on the field.

The Michigan Daily, a student publication, was loud in its denunciation of the attitude of the authorities in this matter. In an editorial in Sunday's issue, it demanded that the university schedule no more games with southern teams, but confine its contacts to schools of Michigan's equal.

Police on Hand

The threatened demonstration on the field to demand that Ward be allowed to play failed to materialize. The reason for this was obvious: Everywhere one looked there were State policeman and Naval Reserves from Detroit. Just what would have happened had the students marched on the field as they had threatened to do is a matter of conjecture, but was apparent that the presence of the policemen and sailors, coupled with the fact that it rained throughout the game, had much to do with the cooling of the ardor of students to fight for a principle.

And so, the game was played with Ward and Franklin Lett, another Race member of the squad, out of uniform. Ward, remaining in seclusion, made no statement for publication, although to several persons who talked with him the impression was given that he felt keenly the insult to himself and his race as a result of the treatment meted out by the Michigan authorities. Georgia Tech, although losing the game, was winner of a moral victory. The Confederate flag had come to Michigan to wave over America's greatest state university. And there was no one in authority with fairness enough or guts enough to drag it down. The two schools—Michigan and Georgia Tech—had come together to bargain, and Georgia had all the better of the bargain in spite of the fact that the game was lost. Like Richard the Third, Michigan had won a crown but lost a kingdom.

Document 9: Trying to Comprehend
Why Professional Football Is All White

During the first half of the twentieth century progressive sportswriters and others spent much of their efforts trying to see that black players were allowed to participate in MLB. It stands to reason why this was the case since baseball had always

*been considered America's national pastime and the most democratic of all sports.
On occasion, campaigns were waged in an effort to integrate other professional
sports. The following selection by William A. Brower from Opportunity magazine sits squarely in this category. He disputes the arguments that there were no
black players talented enough to play in the NFL and that it would be impossible
for blacks and whites to play with and against one another without racial conflicts.
Those were just excuses. There was only one reason for the lack of black players
in professional football and that was the owners of NFL franchises who showed no
commitment to integration.*

In a recent issue of the magazine *Golf*, Bob Considine, young sport sage of
the *New York Daily Mirror*, made this pertinent observation: "One of the
great success stories in the history of sport is the rise of pro football. It has
advanced from the gutters of the gridiron to a position where it is the darling of rich young backers and the alma mater of 5,000 passes a week to a
reluctant public and estimated that only half of them were used. This coming season (the current campaign) the Giants will draw in the neighborhood
of a quarter of a million customers, all of whom will lay their dough on the
barrel head."

Last December, shortly after the championship contest between the
Green Bay Packers and the Giants, Sam Balter, eminently fair and forthright
sports commentator, struck a different note. On one of his daily broadcasts,
heard on a major network, he read an open letter to the magnates of the National Professional Football League, inquiring if it were malice aforethought
that each of the ten clubs neglected to select Kenny Washington, great
Negro half-back of the University of California, Los Angeles Branch, during
their draft session at Milwaukee the day preceding the titular game. If so, he
asked them to make a public announcement, stating unequivocally whether
such practice, which inferentially debars Negro football players from active
engagement in major league pro football, be a permanent policy of their organization. For this purpose he volunteered the facilities of his program and
the network which carried it.

What is the kindred of these two sport items, with the obvious exception
that they pertain to professional football? To the naked eye any other affinity
may appear lacking. But if you explore the nether regions you will find them
linked closely—rather closely together. This relationship may be explained
simply and in a few words: Easy money and prejudice tend to gravitate toward
each other.

The most assailable fault of a Democracy is that whenever symptoms of
prejudice manifested, somebody's feelings are hurt. In this instance, if the mag-

nates have by concerted accord definitely decided to close the door to Negro gridiron stars in big time post graduate football, the feelings of (in round numbers) thirteen million Negro citizens, augmented by an undetermined number of sportsmanlike white spectators are going to be seriously impaired.

But Negro pigskin performers do not have to lean too heavily on sentiments. They have made a cogent case for themselves solely on the basis of merit. Each year several turn in notable, sometimes extraordinary, performances for their alma maters in white collegiate circles. In fact, in recent years a noticeable number have achieved All American recognition. Cornell's Brud Holland twice attained this distinction, in consecutive years. On conference and sectional teams, they have also gained impressive representation. At the conclusion of the 1937 season, members of the University of Iowa team chose Homer Harris, versatile linesman, as their captain. Negro participants in College All-Stars-Professional Champions games have likewise acquitted themselves admirably.

In the Negro collegiate realm, there lies a fertile field still fallow as far as the cognizance of the cash-and-carry magnates are concerned. Here, because of limited numerical strength, a premium is placed on durability. Sixty-minute men, a rarity in white colleges, are not uncommon. Competition among high-ranking teams is taut and stern, the players having to absorb terrific punishment. Despite the recent increase in player-limits, one still must be able to take it to survive in the pro game.

Are the professional football bigwigs cheating Negro players out of the opportunity to participate in their league? One look at the workings of their "draft system" is enough to answer that question.

This system has been in operation for three years in the National Professional Football League. It works very simply. At the close of the regular college and professional schedules, representatives of the ten teams comprising the circuit assemble at a designated site, usually the scene of the championship game, where a prepared list of top college players whose eligibilities have expired is handed around for inspection. These men have been carefully scouted during their careers and the gridiron wheat has been detached from the chaff. Each team is allowed to select a quota of ten men. Inversely, according to the standing of his team at the conclusion of the regulation campaign, each representative picks an individual. (The aggregation lowest in rating having the choice prerogatives, though there are invariably more than enough good men to go around.) This procedure is repeated until the prescribed share has been reached by all.

Coincident with the institution of the draft system came an era in which white colleges produced a bumper crop of Negro players, both qualitatively and quantitatively. The array has been artistically attractive; yet none has been chosen in the brief annals of the selective process. Hearken to this catalogue and you will better get the point: In 1937, the first year of the draft, eligibles included Dwight Reed, Minnesota's fine flankman. In 1938, the contingent contained Holland and Harris; Bernie Jefferson, star halfback of Northwestern; Horace Bell, sterling guard and place-kicking specialist from Minnesota; Ed Williams, better-than-average fullback of New York University; Fritz Pollard, Jr., South Dakota's backfield flash; Roland Bernard, able linesman of Boston University, and Wilmeth Sidat-Singh, accomplished passer from Syracuse. Last season, aside from the illustrious Washington, there was Woody Strode, talented end, whose reputation exceeded just being Washington's teammate. All these admirable performers were blandly ignored in the voluntary conscription of college stars!

In trying to find the logical reason for the apparent prevailing discrimination against the ebony athlete in professional football, one is inclined to wonder if its big-wigs are not tracing the footsteps of the warmer-weather neighbor-baseball. The game that is generally recognized as our national pastime has been kept lily-white since it became an organized sport. The ostracism of the Negro from professional baseball is predicated on untested premises and, thus far, inexorable traditions. Some contend that because the majority of major league teams train in the south during spring conditioning exercises, matters of delicate nature might arise if an attempt to use a Negro were made. Others cite the preponderance of white southern athletes in the big leagues and express the opinion that the infiltration of Negro players might mean the sacrifice of technical efficiency and harmony.

There are no arresting or rational excuses for professional football to follow the dubious precedent set by professional baseball. Before pro football was elevated to its present position of prominence and affluence on the national sporting panorama, Negroes were identified with it in playing capacity without displeasure. Joe Lillard, the old Oregon star, contributed excellent backfield work to the cause of the Chicago Cardinals as late as 1932; Duke Slater, former Iowa All-American, performed superbly at tackle for the same team earlier; and Ray Kemp, who did his collegiate chores on the gridiron at Duquesne, distinguished himself in the employ of the Pittsburgh Pirates at guard. It is a plausible deduction that if players of color were used then with satisfactory and beneficial consequences, they could be used with similar results now.

But that is only a portion of the story. The playing personnel of professional football is by and large constituted of college players from all sections of the country—no single section predominates. All are intelligent young men with a sound sense of human values. Many of them either played alongside of, or face Negro stars, without resentment. It is inconceivable that they would renege when goaded by the additional incentive of receiving cash amounts for their gridiron labors. In fact, if a survey were conducted it is reliably believed that you would discover a minute percentage of conscientious objectors.

Any fear that if Negro athletes shared in the cash-and-carry sport it would create mental rifts and technical discord is sort of a delusion and should be summarily dismissed. It has already been inferred that they play on college squads without embarrassing the mechanical coordination or undermining the morale of the units. There is nothing to indicate that team function and spirit would suffer in the professional phase of the sport. Truthfully such a contingency in the play-for-pay game is diminished because playing football is a job, the primary source of income, for many of the players. They can ill afford to let internecine strife and private predilections interfere with team unity and welfare. Oze Simmons, another former Iowa luminary, recently wrote a letter to Chester L. Washington, sports editor of the *Pittsburgh Courier* leading Negro weekly, concerning this very point. Simmons wrote: "I know whereof I speak. The owners contend that the reason colored stars are not playing in the National Football League is because there are too many southern players in the league. I had the pleasure of playing with the Paterson (N.J.) team in the American Association for two years. And not only did the southern boys block for me, they even fought for me. The players have a job to do—WIN GAMES—and they are out to do their best, because that's what they are getting paid for. And if they can't produce they are fired."

Jimmy Powers, sports editor of the *New York Daily News*, had this to say on the heels of the All-Star-Green Bay Packers game in Chicago: "If I were Tim Mara or Topping, I'd sign Kenny Washington. He played on the same field with boys who are going to be scattered through the league. And he played against the champion Packers. There wasn't a bit of trouble anywhere. Kenny was tackled hard once or twice, especially after he ran a kick-off 43 yards right through the entire Packer lineup. But that's routine treatment for jack-rabbits. You slam your opposing speed merchants about, hoping to wear them down. Kenny took it all with a grin."

Another element in favor of the argument for Negro participation is that every franchise is located in a city where athletic miscegenation is not prohibited. Fans in Detroit, Chicago, New York, Cleveland, etc., are not allergic to one set of players because their skin pigmentation, by whims of birth, is darker than another group, but are largely interested in the skill and capability of their exploits on the playing terrain. A considerable segment of professional patronage is drawn from the college clientele. They demonstrate the same cosmopolitan reaction at a professional contest that they exhibit at a college combat. The same emotional currents circulate. They exude the same instinctive flair for sportsmanship. They emit exhortative yells when the battle conforms to their preference; they sit in frustrated silence when a change of complexion adversely affects them. They show accolades for a deserving deed, no matter who executes it, with the same spontaneity and sincere enthusiasm.

When you simmer everything down there is only one direction in which to look when you go to attach the blame—categorically in the faces of the National Professional Football magnates. There is no record of any authenticated commitment by them on the issue. Professional football is to a large extent autocratic, but it is hard to think that it will continue, premeditatively or differently, to flout fair-minded fans whose cash provides the ways and means for the game's existence. It is hard to think, too, that it can further injudiciously disregard the professional and commercial value of such Negro players of excellence as Kenny Washington, Brud Holland and Oze Simmons.

You realize it is difficult to entertain any particular grievance against Tim Mara, George Halas, George Preston Marshall: 11, Art Rooney and others of the NPFL official-dom. These are gentlemen of estimable character. They purged their game of all the poison with which it was formerly rife. It was their promotional ingenuity, generous and patient investment, courageous perseverance and commendable foresight which proved to be the optimum for the prevalent salutary status of the game. Their combined efforts lifted pro football from a floundering business in the ruck into an aura of respectability as an established enterprise of sports. But the evidence of double-jointed action towards the Negro somewhere along the line is transparent. The professional game of football has flourished with amazing celerity. One hopes that its guardians will not let its prestige continue to be retarded and tarnished by discrimination because of color—the most truculent tentacle of Prejudice.

Document 10: Chronicler of Black Athletes Expounds on the Importance of Sporting Success

Edwin Bancroft Henderson was a prominent Washington, DC, physical educator and civil rights activist who was the first person to chronicle the history of the African American experience in sport through his Negro in Sports *(1939) and subsequent books and essays. In the following document from* Opportunity *maga-*

zine, Henderson expounds on why he believes black athletic success is so important. Although the logic of his thinking here is sometimes difficult to follow, his basic premise is that success in sport was symbolic, testimony to the hard work of black athletes and indicative of the potential contributions that African Americans could make in other professional careers.

Will history record the Negro athlete a significant factor in the moderation of racial prejudice in America? Is our Negro athlete contributing much to an all-round New Deal for the Negro group? On one Sunday morning three years ago, the names of two black boys made great headlines on the first page of many of America's great conservative newspapers, including the *New York Times*. Their pictures glared from millions of front page copies of the world's press. Since then, news columns, sporting sections, and editorial comments have referred to Negro athletic achievement more than to any other artistic, political or educational phase of Negro life.

Sociologists are questioning the extent that this interest in the Negro athlete is affecting race prejudices. Another interesting question is, how have Negro boys made progress against the tide of race prejudice to reach the goals they have attained?

Athletics, in the main, begin with school life. In the South, after we leave the border states, are found the poorest of schools, and in a sampling survey made by the writer, there was found to be practically no physical education programs or athletics in schools for Negroes below the college level. The separate school systems provide little beyond the tool subjects, not much progressive curriculum material, but frequently a lot of worn out traditional educational content largely discarded by contemporary school systems. Time allotment and provision for play, games and other socializing educational media are absent in the great mass of Negro schools. However, the great trek of Negroes northward put a generation of colored boys in the schools of the more liberal states. There, the physical education programs gave them their chance. That they make the teams is due to rugged abilities, social adaptiveness, and the desire of the coach or school to gain prestige through athletics with its accompanying personal or institutional appraisal.

To make a success in team athletics, the colored boy must be definitely superior. Sometimes color aids him by marking him conspicuously in the course of the activity but frequently it identifies him as the bull's eye for the shafts of the opposition. He must make adjustments in realization of the prejudices of teammates, and must learn to "take plenty" from opponents. Often he must find separate lodgement when on tour. He must survive the humiliation of being left behind when his team plays the "Service" schools or the gentlemen of the South. In most such cases, he will receive a compensatory good will gesture as an effort of the coach to offset the humiliation. . . .

Without superior blockers to get him away from the maelstrom of the opposing line and backs, Red Grange would have been just another ice-man. To dim the lustre of a star Negro back, it is only necessary for a blocker to conveniently fail at his job occasionally. That Ossie Simmons would get his team's support during the past season became an item of publicity and that he performed so well was due to the support he did get despite being behind a line not up to the charging strength of some opposing teams. It is also a fact not generally known that where "scholarships" are the means by which many a poor boy gets to and stays in college for athletics, some of the bigger scouting colleges make it a policy not to subsidize college life for more than one good colored athlete per team.

Our professional or money-seeking athletes in the profit making game are up against different problems. Backers and promoters are openly in the game for money. If the color of an athlete is a financial factor of importance, or if he is an exceptional athlete, despite his color, he will be sought and used wherever the mores of the community are not taboo to colored athletes. . . . Although all contact games have the capacity to stimulate the fiercer emotions, the present-day rules of the boxing game and short bouts have put a premium on skill, strength, timing and endurance and probably limits the express of instinctive responses of rage and prejudiced hate. In this as in some other sports, promoters frequently find color an asset, and are inclined to depend a great deal upon the growing sense of American spectator sportsmanship. In some southern cities, the local fight promoters have begun to use colored fighters in non-mixed bouts on the same card with white fighters. In Missouri, the boxing ban against mixed bouts has been lifted. . . .

During the past year there has hardly been a sports commentator or columnist who has not advanced some reason for the unprecedented rise of Negro track and field athletes. For the last ten to twenty years, Negro broad jumpers have practically dominated the records in this event. Only two white athletes and one Japanese have excelled in this event. Theorists, many of them honest, have attempted to prove that Negro athletes were endowed with some peculiar anatomical structure of foot, leg or thigh that enables them to run or jump better than white athletes. Dr. Montague Cobb, associate professor of Anatomy at Howard University, in studies undertaken at the laboratory of Ohio State University, has shown with painstaking research, tests, and x-rays of the body of Jesse Owens that the measurements of Owens fall within the accepted measurements of white men.

Prejudiced thinking as to race and athletic success has served to stimulate further poisoned-pen comments from men like Brisbane of the Hearst press. Brisbane has a wont to compare athletes with "Grizzlies" or gorillas whenever an outstanding Negro athlete looms on the horizon. Recently, a story of Louis' great grandparent overcoming a baboon in a wrestling match on a slave farm in Alabama became a current press fable to account for the descent of strength to Louis. Several generations ago when the dark continent was invaded by explorers, the hunt was on for the "Missing Link," or the man-monkey. If slave-traders and exploiters could have satisfied the world that the Negro was on the border line between man and beast, this would have been justification for his classification as a beast of burden to be worked, enslaved or starved with only the compunction that Christians have been inspired with by the principles of the Society for the Prevention of Cruelty to Animals. The implications of the hunt for the missing link of the 18th century have their counterpart in those of the Brisbanalities of the present day "Negro-phobiacs."

General Hugh Johnson dismisses the question as to Negro supremacy in his brusque language by saying, "They're just too physical for us." Dr. Cobb has scientifically disproved the one and twenty theories that Negro athletes have peculiar anatomical structures. Therefore, the writers' guess is as good as some others. When one recalls that it is estimated that only one Negro slave in five was able to live through the rigors of the "Middle Passage," and that the horrible conditions of slavery took a toll of many slaves who could not make biological adjustments in a hostile environment, one finds the Darwinian theory of the survival of the fit operating among Negroes as rigorously as any selective process ever operated among human beings. There is just a likelihood that some very vital elements persist in the histological tissues of the glands or muscles of Negro athletes.

It is the belief of many students of race phenomena that the Negro athlete is making a considerable contribution to the spread of tolerance and improved race relations. Negro artisans and some intellectuals have risen to high planes of social relationships with individuals of other races through the recognition of values that transcend the physical. But the mass of humanity still is motivated by feelings and emotions. The main springs of action are still located in the glands. Fear, love and hate determine attitudes towards neighbors of foreigners. Our keenest pleasures and most poignant pains are born of feelings rather than of intellect. . . .

Even the most intellectual, no matter how far we strive to appreciate sophisticated music, non-understandable art symbols, or high values in literature, we still respond readily to the call of the chase, the fight, the race or the hunt and live over something our early ancestral experiences when we thrill or despair with the runner, boxer or other athlete. The world still loves a fighter, whether he be the winner or loser.

Joe Louis has thus captivated the fancy of millions. He is to some a symbolic sphinx of Egypt or a human replica of Rodin's "Thinker." In the ring he associates ideas and responds with lightning-like rapier thrusts about as rapidly through the medium of mind and muscle as an Einstein calculates cause and effect in cosmic theory. Jesse Owens, Metcalf, Tolan, and a host of others have likewise provided a feeling of pride and joyful relationship for many. These athletes are American athletes. They claim the loyalty of the thousands of students at this or that university. They are emulated by thousands of growing youth of all races, and above all they gain for themselves and the Negro the respect of millions whose superiority feelings have sprung solely from identity with the white race.

If Negro athletes do contribute to racial respect, and despite its nature, it is conceded by many that they do, then it behooves educators and racial agencies for uplift to make greater social use of athletics. Every opportunity for extending the games and plays of the physical education program of schools should be a part of education for Negroes. School teachers of little one-room school houses can encourage practice in a variety of activities by which the qualities known collectively as good sportsmanship as well as the skills can be learned by Negro youth. More happiness may be brought into the lives of the less-privileged, and at the same time we will be developing future good-will ambassadors through athletics.

Document 11: Rickey, Robinson and The Great Experiment

The integration of MLB was one of the most important events in the quest for racial equality in America. The two central figures in what historian Jules Tygiel referred to as "The Great Experiment" were Branch Rickey and Jackie Robinson. The two men are inexorably bound together in American history, the white baseball executive from Ohio carefully selecting to integrate MLB with the great all-around athlete from UCLA by way of Cairo, Georgia. The following editorial from the May 1947 edition of The Crisis *points out what has to happen if "The Great Experiment" is to be successful. Tellingly, the editorial points out that Robinson needed the support of black fans who could more positively contribute to the integration process if they did not just focus on Robinson and refrained from engaging in arguments about race with white fans.*

To Branch Rickey, president of the Brooklyn baseball team, must go the major credit for the presence of Jackie Robinson in major league baseball at first base for the Dodgers of the National League. Rickey shrewdly picked Robinson during 1945 as the most likely Negro prospect. Jackie was signed to a Montreal contract that fall and played first class baseball in the minor league during 1946.

Rickey did not bring Robinson up at the close of the season not yet at the beginning of the 1947 training season. Instead, he held off the announcement until April 10, just five days before the opening of the season. Rickey knew his man and the indications are that he knows his public and can see the signs of the time.

Robinson is a superb athlete, having starred in baseball, basketball, track, and football at UCLA on the West Coast. He is a competitor, is accustomed to huge crowds, and knows something of spectator psychology. He is accustomed to playing with and against white boys and men. He is acquainted with what may be called "locker room" problems and he knows something about getting along with hostile individuals. In addition, he is an ex-lieutenant in the army, a man who served his country and won his officer status after starting as a private.

Of all the cities with National League teams, Brooklyn seemed most likely to greet Robinson with minimum reservations and give him an even chance to make good on his merits. So Rickey made his plan and carried it through. At this writing it appears that his plan has not mis-fired at any point. The sports writers and the fans have been won over to a fair shake for Jackie. The only remaining question mark is the attitude of some of the Dodger players (not all of them from the South) and of players on other teams in the league.

The solving of this question is largely up to Robinson himself, but he can get valuable aid from the fans and the public. White and Negro fans ought to try and judge Robinson as a ball player, not as a miracle man. He will strike out, commit errors, and have his batting and fielding slumps just as all players do. He is not hired to solve the race problem, but to play baseball. Negro fans, especially, should not embarrass Robinson by their conduct in the stands, by special attention to him and no one else, by booing other players, by loud comments and racial arguments with other fans. Negro newspapers have their duty to perform in this respect, also. In the first game Reiser was the Dodger hero, but from the headlines in one of the larger weeklies one would have thought Jackie was the whole show. This kind of reporting and editing can do so much damage as a drunken, loud-mouthed fan.

Robinson can be an ambassador of racial goodwill to millions of Americans if he is given a chance. The judgment and courage of Branch Rickey and the skill and courage of Robinson himself should be rewarded by thoughtful and sensible reactions on the part of Negro and white Americans.

Document 12: Wilma's Journey from Tennessee to Rome

Wilma Rudolph's story is an inspirational one that has been recounted many times. Growing up in a family of seventeen children in rural Tennessee and suffering physical maladies as a child, Rudolph competed for famed coach Ed Temple at Tennessee State University before capturing three gold medals in the 1960 Olympic Games in Rome. Rudolph's great performance in Rome, which was made visible via an admiring television audience, brought her immediate hero status and lasting fame. In the following document from The Rotarian *magazine, Alex Haley, who achieved his own fame through such books as* The Autobiography of Malcolm X *(1965) and* Roots *(1976), provides an overview of Rudolph's life and career shortly after the games in Rome. It is truly a rags-to-riches story, a black woman from an impoverished background overcoming gender and racial barriers to become a legendary track and field athlete and Olympic hero.*

Wilma Rudolph's spectacular triumphs at the Olympics were to bring her many honors in the United States and abroad. Last December, European sports writers in the annual United Press International poll named her Sportsman of the Year, the first woman ever voted this award. In the U.S. she was voted Woman Athlete of the year by the Associated Press. But more remarkable than all the honors is the triumph which she achieved over a staggering handicap: for one-third of her life she was a cripple unable to walk. Two great personal influences aided her in her struggle: a mother who practiced and counseled the personal philosophy of never giving up, and a coach who taught that notable success demands that one usually prepare himself.

A tiny 4 1/2 pounds at birth, Wilma was the 17th child in the poor home of a Negro store clerk and a domestic in Clarksville, Tennessee. Always sickly, she was 4 when she began to toddle. Then she was stricken with scarlet fever. Soon double pneumonia set in, and her tonsils inflamed dangerously with her condition too desperate for the doctor to chance taking them out. The child lay near death for weeks. Finally she rallied and pulled through, but her left leg had suffered a form of paralysis.

Her mother, a resolute woman, decided that this pitiful child was as deserving of good health as the rest of her youngsters. Wrapping Wilma in a blanket, Mrs. Rudolph took her by bus the 45 miles to the Negro Meharry Medical College in Nashville. Meharry specialists exhaustively tested the baby. They said that years of daily therapeutic massage might restore the use of the leg. "I can't bring her here every day—can you teach me?" the mother asked. The doctors could, under the circumstances, but there had to be scheduled clinic whirlpool and heat therapy, also, with special apparatus.

For the next two years, Mrs. Rudolph, on her weekly day off, made the 90-mile round trip to the Meharry clinic. The six other days, after arriving home tired from work, she prepared the family supper and afterward she carefully massaged the wasted small leg until long after the child had fallen asleep.

When a year after the doctors could detect only slight improvement in the muscular reflexes, passionately determined Mrs. Rudolph taught three older children to massage, and there began four daily shifts of "rubbing Wilma." "She's going to walk," Mrs. Rudolph declared.

By 1946 Wilma could manage a sort of hop for short distances, and then the leg would buckle. By the time she was 8 she was sufficiently improved to walk with a leg brace. That summer the Meharry clinic substituted a specially reinforced high-top left shoe for the brace, and Wilma limped the eight blocks to school happily.

A brother, Westley, had a basketball, and he mounted a peach basket on a pole in the wide, dirt back yard. To the family's surprise and delight, Wilma began playing with Westley. Catching on from watching him, she was soon on the court, and played almost, fanatically. Ignoring the heavy orthopedic shoe, she swivelled and pivoted away from Westley, dribbled in a weaving crouch toward the peach basket, and suddenly sprang up to make her shots. "Not one of all my boys ever played hard as that child making up all the playing she'd missed. I would watch her nearly about to cry," recalls Mrs. Rudolph.

Competing brother-sister teams formed around Westley and Wilma. When the rest tired and dispersed after hot contests she continued with phantom opponents. One day the mother did cry. Returning home from work, she stood slack-jawed with astonishment—Wilma was bounding around under the peach basket barefoot! She no longer needed the shoe. "It went on clear through her grammar school. She was basketballing when I left for work, and when I came back. I've had to start out in the yard with a switch to make her come and eat."

Upon entering Burt High School in 1953, 13-year-old Wilma went out for basketball. She played with such fervor that during one game she collided with Coach-referee Clinton C. Gray. "You're buzzing around like a 'skeeter' whenever I turn!" Gray exclaimed, exasperated. "Skeeter," as Wilma promptly was nicknamed, did make the team, and not long afterward Coach Gray inaugurated girls' track. Burt High had been invited to a state high-school meet to be held at Nashville's Tennessee State University. When Coach Gray saw "Skeeter" run, he timed her—and stared at his stop watch in disbelief. The gangling, unknown "Skeeter" proved the sensation of the state meet, winning the girls' 50-, 75-, and 100-yard dashes. Watching her like a hawk was Tennessee State University's coach of woman's track, Edward Stanley Temple. Temple badly wanted his young co-ed team of "Tigerbelles" to gain wider recognition for the Negro University through winning some of the important national competitions. He was sponsoring this high-school meet and attending others about the country in search of new talent. In "Skeeter" he saw tremendous natural speed hamstrung by grievous flaws in style—correctable flaws if she would work. And she had the perfect sprinter's body, the legs long and powerful, the height—unusual for a woman. He recognized in her a potential champion.

Temple explained that he was developing a "farm system," trying out ten high school girl stars each summer, and those proving of Tigerbelle caliber could receive a work-aid scholarship for four years at Tennessee State. "Be glad to try you out," Temple said casually. Wilma gulped that she would do her best. The news elated the Rudolph household. After several days the mother drew Wilma aside. "You're the first one in this house that ever had the chance to go to college. If running's going to do that, I just want you to set your mind to be the best! You can if you never give up."

The high-school year finally ended, and Wilma arrived at Tennessee State along with nine other bobby-soxed speed stars from Negro high schools about the United States. Welcoming them in the field house, Temple said, "You're going to find it tougher to get invited back." He showed movies of his Tigerbelles winning breathtaking races. Suddenly, he was curt: "O.K. Get togs from the manager, tomorrow be at the track." The girls had come expecting to display speed, but Temple's initial order was cross-country jogging for about five miles over rough farm pastures. About halfway, Wilma was gasping for breath. She had passed other girls sagged down exhausted, some even retching. But she somehow kept going until she stumbled and fell. When all had dragged back to the track after the ordeal, Temple was blunt: "If you want to run here, when you leave this campus for a meet you have to be in condition."

After a night to recover physically, the prep stars were routed from dormitory beds at 5 A.M. the next day. The college Tigerbelles were on the field. Pairing each with a prep girl, Temple ordered 50-yard sprints. Each crack high-school runner finished a humiliating five to ten yards behind. Even most of the other high-schoolers outran Wilma. Back in the dormitory, sick with shame, she anguished that she had ever come. Never could she be as fast as the Tigerbelles.

But she thought of her mother's admonition to "never give up."

Temple knew precisely that he was planning fierce incentives and competitiveness. By week-end, Wilma's starting humility had become fury at him. Relentlessly, Temple criticized the flaws in her style. "Stop digging postholes! Stretch out those long legs—stride! . . . Your elbows look like a windmill! The arms are pumped straight, like this—." Angrily she worked at effecting the changes in style, just to get Temple off her back. "No clenched fists! With open palms, you're running more relaxed! . . . Don't grab that baton, grasp it!" One day when Wilma was ready to explode, he knew. "Look, Skeeter," he said, calming kindness in his voice, "right now, I'd call you a fair runner. Most teams have good runners. But I want great runners. You're hot under the collar because my Tigerbelles make you look bad. You know the reason? They're better prepared than you are. Always remember, on this track, anywhere else, the one who is the best prepared you find at the top. Now I'll tell you, you can go home tonight if you want to. Or you stay and I'll teach you these things that will help you to win races." Pausing, Temple added, "I think you can be a champion if you want to."

Standing there with sweat running down into her eyes, Wilma was speechless. Three days later she was again staggered when Temple quietly read her name among the four Junior Tigerbelles he was taking with his college stars to Ponca City, Oklahoma, to participate in National A.A.U. competition. The junior division 440-yard relay was won by Temple's four prep trainees, including Wilma. With breath-stopping suspense, their big sister Tigerbelles swept all senior-division sprints and the relay. Tennessee State had its first A.A.U. championship!

Wilma returned to her family and schoolmates a heroine—to everyone but herself. Deeply she was convinced that she could never run so brilliantly as Temple's college girls. Her mother figured the trouble; finally she picked it out of Wilma. "It looks like you can't," she said, "but you can't think you can't! You just got to forget everything but trying!"

Through remaining high-school summers, Wilma drilled in the countless details of Tigerbelle style. By the time she enrolled as a freshman at the University, Temple was admonishing his summer trainees, "Watch how Rudolph does it." Training herself, countless times she raced 100 yards, walked back to the starting line, then raced again. She had heard so many starter pistols, and counted her early strides so often, that by now instinct triggered her catapulting takeoffs, then next told her the exact instant to begin straightening up and "floating," and, seconds later, when to start leaning to meet the tape. In the relay, she, Martha Hudson, Barbara Jones, and Lucinda Williams learned to fuse their very reflexes in top-speed exchange of the baton. Temple approached the fanatic about this: "Sloppy baton-passing loses relays!"

Everywhere they raced, the Tigerbelles demolished the opposition. Wilma's permanence on the relay team ranked her among the four fastest Tigerbelles. Yet the other three inevitably beat her in the hotly jealous vendettas of intrasquad racing. "You've got the physical equipment and style—you're supposed to be winning; what's wrong, Skeeter?" Temple asked often. In truthful embarrassment she would say, "I don't know, Coach," for she was trying with all she had to win.

Then in early November, 1959, Wilma began suffering from a sore throat. Gradually her tonsils flared into a swelling agony. Temple hustled her to a Nashville doctor. Immediate surgery was performed. "Those tonsils were terribly infected, Coach," the doctor commented. "They've sapped the girl's strength for years, draining poison into her system." A strange light came into Temple's brown eyes. After three weeks in the University infirmary, Wilma returned to the track—for the first time in her life in full health. In a few days, in the Chicago 1960 Indoor A.A.U. Nationals, she blazed to victory in three races! "I can't believe it! I feel so wonderful!" she exclaimed to flabbergasted sister Tigerbelles.

In Corpus Christi, Florida, she shaved three-tenths of a second off the Olympic and world 200-meter record! In the Olympic tryouts in Abilene, Texas, she took the 100 and 200 meters, and anchored the winning Tigerbelle relay team that would represent the United States. "Somebody'll have to set a new world record to beat her in Rome," the jubilant Temple crowed to Earl Clanton, his assistant. And now he dared to dream of the greatest triumph that a coach and athletes can have—a "clean sweep" of every event entered, against Olympic world competition!

Seven Tigerbelles were among the 310 U.S. athletes who in August flew from New York City to Rome. In the first 100-meter women's sprint, Wilma scorched to a new Olympic record of 11 seconds flat. In the 200-meter trials the following day, Wilma cracked the Olympic time! Then in the finals she blazed to breath-stopping victory over Germany's great 200-meter star, Jutta Heine! Deafening ovation exploded in Stadio Olimpico. Not since the immortal "Babe" Didrikson's phenomenal performance 28 years before had the United States boasted a woman double-Gold Medalist.

No woman ever had won three Gold Medals in track, the Italian morning press reported: "La Gazzelle Nera" (The Black Gazelle) would make that

Olympic history if the Tigerbelles won the women's relay. This they did—despite the bobbled pass.

A new Olympic women's relay record! An unprecedented triple-Gold Medalist! "Gazzelle Nera!" "Perle Noire!" "Wilma!" "Skeeter!" A hundred thousand throats fed the reverberating din of merged accents, and hats, newspapers, programs, and autograph books rained down on the emerald-green field as the lean, brown girl half-circled, slowed, and jogged toward the sidelines. "Coach Temple! Coach Temple!" Wilma was crying as sister Tigerbelles, other athletes, and photographers mobbed her. She was the World's Queen of Track, flooding out tears of gratefulness for Coach Temple's long, persevering training, and for her mother's determination that a puny, crippled daughter must walk.

Document 13: Muhammad Ali in the Congressional Record

Muhammad Ali became one of the most famous men in the world. Amazingly gifted physically, nice looking (he would say pretty), brash, confident, and brave, Ali startled people at home and abroad when he announced he had become a member of the NOI shortly after defeating Sonny Liston for the heavyweight title in 1964. He would incur the wrath of many people for his membership in a group calling for a separate homeland and speaking of "white devils" and further infuriated a large segment of Americans when he refused to enter military service on account of his religious convictions. Over time, however, Ali would become a beloved figure, a result of a combination of factors, including the religious transformation of the NOI, diminishing racial discrimination, and a sea of changes in American politics and culture. All of this is evident in the following 1976 interview that Ali did on the CBS program "Face the Nation" and ultimately printed in the Congressional Record.

Mr. Mansfield, Mr. President, on Sunday last, I had the pleasure of watching and listening to Mr. Muhammad Ali on the CBS program, "Face the Nation." The reporters on that occasion were George Herman of CBS News, Peter Bonventre of Newsweek and Fred Graham of CBS News. I found the interview fascinating. I found it very much worthwhile. I had never seen Mr. Muhammad Ali except in pictures in the public prints before. I was impressed with his performance. I ask unanimous consent that the transcript of the Face the Nation broadcast, which starred Muhammad Ali, be printed at this point in the Record.

There being no objection, the transcript was ordered to be printed in the record as follows:

Face the Nation

Herman: Mr. Ali, you have said that you like to lecture better than you like to box. You've become certainly a very well-known world figure; people know about you in every corner of the earth. You say you want to be a sort of a black Henry Kissinger. What is it you want to do after you stop fighting?

Mr. Ali: Well, I figure that we only have so many hours a day to do whatever we have to do, so many years to live, and in those years we sleep, about eight hours a day, we travel, we watch television; if a man is 50 years old he's lucky to have had 20 years to actually live. So I would like to do the best that I can for humanity. I'm blessed by God to be recognized as the most famous face on the earth today, and I cannot think of nothing no better than helping God's creatures or helping poverty, or working for good causes where I can use my name to do so, to help this country, and other countries where we're having various problems where my influence might help.

Bonventre: Muhammad, what do you think you would have become if you didn't get into boxing?

Mr. Ali: I really don't know. I started boxing when I was 12 years old. I was not that educated in school, and I don't know what I would have done— probably a factory worker, or could have been somewheres dead, wound up in the wrong game, or the wrong life, but if I had heard the Islamic teachings, and if I'd heard the Muslim teachings, which I've accepted, I would probably have been a minister or doing something else good for mankind, but not in a larger way.

Graham: . . . I want to ask you a sort of Walter Mittyish question. Is there ever going to be another great white hope, a white heavyweight that's going to come in and whip all of you black heavyweights?

Mr. Ali: Well, there's a great possibility. We can't foresee him now, like—they come up—we might have one now, might come out of the next Olympics. One might be in some gymnasium now, and he'll knock out somebody next week—we never know until it happens.

Graham: Why are there so few American white fighters? You're going to fight a white man in Germany, but why so few American white heavyweights?

Mr. Ali: I really don't know. One time we had Jack Dempsey, Gene Tunney, John L. Sullivan, Rocky Marciano, Max Baer, Tony Galento, we had good fighters—Carmen Basilio, Gene Foreman, and they're just not here now.

Graham: Well, let me ask you about this Japanese wrestler. Isn't that denigrating your position as a champion to go over and take part in a gimmick like fighting a wrestler?

Mr. Ali: I would say for an ordinary champion, yes, but people expect these things of me, I have a great imagination, I'm always doing something. I don't think you've ever had a boxer on this show, because the things that I've done calls attention, so this is going to be—we're going into the oriental world—these things I want to do for people over the world, and I can get through them through sports, where when I'm out of boxing, they'll all know me. Now we're working on the oriental part of the world for some things we'd like to do there, and we get to meet them through sports, plus I have a family, I'm looking to take care of my family, it's a nice payday and it's interesting. Many people want to know what would a boxer do with a wrestler. Then they'll have a chance to see.

Herman: Now let me ask you about that nice payday. It seems to me that in February of 1975, you said all your fights from now on were going to be free, that you were going to give all the money to various black charities and to help small businesses and so forth.

Mr. Ali: Not just black charities. We have all type charities, all type people, so I want to get that straight now. Yes, the monies that I make after all taxes, I say I like to do all I can to help people and work for charity groups, and I want to say this on the show now—I get millions of phone calls from people thinking I'm the First National Bank. We don't give away monies. I have lawyers, I have attorneys who check the organizations, the movements, and we don't have no individuals in business that have propositions. It's only for groups of people who need, and this is what I want to do.

Herman: Is it lawyers and attorneys who went to that Jewish old people's home in New York, where there are just about 50 people, or was it Muhammad Ali himself?

Mr. Ali: That was me, this was me, but things such as this, I almost don't have to get permission to help, because we know this is right, and there's no greed involved on no part of no individuals.

Bonventre: Muhammad, what would you say to your son if he came to you and expressed a desire to box?

Mr. Ali: Well, I would—I think I'm going to control him, or help my wife to control him, and let him get educated first and get his mind together, and I wouldn't encourage him to box. I'd let him do it as a game, a sport, for health, but not as a livelihood because it's too dangerous, but teach him foreign language and get him—see, we are all born for a purpose, every tree, the moon, rain, snow, everything God created has a purpose, and man has a purpose, and the wise man is he who finds his life purpose and we want to help him find his purpose in life, which I'm sure is not boxing.

Bonventre: Are you worried about the burden he'll have to bear, being the son of Muhammad Ali? You're a tough act to follow.

Mr. Ali: Well, if my act is not a good act, and if I'm not doing nothing right for people, and if my image is bad, it'll be bad. But if I can do the things that I'd like to do for God and the service of mankind, then I'm sure he'll be honored to be known as my son, and he would like to follow in my footsteps and people will admire him for that, but if my image is bad, then it's bad for him.

Graham: Can I go back to the question of money we were talking about before. By a rough estimate you've made almost $25 million in purses since you came back to fight. Now we've had the spectacle of some former champs who end up in the gutter. What are you doing to avoid that? Are you going to avoid that?

Mr. Ali: Yes, sir. I pray to Almighty God Allah I do. I think the best thing that I can do, or anybody can do, is to save their money—

Graham: What's your money in?

Mr. Ali: Government tax-free bonds is the best thing, I think a man can put his money in. Investments are bad, there are no real good investments, all of them are gambles. And we pay the government all its taxes before I get mine, but this is why we fight so regular, because I think two halfs is better than just one, so we plan to save as much as we can, and—

Graham: You are a conservative, aren't you, champ? Government tax-free bonds—you're a pretty conservative man with your money.

Mr. Ali: Well, I have a lot of conservative fellows advising me.

Herman: Let me ask you about something you said just a moment ago in reply to a question by Pete. You said, advising your son, you would say boxing was too dangerous. Has it been dangerous for you? Have you been hurt, have you been injured, have you been damaged in any way?

Mr. Ali: Oh yes, my jaw's been broke, and one nerve is just coming back from under here where I couldn't feel for about a year or two, and right now my eardrum in Manila with Joe Frazier—training for Frazier—and I just had it rebusted, the same one again in Italy—healed itself in about two weeks, but this is about all. I've had a few sore ribs.

Herman: I asked because there's been some belief in some quarters that boxing was a dying sport in the United States. I noticed it dropped out of a lot of schools and a lot of colleges. I'm told that now it's coming back in some colleges. What do you think of boxing as a sport for amateurs?

Mr. Ali: I think boxing is dangerous. Any man been hit in the head and the brain's a delicate thing—I think you should be well protected. If a fellow is not qualified, he shouldn't be allowed to fight, but football is proven to have more deaths, baseball, ice hockey, horse racing—car racing is much more dangerous, but I would advise nobody to box if they get hit too much and it's too dangerous. . . .

Graham: . . . I know you have more of an interest in religion, and you've said that's one of the things you want to devote a lot of time to later, but now, Mr. Ali, what about this image also as a womanizer that you also have. Is that-you're looking at me a little incredulously here, I don't know why, but—

Mr. Ali: I'm trying to figure out what you mean by womanizer.

Graham: Well, you have a reputation as—you're separated from your wife, and you have a reputation as a man who has a sharp eye for the ladies. Now, how is that going to be consistent with your role as a religious leader in the years ahead?

Mr. Ali: Well, as far as my personal beliefs are concerned, I don't talk about them in public, as far as my personal problems with family, these are things I don't discuss in public especially on high-class shows like I was told yours would be so, I don't even expected to talk about that here.

Herman: You said from time to time that a wise man can play the fool but a fool can't act like a wise man, and then you've said, "I've always got to talk. People expect it of me." Is that a role that you play? Are you trying to be an actor?

Mr. Ali: What I was talking about, I used to watch a wrestler named Gorgeous George, and he would always talk about how he would do this and do that, and people came to see him get beat. And this is where I got the idea. So the talking and the gimmicks and the predicting, which I don't do nowadays like I used to, was only to promote the fights which has now elevated me over all athletes in the history of the world as far as drawing power and world attractions in a sense. This is just a purpose of publicity, all the talking. That's why I did that. I don't have to do it.

Herman: You kind of disappoint me, I have to admit. I sort of thought this poetry, this float like a butterfly, sting like a bee, was the real Ali, not some kind of a commercial gimmick.

Mr. Ali: No, that's all. It wasn't a commercial gimmick, but it was promotion, and it was the real Ali. I do float like a butterfly, sting like a bee. But the little poems and the gimmicks were just to promote the fights. Newspapers, gave them something to write about.

Graham: If I can go back just for a minute, and this is obviously meant in a spirit of friendliness. The question of the Islamic religion and your future in that—do you, the impression one gets is perhaps it is loosening up a bit after the death of Elijah Muhammad. Do you think it's changing now, and that your role in it can change?

Mr. Ali: Well, what the honorable Elijah Muhammad taught was good for the time, during the thirties when black people were being castrated, lynched, deprived of freedom, justice, equality, raped. He had to teach that the white man is the Devil, his actions towards us is that of the Devil. Now that we're no longer being lynched, raped, castrated, we're given equal justice, we can go anywhere to live, even the North fights the South to have, so we can have certain rights. People are not acting this way today. So honorable Wallace Muhammad is on time. He's teaching us it's not the color of the physical body that makes a man a Devil. God don't look at our colors. Minds, hearts have no color, God look at our minds and our actions and our deeds. So we have white Muslims, brown Muslims, red Muslims, yellow Muslims, all colors. So it's the color. So the big thing in the change now, we have white people who have accepted our faith and we now recognize all men as brothers and we look at them according to their works. Some blacks can do evil, and whites. So it's not the color now, we look at the actions. . . .

Herman: Okay, thank you very much, Muhammad Ali, for being with us today on Face the Nation.

Document 14: Anita DeFrantz
Provides Her Perspective

Anita DeFrantz has made major contributions to the world of sport. Captain of the 1976 Olympic bronze medal winning rowing team, DeFrantz became the only woman on the International Olympic Committee and President of the LA 84 Foundation (previously the Amateur Athletic Foundation of Los Angeles). In the following selection from the August 12, 1991, issue of Sports Illustrated, *Defrantz describes her own difficulties as a black woman athlete and points out her belief that the lack of African American women in coaching and administrative positions was a result of the intersection between racism and sexism. She makes clear her view that African American women had to be "twice as good" if they were going to be offered coaching and administrative positions.*

In 1976, I rowed seven seat in the U.S. eight-oared shell that won a bronze medal at the Montreal Games. Since 1986, I have been a member of the International Olympic committee. My term of office lasts until I turn 75 in the year 2027. Only 10 years passed between my becoming an Olympian and my election to the IOC. But for me, an African-American woman, reaching the top of international sport seemed like the accomplishment of 10 generations.

Even in those sports that are largely sustained by black athletes, the guiding decisions are still made by white males. As a consequence, any African-American woman who finds herself in a position of influence in U.S. sport is a magnificent overachiever.

And the number of such women, always small, is dwindling. A remarkable resource is in danger.

When I was growing up in Indianapolis, I became curious about the energy and endurance of my great-grandmother, Laura Ethel Lucas. She was in her mid 70's, yet she carried sacks of groceries that I—at nine—could not lift. When I asked her how she got so strong, she said, "I wanted to be a nurse. But because I was a colored girl, they wouldn't let me go to school and get the necessary training. So worked in white people's homes, cleaning, washing their clothes and preparing their meals. It was hard work, so I had to be strong. But things are changing. You can get an education. You can be whatever you want to be."

I knew right then that I wanted to be strong, strong as Grandma Lucas was, strong enough to take on a world I knew would be hostile to me simply because of the color of my skin.

I saw other black females who were not able to sustain that strength. As a child, I swam during the summers for the Frederick Douglass Park team. All of us were black. A teammate of mine won almost every race, even against the white kids who trained year-round at the Riviera Club. The mostly white crowds on such occasions received this gifted girl in silence. Eventually she quit the team.

At Connecticut College, I discovered rowing, a discipline that would take all the strength I could muster. My skin color made me conspicuous in the sport. As a result, I never pulled at half pressure. I knew that I had to be better than my teammates. Today, that is the creed of every black female coach or administrator. "Twice as good?" says former USOC vice-president Evie Dennis. "Try five times as good."

I know from experience that it is painful to acknowledge that you are the target of racism or sexism, but I believe it is essential to call people on it. So here are some hard facts: A survey of 106 Division I schools that field women's basketball teams found that only 11 are coached by black women.

In those 106 schools, there is only one athletic director who is an African American woman.

There are no black women among the executive directors who lead the 50 governing bodies for U.S. Olympic sports. There has never been a black woman on any U.S. Olympic basketball coaching staff.

Even worse, in U.S. amateur sport, there are fewer female coaches today, black or white, than there were only 10 years ago. Decisions on women's staff and spending used to be the province of the female administrators who were responsible for women's athletics. Now decisions are usually made by white male athletic directors, whose imperatives are football and the bottom line. Cost-cutting has led to a shrinkage of non-revenue sports and the coaching jobs that go with them. In response, black female student-athletes are turning their backs on programs that would prepare them for jobs in those fields. The obstacles are too formidable.

Marian Washington, a black woman who is in her 19th season as the women's basketball coach at Kansas, says, "You constantly believe people will judge you by your work. It's such an unhappy surprise when they don't."

And, ultimately, it's enormously debilitating. After many years of watching other coaches receive opportunities to coach in international competitions, Washington finally decided to stop caring about it. "When I started to question myself and my capability because I wasn't being chosen, I decided not to allow myself to remain in that environment," she says.

Two American traditions collide here: Black women's belief in our own strength slams head-on into society's refusal to let us choose where to employ that strength. Sport doesn't lead society, it reflects it. To bring African-American women fully into American sport, attitudes must be changed. Sports executives must search their souls to see whether they are judging black women coaches and administrators fairly on their work, not dismissing them on the basis of their sex and the color of their skin.

Read about the obstacles faced by men—the stacking, stereotyping, discouraging and dumping—described in this magazine's series on the black athletes, then take my word for this: It's worse if you're female. And those who would deny all women their rights will oppose black women even more.

The strength and leadership ability of African-American women has been tested for centuries, and we have never failed to perform. Harriet Tubman escaped enslavement, led others to freedom and became a scout for the Union Army. Today's African American women are ready and able to contribute to this nation through sports. But only if given the opportunity, only if given the chance.

Document 15: Dreams Deferred on the Hardwood

Hoop Dreams was a very engaging, popular, and thought provoking documentary. It portrayed the lives of two black athletes, Arthur Agee and William Gates, as they strove to achieve success in basketball. Particularly noteworthy were the insights provided on the families and friends of Agee and Gates and how the African American community pinned its hopes and dreams on the power of sport to both improve the lives of young blacks and potentially lead to financial rewards. The following selection is a review of the documentary written by bell hooks, a noted writer and cultural critic. Appearing in the April 1995 issue of Sight and Sound *magazine, hooks argues persuasively that the filmmakers at once undermined and perpetuated deep-seated stereotypes about the black family. She also makes clear that victory in sport, if that is the only pursuit of talented black athletes, is a tragic circumstance and ultimately demoralizing.*

Entering a movie theater packed tight with bodies of white folks waiting to see *Hoop Dreams*, the documentary about two African-American teenagers striving to become professional basketball players, I wanted to leave when it seemed that we (the two black folks I had come with—one of my five sisters and my ex-boyfriend) would not be able to sit together. Somehow I felt that I could not watch this film in a sea of whiteness without there being some body of blackness to anchor me, to see with me, to be a witness to the way black life was portrayed.

Now I have no problems with white filmmakers making films that focus on black life: the issue is only one of victim perspective. When you're living in a white-supremacist culture the politics of location matters, no matter who is making a film about people of color. In the United States, when white folks want to see and enjoy images of black folks on the screen, it is often in no way related to a desire to know real black people.

Sitting together in the packed crowd, every seat in the house taken, we joked about the atmosphere in the theater. It was charged with a sense of excitement and tension, the anticipation normally present at sports events. The focus on basketball playing may have allowed the audience to loosen up some, but without knowing much about the content and direction of the film, and whether it was serious or not, folks were clearly there to have fun. As it began, a voyeuristic pleasure at being able to observe from a distance the lives of two black boys from working-class and poor inner-city backgrounds overcame the crowd. The lurid fascination involved in the "watching" of this documentary was itself profound documentation of the extent to which blackness has become commodified in this society—the degree to which black life, particularly the lives of poor and working-class black people, can become cheap entertainment even when the filmmakers don't intend anything like this. Filmmakers Peter Gilbert, Fred Marx and Steve James make it clear in interviews that they want audiences to see the exploitative aspects of the sports systems in America even as they also wish to show the positives.

Gilbert declares: "We would like to see these families going through some very rough times, overcoming a lot of obstacles, and rising above some of the typical media stereotypes that people have about inner-city families." Note the way in which Gilbert does not identify the race of these families. Yet it is precisely the fact of blackness that gives this documentary popular cultural appeal. The lure of *Hoop Dreams* is that it affirms that those on the bottom can ascend this society, even as it is critical of the manner in which they rise. This film tells the world how the American dream works. As the exploitative white coach at St. Joseph's high school puts it while he verbally whips these black boys into shape: "This is America. You can make something of your life."

White Standpoint

In the United States, reviewers, an overwhelming majority of whom are white, praised *Hoop Dreams*, making it the first documentary to be deemed worthy of an Academy Award for best picture, by critics and moviegoers alike. Contrary to the rave reviews it has received, though, there is nothing spectacular or technically outstanding about the film. It is not an inventive piece of work. Indeed, it must take its place within the continuum of traditional anthropological and/or ethnographic documentary works that show us the "dark other" from the standpoint of whiteness. Inner-city, poor, black communities, seen as "jungles" by many Americans, become in this film a zone white film makers have crossed boundaries to enter, to document (over a period of five years) their subjects. To many progressive viewers, myself included, this film is moving because it acknowledges the positive aspects of black life. It also encouraged us to look at it critically. . . .

By comparison with many films examining the experience of black Americans which have overtly political content and speak directly about issues of racism (such as documentaries on Malcolm X, or the Civil Rights series *Eyes on the Prize*), the focus of this film was seen by reviewers as more welcoming. It highlights an issue Americans of all races, but particularly white Americans, can easily identify with: the longing of young black males to become great basketball players, and to play for the National Basketball Association. No doubt it is this standpoint that leads a review like David Denby's in *New York* magazine to proclaim it "an extraordinarily detailed and emotionally satisfying piece of work about American inner-city life, American hopes, American defeat." Such a comment seems highly ironic given the reality: that it is precisely the institutionalized racism and white-supremacist attitudes in everyday American life that actively prohibit black male participation in more diverse cultural arenas and spheres of employment, while presenting sports as the one location where recognition, success and material reward can be attained. The desperate feeling of not making it in American culture is what drives the two young black males, Arthur Agee and William Gates, to dream of making a career as professional ballplayers. They, their family and friends never imagine that they can be successful in any other way. Black and poor, they have no belief that they can attain wealth and power on any playing field other than sports. Yet this spirit of defeat and hopelessness, that informs their options in life and their choices, is not stressed. Their longing to succeed as ballplayers is presented as though it is no more than a positive American dream. The film suggests that it is only the possibility of being exploited by adults hoping to benefit from their success (coaches, parents, siblings, lovers) that makes their dream a potential nightmare.

The film's most powerful moments are those that subversively document the way in which these young, strong, black male bodies are callously objectified and dehumanized by the white-male dominated world of sports administration in America.

Hoop Dreams shows audiences how coaches and scouts, searching to find the best ball players for their high-school and college teams, adopt an "auction block" mentality that has to call to the mind of any aware viewer the history of slavery and the plantation economy, which was also built on the exploitation of young, strong, black male bodies. Just as the bodies of African-American slaves were expendable, the bodies of black male ballplayers cease to matter if they cannot deliver the desired product. In the film, the filmmakers expose the ruthless agendas of grown-ups, particularly those paternalistic, patriarchal white and black males, who are so over-invested, emotionally or otherwise, in the two teenagers.

While the trials and tribulations Agee and Gates encountered on the playing field give *Hoop Dreams* momentum, it is their engagement with family and friends, as well as their longing to be great ball players, that provide the emotional pathos. In particular, *Hoop Dreams* offers a different—in fact unique—portrayal of black mothers. Contrary to the popular myth of matriarchal "hard" black women controlling their sons and emasculating them, the two mothers in this film offer their children all necessary support and care. Agee's mother Sheila is clearly exemplary in her efforts to be a loving parent, providing vital discipline, encouragement and affection. Less charismatic (indeed she often appears to be trapped in a passive and depressive stoicism), Gates' mother is kept in the background, the single mother raising her children. The film does not throw light on how she provides economically. . . .

Even though one of the saddest moments occurs as we witness Agee's loss of faith in his father, and his mounting hostility and rage, he is never interrogated by the filmmakers about the significance of this loss, as he is about his attitudes toward basketball, education and so on. And there is even less exploration of Gates' problematic relationship to his son. Without any critical examination, these images of black father-and-son dynamics simply confirm negative stereotypes, then compound them by suggesting that even when black fathers are present in their children's lives they are such losers that they have no positive impact. In this way, a cinematic portrait is created that in no way illuminates the emotional complexity of black male life. Indeed, via a process of oversimplification the film makes it appear that a longing to play ball the all-consuming desire in the lives of these young black males. That other longings they may have go unacknowledged and unfulfilled is not addressed. Hence, the standpoint of the filmmakers is no way to see how these states of deprivation and dissatisfaction might intensify the obsession with succeeding in sports. Audiences are surprised when we see Gates with a pregnant girlfriend, since until this scene the narrative has suggested basketball consumes all his energies.

Competition Rules

This suggestion was obviously a strategic decision on the part of the filmmakers. For much of the dramatic momentum of *Hoop Dreams* is rooted in its evocation of competition, through the documentary footage of basketball games where audiences are able to cheer on the stars of the film, empathically identifying with their success or failure, or via the rivalry the film constructs between Agee and Gates. Even though we see glimpses of camaraderie between the two black males, the film, constantly comparing and contrasting their fate, creates a symbolic competition.

On one hand, there's the logic of racial assimilation, which suggests that those black folks will be most successful who assume the values and attitudes of privileged whites; opposing this, there's the logic of narrow nationalism, which suggests that staying within one's own group is better because that is the only place where you can be safe, where you can survive. This latter vision, of narrow nationalism, is the one that "wins" in the film. And it is perfectly in synch with the xenophobic nationalism that is gaining momentum among all groups in American culture.

~

About the Author

David K. Wiggins, professor in the School of Recreation, Health, and Tourism and affiliated faculty member in the Department of History and Art History at George Mason University, is the author of *Glory Bound: Black Athletes in a White America* (1997), co-author of *The Unlevel Playing Field: A Documentary History of the African American Experience in Sport* (2003), and editor or co-editor of *Sport and the Color-Line: Black Athletes and Race Relations in Twentieth Century America* (2003), *Out of the Shadows: A Biographical History of African American Athletes* (2008), and *Separate Games: African American Sport Behind the Walls of Segregation* (2016). He is the former editor of the *Journal of Sport History* and currently president-elect of the North American Society for Sport History.